FROM HERE TO THERE

An Astrologer's Guide to Astromapping

*Edited by
Martin Davis*

The Wessex Astrologer

Published in 2008 by
The Wessex Astrologer Ltd
4A Woodside Road
Bournemouth
BH5 2AZ
England

www.wessexastrologer.com

Copyright © Martin Davis

ISBN 9781902405278

A catalogue record of this book is available at The British Library

Cover design by Iris de Leeuw

Printed and bound in the UK by Biddles Ltd, Kings Lynn, Norfolk.

Astro*Carto*Graphy (A*C*G) and Cyclo*Carto*Graphy (C*C*G) are registered trademarks of Jim Lewis.
Local Space (LS) is a registered trademark of Matrix Software.
Most of the charts and maps used herein are from Horizons, the mapping software by Matrix Software, Big Rapids, MI, USA.
The A*C*G maps in Chapter 4 were created by Robert Currey
The Geodetic World map, page 114, is from Kepler Software, Cosmic Patterns, Gainesville, FL, USA
The Local Space Compass, page 211, and LS global view, page 212, are from Solar Maps, Esoteric Technologies, Australia.

Martin Davis can be contacted through his website:
www.astrologymapping.com

All rights reserved. No part of this work may be used or reproduced in any manner without written permission. A reviewer may quote brief passages.

Acknowledgements

Thank you to Lucy Dixon for copy-editing, Iris de Leeuw for the cover art and help with the illustrations, Arlan Wise for review and feedback on the manuscript, Kyle Pierce of Matrix Software for technical assitance and to my publisher Margaret Cahill, who is always encouraging me.

Then of course there are those who so generously contributed to this collection. They are (listed in alphabetical order):

Bernadette Brady, Kathryn Cassidy, Faye Cossar, Donna Cunningham, Robert Currey, Dennis Flaherty, Arielle Guttman, A.Tad Mann, Chris McRae, David Meadows, Dale O'Brien, Angel Thompson and Maya White. Thank you one and all!

Dedication

This book is dedicated to all those who have ever played a role – large or small – in the furthering of the locality techniques.

Contents

Preface

Introduction

1
History
Martin Davis 1

2
The Astro*Carto*Graphy Book of Maps
Jim Lewis and Arielle Guttman 25

3
The Uses of Astromapping in Astrology
Martin Davis 31

4
Relocation can be a Career Move
Robert Currey 58

5
My Summer Vacation
Maya White 77

6
Between Heaven and Earth: The Influence of Astrology on Earth
Angel Z. Thompson 87

7
Reincarnation in Local Space & A*C*G Maps
A T Mann 93

8
Looking at the World Geodetically
Chris McRae 113

9
Would Relocation Change Your Life?
Donna Cunningham   130

10
Jyotish Locality
Dennis Flaherty   142

11
A Locality Tale
Kathryn Cassidy   162

12
The Stars and Stripes
Bernadette Brady   168

13
The Solar Return Astro*Carto*Graphy Map
David Meadows   196

14
The Business of Place and The Place of Business
Faye Cossar   203

15
Locality and the Question of the USA Birth Chart
Dale O'Brien and Martin Davis   220

16
A History Lesson: The A*C*G, Geodetics and Local Space of the George W Bush Presidency
Arielle Guttman   251

Index 269

Preface

"And, at the round earth's four imagined corners, blow your trumpets, angels."

John Donne (1572-1631)

The astromapping techniques of Astro*Carto*Graphy (A*C*G), Local Space (LS) and Geodetics have become widely available to all through their inclusion in contemporary astrological software. This is surely one of the most revolutionary developments of modern astrology, for, with their help, we now have the tools to identify significant earth locations and directions. Some call this an "archaic revival" as it is a modern equivalent of the ancient craft of earth divination. This development has been possible because of the speed and graphical capabilities of modern computers. It makes astromapping a perfect fit for this era of technology and information, and when the world is experienced as a 'global village'. Nowadays, we are often required to move due to family, professional or social necessities. Equally, we can expect people and events to come to us or at us from almost any location in the world. It becomes imperative to know our significant directions and global hot spots. Astromapping tools answer this need. Furthermore, these tools and techniques are no longer limited to the study of nations or world regions; they can now be applied to individual data for personal relocation information. This opens up a new potential for human development as we come to understand our connection with Mother Earth through the influences offered to us from her various earth locations and directions. Our birth charts no longer reflect isolated birth locations. *With astromapping our horoscopes become the whole world and we become potential global citizens.*

Introduction

I was delighted when I received my first Astro*Carto*Graphy map from Jim Lewis in the late 1970s. The lines – each with their own astrological symbolism – clearly matched much of what I had experienced roaming the planet in my travelling years. I, like many others, went back to Lewis to obtain maps for friends and family. Evenings were spent pouring over the lines and reading his detailed text from beautifully produced booklets.

Under the spell of the maps and Lewis's lucid text, the essence of astrology expanded for me. Astrology's connection with earth location became evident: it was no longer limited to something vaguely psychological and out there in the sky; it was also right here where I stood, where I had travelled and where I longed to visit one day. My natal horoscope had metamorphosed from a chart limited in time into a world map describing qualities of my past, present and possible future, all in terms of location (space).

Soon after this, I came across Michael Erlewine's articles on Local Space. By 1984, I was able to explore the technique using the program he had written for early Commodore computers. This was really magic! We now had a tool to describe the significance of earth directions in our lives, be it for our natal planets or any other object placed on earth or in the sky.

In the mid 1990s another mapping system, Geodetics, was brought to my attention. It came from the work of Canadian astrologer Chris McRae, who, by 1988, had worked out how to present it on a world map using the computers and software of that time. Geodetics represented a unique world horoscope, with the zodiacal signs wrapped around the earth itself. McRae showed how Geodetics could be employed to give meaning to both global events and personal relocation. I was impressed at how the Geodetic world map seemed to identify the varied cultural patterns we find around the world, as if they had arisen from the earth itself.

By the early 1990s, it was clear that a great maturing in the astromapping field was under way. Computer power was all but exploding, allowing maps to be calculated quickly and with stunning graphics, important books had been published, and, most of all, some of the finest astrologers and astrological minds had begun employing the astromapping techniques in their studies. There was a growing corpus of work that was notable for its richness and detail. It was, in a way, substantiating astrology itself, as specific locations could now be added to timings of events.

By 1998, as my lecturing experience grew, I saw a need for a textbook to document the details of each of the locality techniques. I felt the book should become a central resource for students, augmenting the separate, varied sources I had found. The absence of such a book felt to me like a void that needed to be filled. I acted upon this and in 1999 my book, *Astrolocality Astrology – A guide to what it is and how to use it*, was published in Great Britain.

Some years have passed since the publication of *Astrolocality Astrology* and the writing of this, my next book on mapping. In this time, astromapping techniques have achieved acceptance and become mainstream in astrological use. The techniques are routinely found in astrological books, magazines, workshops and conference lectures. They have become a requirement in mundane (world) studies and a great addition to other types of astrological enquiry. In other words, astromapping has arrived!

Why this book? Yet again, I feel a void exists in contemporary astrological literature. It's time we pause to reflect upon what has happened since the use of astromapping became widespread. This reflection includes reviewing the history of the field (telling its story) and presenting a cross-section of examples from the work of the contemporary astrologers who employ astromapping today. To this end, this book is an anthology of astromapping examples. The word 'anthology', by definition, is a collection, and, sweetly, the derivation of the word from the Greek means, 'flower gathering'. So here, kind reader, we offer a bouquet of locality flowers!

1

History

The Beginning
What we know today as Locality Astrology started with the yearning of astrologers over the centuries to associate terrestrial location with the qualities of zodiacal signs. The first known efforts at this can be traced back to Babylonian and Assyrian tablets.[1]

The first known classical attempt, ascribing zodiacal rulerships to nations, is found in Marcus Manilius' work, *Astronomica*, written around the beginning of the Christian era. An early attempt that survives was by Claudius Ptolemy in the first to second centuries AD and published in his work *Tetrabiblos*.[2] Muslim astrologers of the ninth to twelfth centuries added to these attempts, most notably Al Biruni, writing in 1029. Medieval astrologers followed, most borrowing heavily from the work of Ptolemy. Of note was the work of William Lilly who published in 1647. Further lists were produced by Raphael, Green, Sepharial and Charles Carter, each adding their insights to the correlation of zodiacal qualities with locations on Earth.

Early Influences
In the early twentieth century, works appear that, in hindsight, can be seen as inspirations for the mapping techniques that would follow. For example, there is Sepharial's work, *The Geodetic Equivalent*, published c.1924, and Edward Johndro's book, *The Earth in the Heavens*, published in 1929, which was about calculating and using "ruling degrees of cities". In the introduction to his work, Johndro writes about investigating "the important problem of aiding the individual to find his place in the world", and he concludes, "who among professional astrologers and students has not felt the need of coordinating the heavens and the earth?"

The First Maps[3]

The earliest locality maps that we would recognise as such were astronomical diagrams of eclipse paths over the Earth. Appearing in astrological magazines, it is possible that Charles Jayne[4] published the first one in 1941.[5]

- In 1957-58, Donald Bradley, in *American Astrology Digest*, published a hand-plotted map showing the rising, setting and culminating lines of all the planets over the entire world for the 1958 sidereal[6] ingress of the Sun into Capricorn. His transformation of this mundane[7] chart into a world map was probably a first.

- In July 1962, Roy Firebrace, first president of the British Astrological Association and editor of *Spica*, the British siderealist journal, also published a hand-plotted map, this time of the Sun's ingress into sidereal Cancer. Though not a first, this further demonstrated the usefulness of astromaps in mundane studies.

- In 1966, a computerised astromap created by programmer Gary Duncan was published in the *Llewellyn Annual* for that year. It was the first computer-generated map ever published. Again, the map was of a mundane (worldly) moment, affecting large numbers of people.

- Also in 1966, Cyril Fagan (a siderealist) writing in his *Solunars* column of *American Astrology* magazine described the mathematics and interpretive methods that were to become so important in Astro*Carto*Graphy. Though he didn't include an actual map, he spoke of the case study of a young woman who could improve her life by moving to locations where *benefic* rather than *malefic* planets were angular.

The Stage is Set: Jim Lewis

In 1969 Jim Lewis comes into this narrative. His work was to become a key contribution to astromapping. That year Lewis joined the Personal Service department of *American Astrology*. There, he became acquainted with the mundane work of Bradley and Fagan, and especially their emphasis on the importance of angularity in charts and maps.[8]

The Big Leap

At this point, the big leap occurred in the development of astromapping techniques. Jim Lewis recognised and seized upon the potential of astromapping as the best tool to use in his consultations. He began offering natal A*C*G maps to his clients, arduously drawing each one by hand.

Along with this, and as a necessity of his consulting service, Lewis developed a complete interpretive system, using both the natures of planetary energies themselves and feedback from his clients on their relocating experiences.

Though Lewis was not the inventor of the mapping approach, he was certainly the first to develop a complete system of interpretation for it, transforming a natal chart into a world map of rising, setting culminating and anti-culminating lines. This had not been done before in natal astrology. It was a true first.

In my book, *Astrolocality Astrology*,[9] I note that his work brings space into our usual time-oriented astrological perspective, thereby better matching the modern view of existence as a space-time continuum. I also point out that his system strengthens astrology itself, emphatically showing us the connection of planetary energies and influences directly upon the earth, where we live and roam.

A*C*G Introduced to the Public

- In 1975, Lewis approached Gregg Howe of Astro Numeric Service (ANS)[10] "to automate the production of A*C*G maps". ANS successfully employed a breakthrough combination of hardware and software (especially for the computers of the time) to create plotted A*C*G maps. With this setup there was now a precise map, at an affordable price, ready to offer to the wider public.

- In 1976 Lewis published a 44-page booklet entitled *Astro*Carto*Graphy*. The booklet was "dedicated to the astrologers who pioneered understanding of planetary influence, and particularly to the late Donald A. Bradley". It introduced the Astro*Carto*Graphy name itself, suggested how to use the map, defined the planetary symbols used, gave the general meanings for each of the four angular positions, and most importantly, it contained interpretations for each planet at its angular positions. The booklet finished up with interpretive text for planetary crossings – which he later referred to as Parans.[11] The interpretative texts were written with such insight that even today, decades later, they remain among the best available. It was this package of map and booklet that Lewis offered to the astrological community.[12] It was, and still may be, the single most revolutionary development in modern astrology.

- In 1978, Jim Lewis received the Mark Edmund Jones award for his work on A*C*G.

- In 1979, at the suggestion of the late, eminent British astrologer, Charles Harvey, Lewis published his first *Sourcebook of Mundane Maps*. This was to become an annual publication for the year ahead, which included the coming year's four ingresses, New and Full Moons and solar and lunar eclipses. Harvey called it a "totally indispensable publication".[13]

The Stage is Set: Michael Erlewine
In the early 1970's another astrologer, Michael Erlewine, began to investigate the spatial side of things to see how it could be brought into astrological practice. Erlewine, who is also a musician, computer programmer and businessman, was influenced by the 'whole system' writing of Edward Johndro and by his mentor, Charles Jayne. Together, their view was that the three great co-ordinate systems comprising our natal charts, i.e., Ecliptic, Horizon and Equatorial, be studied separately as different reality views.[14] Jayne also felt the Horizon system was so important that it should be studied around its entire plane and not just at the points that intersect the Ecliptic to give us the ascendant and descendant of our natal charts.[15]

Initially spurred on by the desire to better understand house systems, Erlewine began working with sky maps. Laying out his natal horizon system on an equatorial star map allowed him to identify the chart's sensitive points (e.g., house cusps, ascendant, descendant, vertex etc., as well as the planets) etched in the sky. As the result of what he called "a grace", Erlewine came to see that the sky map was a reflection of the map of the earth – or vice versa. He observed "that heaven and earth are interchangeable, or in the last analysis one living entity – a single whole".

Further natal investigations utilizing the Horizon co-ordinate system with both the earth and sky perspectives led him to what he called the Local Space chart, "where every object in the universe, celestial and mundane, has an equal and valid position."[16] Erlewine's first steps in Local Space (LS) were similar to Lewis' in as much as they both had to rely on hand drawn maps. In an email to me, Erlewine writes, "I originally was doing Local Space lines on a hand-held calculator. It could take me an entire day to plot the basics of a LS map that can be now done in seconds. I don't think folks have any idea of what it was like to have none of these tools. [For example] I had to design and print my own heliocentric ephemeris in order to study that." Here's a timeline of some of these developments:

- 1975 – Michael Erlewine published *The Sun Is Shining: Helio Ephemeris 1653-2050*. This is astrology's first ephemeris from a Sun-centred perspective.

- 1977 – *Astrophysical Directions* was published. This book, co-authored by Michael and Margaret Erlewine, introduced astrologers to the major co-ordinate systems used in astrology. It is a detailed catalogue of deep space objects of all kinds, and it delineates the methods for astrologers to plot their natal charts on sky maps. To this day, it is the only work of its kind.

The First Astrology Programs for Personal Computers

- In 1977, Michael Erlewine released the first astrology programs for personal computers[17] (including one for LS). Thus, we can say that in 1977 a new era in astrology had begun. Initially loaded from cassette tapes (and later floppy disks), the programs performed accurate calculations more quickly than possible by hand. In 1978 Erlewine founded Matrix Software to sell his programs.[18] A few years later, in 1980, he was to publish *The Manual of Computer Programming for Astrologers*. This innovative work provided the routines necessary to calculate planetary positions. Some astrologers credit this work as having started them in the computer programming field.

Local Space Introduced to the Public

- 1977 – Local Space was introduced to the public when Michael Erlewine's article, 'The Astrology of Local Space', was first published in Charles Jayne's *Cosmology* bulletin #6. Soon afterwards Erlewine made calculator routines available for other astrologers to discover their own Local Space directions. It must be emphasised here that this work was about as complete a one-man project as could be. Inspired, and on what he called "a voyage of discovery", he had conceived the idea of what might be possible from the horizon perspective, then programmed the calculator routines to get the necessary information and finally, identified the significant indicators within it.

- 1978 – Erlewine published another article on Local Space in the *Circle Books Astrological Calendar*. In that article more was revealed about his own experiences and insights accompanying the development of Local Space.

Local Space: The Word Spreads Slowly

- The dissemination of Local Space into the astrological community was much slower than that of the technique of A*C*G. There was no specific LS booklet or finished product that could be offered directly to the public. Rather, it remained with a small group of enthused technical astrologers. Erlewine had discovered that the tracing of Local Space directional lines onto world maps uncannily revealed the actual routes individuals had taken on their travels. The technique gave individuals their significant *directions*, just as A*C*G yielded their significant *locations*. With Local Space, astrology now had the means to re-create the magical circles of the mystery traditions, uncovering one's personal *Feng Shui*,[19] directional patterns in the home, the community and around the entire globe.

Jim Lewis' Work Goes on: Cyclo*Carto*Graphy (C*C*G), 1982

- In 1982 Jim Lewis published a 55-page booklet on Cyclo*Carto*Graphy. C*C*G is the mapping of one's transits and progressions onto the A*C*G map.[20] In the booklet, each transiting or progressed planet is described in terms of its rate of motion across the map, the duration of its influence and, importantly, the nature of its effects. As in his first booklet, the writing is informative and unsurpassed to this day. Lewis presented the C*C*G planets to clients on a transparent overlay made to fit over their natal A*C*G map. This way the original factors of the A*C*G map could be visually compared with the temporary influences of transits and progressions. With this new development, Lewis brought time or, more aptly, 'an unfolding' into the static A*C*G map. Clients were encouraged to obtain overlays periodically to better follow the changing patterns and influences. C*C*G was another masterly development by Lewis and a first of its kind. We can say he completed the major part of the technical side of his work with the publication of this booklet.

- Through the rest of the 1980s, Jim Lewis wrote and lectured widely on A*C*G. The maps and booklets sold very well, bringing more and more recognition to the technique, ever widening the sphere of those who felt its impact. Meanwhile, at the Heart Centre in Big Rapids, Michigan, Michael Erlewine held summer gatherings on Local Space and other cosmological issues, which attracted a small but growing group of excellent astrologers.[21] As the tools of A*C*G and Local Space were being discovered by an increasing number of astrologers, Lewis, Erlewine and their colleagues continued refining their work.

1984

- In 1984, *Mundane Astrology*[22] was published in Great Britain. This book, written by historian Michael Baigent[23] and astrologers Nicholas Campion and Charles Harvey (1940-2000),[24] was the first of its kind, presenting a comprehensive survey of the mundane field. Of importance to the astromapping perspective are chapters

10 and 11, on Astro*Carto*Graphy and Earth Zodiacs, respectively, both written by Charles Harvey. Harvey establishes the tool of A*C*G as vital to mundane investigations. He states that A*C*G's ability to point out where a particular configuration may manifest or find expression "transforms" things such that mundane forecasts no longer need be "vague, unfocused and lacking any real conviction."[25] His chapter on Earth Zodiacs is well researched, and is a standard-setting survey of the field.

- Neil F. Michelson (1931-1990)[26] of Astro Computing Services,[27] began offering "Astrolocality Maps" in 1984. These geographic maps of angularity (similar to A*C*G maps) were notable for their inclusion of aspect lines (60, 90 or 120 degrees) from the Midheaven or Ascending lines.[28] Locality maps were now available to astrologers from two sources: Gregg Howe's Astro Numeric Service and Michelson's Astro Computing Services.[29]

1985

- In 1985, Lewis inaugurated a program to create a network of A*C*G practitioners. His idea was to offer training and certification to a core group who would be proficient in the application of his techniques.[30] To this purpose, with Jeff Jawer assisting, he held the first training and certification seminar in San Francisco that year.[31] A major part of the certification was to sit an exam. Some passed it, successfully graduating as the first certified A*C*G practitioners.[32] Maya del Mar (1928-2006) held Lewis' certification #1 from the seminar.

1986

- Lewis, this time with Ariel Guttman assisting, held the second A*C*G certification seminar in Laguna Beach California; more astrologers were certified and ideas for new projects came from this focused meeting of minds.[33]
- So too, the advance of technology was offering new opportunities. Data was being gathered that correlated planetary positions with

location. Blue Star, Matrix's DOS program (designed by Michael Erlewine with a small group of colleagues), Nova from Astrolabe (designed by the noted astrologer, Robert Hand) and other DOS astrology programs[34] were available to run on IBM's XT computer, allowing more individuals to do their own research with speed and accuracy.

1987

- In 1987 Jim Lewis completed the text for a computerised astrological report to be made available to the public. Customers could now purchase his map with the informative booklet and get his computerised interpretive text for three locations of choice. As with his previous writing, the text, to this day, remains outstanding for its insight into planetary effects and influences on Earth. Soon after, a version of his text was offered to the general public as a DOS program. It continues to be available today in Windows, as Matrix Software's 'Astro*Carto*Graphy Explained' report-writing program.[35]

1988-1989

- Many of the fruits of the activity of the 1980s seemed to burst upon the astrological landscape in 1988-9, with four significant events:

    1. The publication of *The Astro*Carto*Graphy Book of Maps*, by Jim Lewis and Arielle Guttman[36] was a milestone almost on a par with the publication of Jim's original material in 1976. The book was comprised of the charts, the corresponding A*C*G maps and interpretive text for 136 famous people. It clearly and definitely showed the correlation of planetary lines (location) with significant events in the subjects' lives and their personal history. With this book, those who had not heard Jim's lectures could see the power of A*C*G. In one swoop, the book showcased A*C*G for its modern and revolutionary approach, it showed our connections to cosmic rhythms in space as well as time, and it was impressive as evidence for the effectiveness of astrology itself. *The A*C*G Book*

of Maps set a standard in the superb presentation of its maps, the high quality of the writing, the care taken with the data[37] and its helpful appendices. It was truly an impact book. Guttman reports that it was a great sadness to Lewis that the book was never reprinted after the initial print run of about 3000 copies quickly sold out.[38]

2. *Hi Res Astro Maps.* In 1988 Michael Erlewine completed programming the first DOS mapping program, *Hi Res Astro Maps*,[39] offering it to the astrological public that year. This was quite a feat considering the technical limitations of the time. With it, users could display and print A*C*G and LS natal or event maps on their desktop computers. The program included C*C*G lines of transit and progression for user-selected dates, and, to top it off, Michael had incorporated his database of deep space objects and cosmic points (from his book, *Astrophysical Directions*) to plot on both Earth and sky maps. Technically, for its time, the program was a *tour de force*. Technical features aside, the availability of Hi Res Astro Maps to all astrologers represented a significant turning point in the history of the field – though its significance might not have been apparent right away. For the first time, astrologers could independently create their own maps – as many as they might want – to use for their projects and general research. Though Jim and Michael still led the way, exploration of the field was now open to all. An example of this was my own experience with the program. Within the first hour of receiving it, intuitively, I set out to see where on earth my Local Space lines of direction and A*C*G lines of location would intersect when mapped together. I was stunned to see how meaningful those places of crossing had been in my life! Soon afterwards, I named the intersections Destiny Points, or more technically, Bi-Parans (crossings from two systems). In 1989 I published this finding as part of an article entitled, 'Local Space Astrology'[40], where I first proposed the mixing of LS and A*C*G information on one map.

3. *Planets in Locality*,[41] Steve Cozzi's book on Local Space, was published in 1988. It was the first book offered to the public on the technique. Selling well, it took Michael Erlewine's system into

wider public awareness. Cozzi is well versed in the esoteric traditions of the world. Bringing this perspective into the book, he emphasised what could be seen as the system's magical or near magical properties. Cozzi showed how the LS chart could be used as a Feng Shui type tool to find preferred directions in one's home, community or city. Using the LS chart this way, one creates what he called a "Geomantic Compass". Also of interest, he illustrated how a city's "birth" or incorporation time could be turned into a LS map for itself, thereby pointing out the significance of neighbourhoods according to its own inherent planetary energies. The book also includes discussions of other systems that are not specific to Local Space, such as esoteric grid systems, a secret geometry of the pyramids and Jose Arguelles' Holonomic model of knowledge.[42]

4. The Geodetic World Map. Also in 1988, Chris McRae, published her book on Geodetics, *The Geodetic World Map*.[43] McRae describes herself as a curious person who tries "to probe the secrets of astrology". Her interest in correlating astrological signs with earth location and earth events was rewarded when she came across a reprint of Sepharial's little book, *The Geodetic Equivalent*.[44] Working with a calculator and drawing by hand, she created a world map for the system and then began to explore it for events of all types. She found meaningful applications in client relocation studies, Geodetic identities of nations, weather prediction, and global upheavals, especially for great disasters such as volcanic eruptions, earthquakes, fires, storms and the like.

Finally, in 1988, the technological advances of the time allowed her to computerise her Geodetic material. Using both Digicomp DR-70 and IBM XT computers, along with Michael Erlewine's Blue Star calculation program, she was able to create an accurate geodetic world map and thereby publish her work.

1990

- At the beginning of the last decade of the twentieth century, Charles Harvey teamed up with the British astrologer Michael Harding, to write a book on what they believed to be the most important contemporary advances in astrology. The book, *Working with Astrology*,[45] included a full description of A*C*G, as one of the three most important advances of that time – the other two were Harmonics and Midpoints.

1991

- Edith Hathaway's book, *Navigating by the Stars*, was published in 1991.[46] In the chapter entitled 'Where on Earth?' she presents A*C*G and then includes the A*C*G maps of many interesting cases. Jim Lewis liked this work. In a blurb on the first page, he wrote: "For those who have never attended one of my seminars, this book may be the next best thing; for those who have, Edith Hathaway has added depth and insight to standard A*C*G interpretation techniques, plus suggesting some new ones!"

- Also in 1991, Matrix Software added, *Quick*Maps* (a mapping module) to its DOS program, Blue Star. Quick*Maps was endorsed by Jim Lewis who allowed his trademarked name of A*C*G* to be used on the 'hi resolution' printed output.

1992

- In 1992, the astrological community honoured Lewis by awarding him the Regulus Prize[47] for his excellence in research and innovation. Jim also received the Matrix Pioneer Award for outstanding contributions in the area of marketing astrology to the general public.

- In 1992 the first full-featured Windows astrology programs became available. From the locality perspective, this was to be great news. The visual Windows environment was ideal for the display of maps and for quality printing. *Solar Fire* from Esoteric Technologies and *AstrolDeluxe for Windows* from Halloran Software hit the market first, followed in 1993, by Matrix software's *WinStar* (which included a full-featured mapping module) and then good products from other companies followed. Soon, Solar Fire (Solar Maps) and others joined Win*Star (Win*Maps), with innovative mapping modules integrated into their offerings. From this time on astrologers had the astromapping tools on their computers and therefore, at their fingertips. With Windows and fast computers, the technology had caught up and could now deliver high quality astromapping tools for use in a wide variety of astrological studies.

- Also in 1992, Robert Currey[48] made improvements in the 'official' A*C*G maps sold from his London-based business, Equinox.[49] The Nodal and Chiron lines were now added to the maps, as were coloured planetary lines and planetary glyphs.

1995

- *Lewis passes away.* On the 21st of February 1995, Jim Lewis died, his life cut short at age 54 by a brain tumour. The astrological community mourned his passing. Robert Currey summed it up well: "God, we astrologers were lucky to have a mind like his among us and by heaven, we will miss him."

- *CONTINUUM is founded.* As Lewis' life was slipping away, he arranged his affairs and dictated his last wishes to astrologer Angel Thompson. At his direction she became the sole trustee for all of his intellectual properties, a role she maintains to this day. After his passing, Thompson pondered how to best fulfil the promises Lewis had made to those he trained and tested. On the 1st of August 1995, she, along with Karen McCauley and a small group of friends, brainstormed ideas around the suggestion that a network should be created to maintain and support the A*C*G practitioners that Jim Lewis fostered. They came up with *CONTINUUM* as the name and thus, the organisation was born.[50] As a mission statement, *CONTINUUM* set out to: 1) transcribe Jim's 1993 training seminar, 2) create a curriculum to help those involved in independent study, 3) reconstruct Lewis' original certification test, 4) offer A*C*G proficiency testing and certification and, 5) maintain a list of certified practitioners on their website.

- *More on CONTINUUM.* Since that time in 1995, *CONTINUUM* has been a great success, supporting the field with donations, scholarships and grants. Its website has become the focal point for spatial astrology,[51] identifying the network of A*C*G practitioners, providing proficiency testing, certification and copyright protection. A full description of activities can be found on their website: http://continuumacg.net. Presently, *CONTINUUM* remains under the direction of Angel Thompson, with the administrative help of Karen McCauley, and the cyberspace talents of noted astrologer, Donna H. Cunningham,[52] who is the designer and web master of the current *CONTINUUM* website.

- Also in 1995, Esoteric Technologies of Australia[53] launched its stand-alone mapping program, Solar Maps. The program had animated C*C*G capability and it included Local Space and Geodetic features.

1997

- Dennis Flaherty's article entitled, 'Jyotish Locality', was published in the 1997 August-September issue of *The Mountain Astrologer*. Flaherty[54] showed how Vedic astrologers could use the locational techniques just as easily as Western practitioners. He also pointed out that various Vedic tools – such as preferred lines of angularity for each planet – could "enrich" Western interpretations.

- In 1997 *The Psychology of Astro*Carto*Graphy*[55] was published. Written by Kenneth Irving with Jim Lewis' notes, it is the definitive work of Lewis' approach, especially from the perspective of depth psychology. Erin Sullivan edited the work and, more importantly, was the active intermediary in it all: getting Jim to release his notes (as his health deteriorated), convincing the publisher to take the proposed book and encouraging Irving to take on the task of writing it all down, blending Lewis' material with his own.[56] The book ably explains the essence of A*C*G; it provides fundamental descriptions of planetary energies in relation to the earth and, it presents important historical and technical notes.

1998

- In 1998 (and 1999) Robert Hand and Arielle Guttman held professional astromapping seminars in Santa Fe, NM. At these seminars they applied the traditional astrology Hand had translated from Latin texts[57] to A*C*G and locational astrology in general.[58]

- Sasha Fenton's book *Astrology on the Move* was published in this year also.[59] Fenton is an experienced astrologer and best-selling UK author of popular books on subjects such as Sun sign astrology, tarot and palmistry. Here she turned her attention to locality and in doing so, brought it to a wider, non-astrological public. The book features her interpretations.

- In 1998, David Meadows' book, *Where in the World with Astro*Carto*Graphy*[60] was published. This is a big book. It is a detailed, technical analysis of almost every imaginable A*C*G & C*C*G technique. The book is notable for its presentation of A*C*G and C*C*G for Solar Returns. Using an A*C*G map for a Solar Return (SR) chart solves a few problems. One is that you don't have to worry about which house system to use, and, there is no longer the issue of whether to relocate a SR to the current location of the native, or to keep the birth location. Meadows comments that Jim Lewis did approve the use of A*C*G maps for Solar Returns, and that both he and Lewis used precession correction[61] in the calculation.

1999

- In 1999, Erin Sullivan published *Where In the World?*[62] Her book is comprised of the transcripts from two seminars given in London in 1997 at the Centre for Psychological Astrology. Part one of the book covers the essentials of A*C*G and part two relocation. With this book, Sullivan adds her knowledgeable voice to the literature of the field.

- In 1999, my book, *Astrolocality Astrology* was published.[63] I took on the project because I felt that a 'how to' textbook was needed for the techniques of A*C*G, Local Space and Geodetics. Furthermore, I proposed they be seen and utilised as one synergistic system of locality, each bringing their different perspectives to the same issue of the space around us. For A*C*G, I approached the development of the map from a sky perspective, with planetary energies "imprinting" the earth. For Local Space I gave detailed procedures for using LS charts and maps – along with A*C*G – to pinpoint significant Earth locations. For Geodetics, I added some new examples and proposed investigating something original, the *resonant location*, where the natal and Geodetic charts match one another. The appendices of *Astrolocality Astrology* included new A*C*G interpretations by Jeff Jawer, Local Space interpretations by Angel Thompson and myself, and an obituary of Jim Lewis by Robert Currey. Feedback has been encouraging. The book won the British Spica award in the year 2000, for the best astrology book of the previous year. And, I was very pleased when Michael Erlewine wrote in an email to me that I had "accurately presented the concepts and the techniques (of Local Space) in a clear, concise, and meaningful way."[64]

2002

- Jim Lewis' posthumous book, *Peter Pan in Midlife and the Midlife of America: A Personal and Collective Memoir*, was edited and offered by Erin Sullivan.[65] This material was very close to Lewis' heart, and he was disappointed not to see it published in his lifetime. The book is philosophical and analytical and not directly related to locality.

2004

- In 2004, Robert Currey added Chiron interpretations[66] to the A*C*G booklet he offers from Equinox in London.[67] This booklet is only available with the authorised A*C*G maps he provides, and not sold separately. In spite of this, in terms of numbers, it can be considered a best seller, on a par with any of the popular Sun-sign books.

2006

- In 2006, Matrix Software launched its stand-alone mapping program, Horizons.[68] Along with many features it has the first published interpretative Local Space text written by Michael Erlewine. John Townley wrote the A*C*G interpretive text, bringing his experienced voice to the field.

2007

- As I write this, I hope this work, *From Here to There*, will be a significant addition to the locality field. For a starter it includes this first complete history of all the techniques in one integrated timeline. It then offers the reader a variety of astromapping examples from a group of experienced astrologers. This should be both an inspiration and guide to others for utilising the techniques.

What's Coming Next for Astromapping?

- Computer advances should allow us to work with three-dimensional images, and offer ever more clarity, topographical accuracy, speed and beauty of presentation.
- We should be able to merge astromapping lines with the detailed maps of Google Earth. We would then be able to identify neighbourhoods, city streets, or even a specific house for our relocation studies.
- We can expect the development of effective mapping procedures for handling the relocation of couples and whole families.[69]
- All mapping programs should have an inbuilt filing system that will save maps – as well as charts and any notes – storing them under a person's or project name. This would be the workbook approach in saving maps for retrieval and future use.
- Perhaps it will be possible to create a database that includes locality interpretations written by different astrologers. I realise there are copyright issues here but let's not have this block our thinking about the possibility. Some might like to see Lewis' interpretations as he first wrote them, next to those with his depth psychology slant, next to those of others.[70] The same could be said for interpretations now available for Local Space from Erlewine and

others too. We all hold pieces of the puzzle of understanding and though some may hold larger pieces, all can help in fitting things together. As Goethe said, "Only everyone can know the truth".[71]

- The arrival of a developed "Internet2",[72] with its advanced networking and research capabilities could play a role in locality research one day that can only begin to be imagined right now. For example, a research program could be created that would list and compare information from maps stored at different information nodes around the globe. With such a program we should be able to investigate our geographical patterns more closely and see our earth connections in a new light.

- As good as our mapping tools become, perhaps one day better maps will no longer be the real purpose of things. Rather, we may discover that we ourselves are being changed by a new attention to Mother Earth, that they bring to us. Though it is said, "the map is not the territory",[73] perhaps through changed consciousness, the maps can lead us to new and magical connections with it.

NOTES

1. For an account of the history of earth zodiacs see Appendix 9, *The Book of World Horoscopes*, by Nicholas Campion, The Wessex Astrologer, 2004.
2. ibid page 455.
3. For a complete narrative of the developments leading to A*C*G, see Ken Irving's website: http://www.planetlines.com/acgbook/intro.htm and/ or his book, co-authored by Jim Lewis, *The Psychology of Astro*Carto*Graphy*, Arkana, 1997.
4. Jayne (1911-1985) was a brilliant technical astrologer.
5. Astrologer Bill Meridian attributes the first published eclipse-path maps to Jayne.
6. In the Sidereal Zodiac the twelve signs are based upon the constellations of fixed stars. Though usually only used by Eastern astrologers, Bradley and Firebrace employed it in their calculations, rather than the Western Tropical system, which starts at the vernal point.
7. Mundane: From the Latin *mundus* meaning worldly or profane. In astrology it refers to studies of world, regional or national events, including large groups of people.

8. Lewis rejected their siderealist approach for his own astrological work, but he pointed out that A*C*G worked in both the Tropical and Sidereal systems.
9. The Wessex Astrologer Ltd, 1999, UK.
10. See Gregg Howe's website for Astro Numeric Service, http://www.astronumerics.com/index.html

    Prior to 1973, many astrologers used the ANS computational services of Gregg's father, Horace A. Howe, who, among other accomplishments, was a noted physicist and computer programmer. In an email to me, Gregg writes: "I came to ANS in 1973 when my father (Horace A. Howe) died in a vehicle accident. Jim Lewis did not approach ANS to do his work until two years later. At first, Jim just wanted planetary positions, which he would then plug into his own program to produce the maps. Then he asked us to make a map-making program when his programmer left him taking the program too! It took us (my staff programmer and myself) only about two weeks to build the program which is, essentially, the same as that used today. Don't ask me how we did things so quickly in those days... youthful energy, I guess!" In another email, Howe wrote to me about the technical side of this event: "When Jim Lewis came to Astro Numeric Service in 1975 to automate the production of ACG maps, we had just converted our entire calculation service from an IBM 360 (FORTRAN) to a Data General Mini-computer with all of 16K bytes of memory! The computer language was FORTH, which I had learned while working at Kitt Peak Observatory in Arizona. FORTH went on to become a fairly successful language in imbedded, laboratory automation, particularly in scientific instrumentation. And yes, the maps were actually drawn with a Tektronix desktop pen plotter for many years".
11. According to Rob Hand, the word 'Paran' was coined by Cyril Fagan as a shortening of 'paranatellon', a Greek word meaning 'co-transit'. The term first appeared in *American Astrology* magazine.
12. I believe every serious student of A*C*G should obtain the booklet which is filled with Lewis' wisdom. This package of A*C*G map and booklet is still offered today at three main locations:
    - In North America, Gregg Howe, Astro Numeric Service, Oregon, http://www.astronumerics.com
    - In the French and German languages, Claude Weiss, Astrodata AG, Switzerland, http://www.astrodata.com
    - In the UK – and the rest of the world – Robert Currey, Equinox, London, http://www.equinoxastrology.com
13. *Mundane Astrology* by Baigent, Campion and Harvey, 1984, Aquarian Press, UK. Page 282.

14. Johndro probably was the first modern astrologer to study the differences between the Ecliptic and Equatorial systems. Jayne emphasised the importance of the Horizon system and suggested it be added to any whole system investigations.
15. Erlewine writes: "The actual distinctions between these different systems of coordinates are lost to most of us, and they are jumbled together to form some kind of Zodiac pie." See *Astrolocality Astrology*, Appendix Four, 'Two Articles By Michael Erlewine', page 203.
16. Ibid, page 213.
17. The first hardwired, pre-programmed natal chart computer was introduced at the 1976 AFA Astrological convention.
18. Along with Microsoft these are the two oldest software companies on the Internet still in existence.
19. Feng Shui idiomatically means, 'perfect placement'.
20. A Cyclo*Carto*Graphy map always refers back to an original, fixed-line A*C*G map. The C*C*G map displays the moving, changing positions of transiting, progressed, and/or directed angular planetary lines at any given time. Jim Lewis wrote: "Astrology is comprised of two major dimensions – time and space, and it is the purpose of Cyclo*Carto*Graphy to add to the information about locations given in the Astro*Carto*Graphy map the vital information about when in time the potentials might be expected to manifest." (From the booklet that accompanies C*C*G overlays, 1982, Chapter 1)
21. Participants included: Dane Rudhyar, Michel Gauquelin, Charles Harvey, Charles Jayne, Robert Hand, Theodor Landschiedt, Noel Tyl, Roger Elliot, Geoffrey Dean, John Townley, Robert Schmidt, and scores of others.
22. *Mundane Astrology*, by M. Baigent, N. Campion and C.Harvey, 1984, Aquarian Press, Great Britain.
23. Michael Baigent is the author of many historical books, one of which is *The Holy Blood and the Holy Grail* (with Henry Lincoln and Richard Leigh), Penguin, NY.
24. Both Campion and Harvey are past presidents of the British Astrological Association.
25. *Mundane Astrology*, page 275, Chapter 10.
26. Neil Michelson's wife, Maria Simms, writes in an email: "Neil was born May 11, 1931, 5:34am CST, Chicago, IL. He died on May 15, 1990, at approximately 4:00am in San Diego."
27. See: http://www.astrocom.com for their current products. Maria Simms writes in an email:
"The original birth data for ACS is March 20, 1973, 1:30pm EST, White Plaines, NY." She then goes on to point out that Neil waited in line to register his business, noting the time his papers were handed over and stamped. It turned out that the moment was exactly at the Spring Equinox, so the Astro Computing Services business chart has Sun at 0 Aries 00.

28. Jim Lewis rejected the addition of aspect lines to his A*C*G maps. Gregg Howe writes: "He (Lewis) saw their inclusion as a heresy because they violated his emphasis on strictly angular relationships to a new location." Others have pointed out that aspects should be calculated by Ecliptic ascension and not Equatorial degrees. My own experience is that aspect lines, especially squares, do 'work', showing locations of some tension for the native. Some aspect lines are always there within planets themselves. In my chart, for example, my natal Sun squares Mars. Wherever I have a Sun line it will always carry the tension of a square from Mars energy, and vice versa. In an email, Gregg Howe (of ANS) writes positively of his competitor's (ACS) locality map: "If only Jim lived now, he could appreciate ACS for their old-fashioned business ethics. They used a different name for the product, they produced their own map, and they computed the map differently."

29. In an email to me, Gregg Howe adds a fascinating historical footnote about the rivalry of his father, Horace Gregg, founder of ANS, and Michelson (ACS). He writes: "In the early 70s I used to talk to my father about his budding business. He said he had several small competitors. But the only one he was concerned about was an IBM programmer in New York, whom he said "really knew what he was doing." This was, of course, Neil Michelson. During the mid-70s ACS (Michelson's service) and ANS had a mild "arms race" of astrological computations. Each wanted to make sure they had the most extensive set of services for every kind of astrological practice. Astrologers would come to either company with an original way of computing charts and, particularly if they had written a book, we would be eager to provide calculations in just the manner they wanted. I would say that the rivalry between ANS and ACS was great for astrology, and helped expand the market enormously. All this programming was expensive, of course, so when ANS became heavily involved with Astro*Carto*Graphy, we took a different tactic. To appeal to a broader, less technical audience, we felt it was important not to have dozens of different ways to compute the horoscope. So instead we started focusing on some basic, core calculations that most of our professional clients used, and that our new customers, largely attracted to astrology through Astro*Carto*Graphy, could easily grasp. This meant backing away from asteroids, Uranian planets, harmonics, and a host of other techniques, which, at the time seemed too technical to have broad appeal."

30. A friend of Lewis comments: "Jim did not like to do much personal counselling with A*C*G and this was partly why he set up seminars to train interpreters."

31. The 1985 seminar was facilitated by Jim Lewis and Jeff Jawer. Jawer can be reached at: jjawer@stariq.com.

32. Arielle Guttman was in the first group to be certified. In an email, she writes: "In 1985 I received an invitation to the very first Certification

Seminar in A*C*G given by Jim in San Francisco. I signed up immediately, took the exam and became certified (that exam was not easy!) I hold Certificate of Proficiency #9 given to me by Jim in March 1985."
33. One such idea took form three years later as *The ACG Book of Maps*.
34. See Wikipedia, Astrology and Computers: http://en.wikipedia.org/wiki/Astrology_and_computers
35. Matrix Software, Big Rapids, Michigan. http:// www. astrologysoftware.com
36. *The Astro*Carto*Graphy Book of Maps: How 136 Famous People Found Their Place*, by J Lewis and Arielle Guttman, 1989, Llewellyn Publications, Minnesota, USA.
37. All data sets were categorised by what was called, at that time, 'The Rodden Code of Accuracy'.
38. The book was later translated into German (Astro Data 1990) and French (Editions du Rocher, Jean-Paul Bertrand, ed., 1994). It is the only astrological locality book translated into two other languages to date.
39. Matrix Software, Big Rapids, MI, USA.
40. *The British Astrological Journal*, November/December 1989, Vol. XXXI No.6.
41. *Planets in Locality*, by Steve Cozzi, Llewellyn Publications, 1988, St Paul, MN, USA. Later reprinted in 1997, American Federation of Astrologers, Inc., Tempe, AZ.
42. See appendix B of *Planets in Locality*.
43. *The Geodetic World Map*, by Chris McRae, 1988, American Federation of Astrologers, Inc., Tempe, AZ, USA.
44. First published c.1924, W. Foulsham, UK. Reprinted by The American Federation of Astrologers in 1972. Sepharial was Dr Walter Gorn-Old, (1864-1929).
45. *Working with Astrology*, by Harding and Harvey, Arkana, 1990, London.
46. *Navigating by the Stars*, by Edith Hathaway, 1991, Llewellyn Publications, MN, USA.
47. United Astrology Conference, Washington, DC.
48. http://www.equinoxastrology.com/RobertCurrey.htm
49. http://www.astrocartography.co.uk/
50. In addition to Angel Thompson, the founding group included: Karen McCauley, Lawrence Walters, Arielle Guttman, Madalyn Hillis, Donna Cunningham, Ken Irving, Erin Sullivan and Gregg Howe.
51. Thompson is well known for her writing and lecturing on Local Space and her support for spatial astrology.
52. For information on Donna Cunningham and her work, see: http://www.moonmavenpublications.com/bio.html
53. http://www.esotech.com.au/products/solarmaps.html

54. See the website for his organisation, Northwest Institute of Vedic Sciences. http://www.vedicsciences.com/
55. *The Psychology of Astro*Carto*Graphy*, by Jim Lewis and Kenneth Irving, 1997, Arkana, London.
56. In the 'Author's Preface', Irving writes: "We would not even have had a book now if it had not been for Erin Sullivan..."
57. Robert Hand's organization is called AHRAT, Archive for the Retrieval of Historical Astrological Texts. See his website: http://www.robhand.com/
58. In an email to me, Hand writes: "The main thing we explored that might have been a little different from your point of view was the effect of essential and accidental dignities upon planets in locality analysis. There is a tendency to regard benefics as always good in locality and malefics as bad, but the dignities do appear to make a difference... if one does case studies involving people who did well or badly in places where one might have expected the opposite, that would be a way of looking for the effect."
59. *Astrology on the Move*, by Sasha Fenton, 1998, Zambezi Publishing, Brentford, UK.
60. *Where in the World with Astro*Carto*Graphy*, by David Meadows, 1998, AFA, Tempe, AZ, USA.
61. For a good explanation of precession correction, see *Planets in Transit*, by Robert Hand, 1976, Whitford Press, PA, USA, pages 29-31.
62. *Where in the World?*, by Erin Sullivan, 1999, The Centre for Psychological Astrology Press, London.
63. *Astrolocality Astrology*, by Martin Davis, The Wessex Astrologer Ltd., 1999, Bournemouth, UK.
64. "As the originator of the Local Space technique, so valuable to me in understanding myself and my personal place in this world, I had always hoped that some writer would take the time to document this most useful and wonderful astrological technique. I had to wait some 25 years for a book to accurately present the concepts and the techniques in a clear, concise, and meaningful way. I want to thank Martin Davis for making this possible. Good job! – Michael Erlewine"
65. To order the book see: www.ErinSullivan.com
66. Currey comments that living on Chiron lines is best handled by following an impulse to become whole. By this, he means that Chiron will reveal and test inner contradictions, in ourselves and in others. Where an individual is fragmented into separate sub-personalities, pressure and conflict result. The additional force on these natural fault lines in our psyche leads to stress or emotional or physical wounding and eventually illness. The solution lies in synthesising these sub-personalities into one healthy, centred whole. Thus, locations on Chiron lines provide an opportunity to

become conscious of our inner fragmentation. With this understanding we can enter into a process of healing both physically and psychologically, through the experiences and encounters depending on the lines. This process may involve healing others, an adjustment of life-style and diet and a heightened attunement to nature, natural phenomena and the environment.

67. http://www.equinoxastrology.com/
68. www.astrologysoftware.com
69. Gregg Howe of ANS writes in an email: "Here is a topic that is probably the #1 issue among our customers: How do you use Astro*Carto*Graphy for relationships? We need a lot more work from a theoretical point of view in that area. Jim worked on several techniques: composite maps, relationship maps (Davison), several types of overlays (lines of two charts on one map), but he never found anything that he felt worked well in analyzing how a couple or family would do in a new location."
70. The works of Jeff Jawer, John Townley and Stephanie Johnson come to mind.
71. Johann Wolfgang von Goethe, 1749-1832.
72. http://www.internet2.edu
73. Coined by Alfred Korzybski.

2

The Astro*Carto*Graphy Book of Maps[1]
Jim Lewis and Arielle Guttman

This book, subtitled 'The Astrology of Relocation and How 136 Famous People Found Their Place', was a major step in the acceptance of A*C*G as the mainstream technique it is today. Published in 1989, the 136 biographies demonstrated that a revolutionary development had emerged in modern astrology. The biographies were of people from all walks of life. Each consisted of a birth chart, the corresponding A*C*G map, and a historical and/or personality profile. The book was written by a committee of two: Jim Lewis and Arielle Guttman. Lewis of course, had developed the technique itself and had a mountain of files on the personalities. Guttman supplied the research and organisation to help bring it all together. She writes of this time:

> "Jim Lewis and I met at an astrological conference in southern California in the early 1980s, say about 1981, I think. I loved his talk and his product and began ordering the maps from him for my clients immediately. A few years passed and I continued to see him at conferences and promote him in southern California where I lived at the time (San Diego). In 1985 I received an invitation to the very first Certification Seminar in A*C*G given by Jim in San Francisco. I signed up immediately, took the exam and became certified (that exam was not easy!) I hold Certificate of Proficiency #9 given to me by Jim in March 1985. The second certification seminar was held in Laguna Beach, California in 1986, which I helped Jim organize and co-teach. After that seminar, he said to me, 'You know as much as anyone else in the world about A*C*G besides myself and one other person.' I was thrilled. I never asked him who the other person was. Jim was always being hounded by seminar attendees for a book. At that time I coaxed him into doing something. Jim was so busy running his

business, lecturing and travelling, that he just never seemed to have time to write as much as he would have liked to. Nevertheless, he succumbed to the pressure and invited me to his office/penthouse apartment in the Haight Ashbury district of San Francisco for the purpose of sorting through hundreds of maps in his research files. Those got pared down to the 135 or so that we used in *The A*C*G Book of Maps*. I spent hundreds of hours in libraries, researching biographies of the people we used. I then jotted down notes to go along with the maps, typed them up and sent them to Jim for his editorial work. Thus was born *The A*C*G Book of Maps,* published by Llewellyn in 1989. About 3,000 copies were initially printed. It sold out in two or three years and was never re-printed which greatly saddened Jim in the years before his passing."

For those readers who are relatively new to astrology, it is valuable to recall how it was before the advent of A*C*G. In the introduction of *The A*C*G Book of Maps,* Lewis and Guttman quote from a client's letter: "Under Saturn's influence in Colorado, I worked very hard on a ranch for low pay and spent my spare time rock climbing". They then comment:

"Prior to 1976, few astrologers would have been able to make much sense out of this statement. But since then, astrology has been augmented by a new technique, which has more to do with *where* than *when*. Saturn used to be found only in the sky as a malefic, wizened killjoy, spending two and a half years making natives of any one astrological sign miserable as he 'afflicted' them. How did he get to Colorado?"

Lewis and Guttman go on to answer this, stating that A*C*G, "enables a person to determine which parts of the natal chart potential will be accented, highlighted, or brought into consciousness in a new location."

In doing her research, Guttman states that one of her favourites was the biography of Jacqueline Onassis. As in the book for each personality, we will present her birth chart, A*C*G map and profile. Figure 1 is Jacqueline's birth chart.[2] Figure 2 is her equivalent A*C*G map. Note how, with A*C*G, her localised birth chart becomes a world map, with much of her life story etched upon it! Along with displaying her chart and map, Lewis and Guttman write:

> "With natal Neptune directly overhead at birth, Jacqueline Bouvier has embodied several archetypes and acted out collective fantasies on a national stage. The public's curiosity about her intensified the more she tried to shroud herself in an aura of mystery. While married to her first husband, President John F. Kennedy, the public was able to project onto her the Arthurian fantasy of Camelot. The Kennedy's seemed to represent a new era in American politics, bringing youth, style and glamour into a heretofore stuffy White House. The act had a very short run, however, and her next role was that of *mater dolorosa*, the wounded, but glamorous widow.

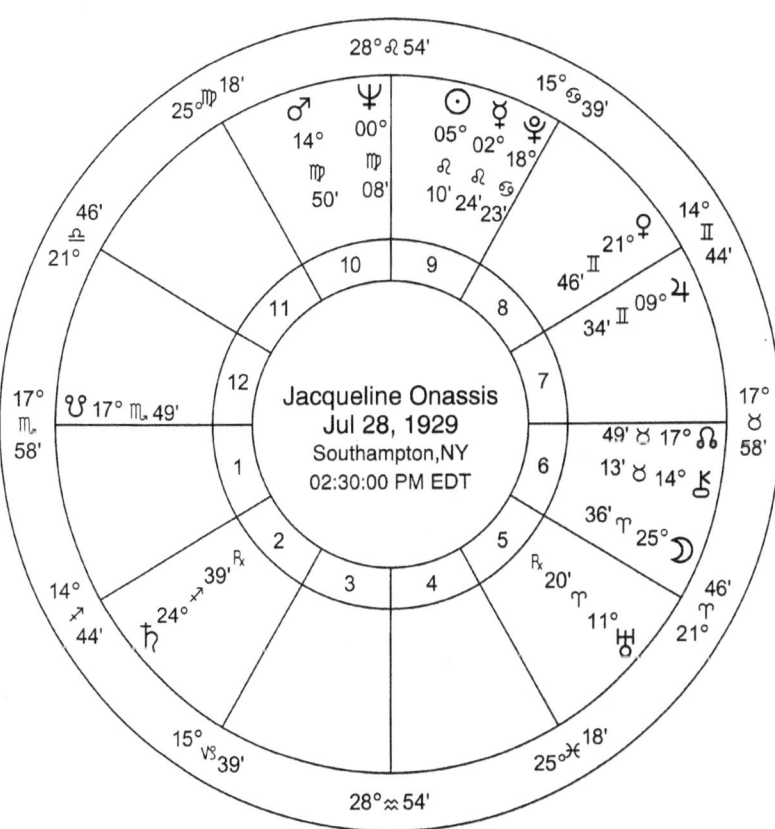

Figure 1 – Jacqueline Onassis birth chart

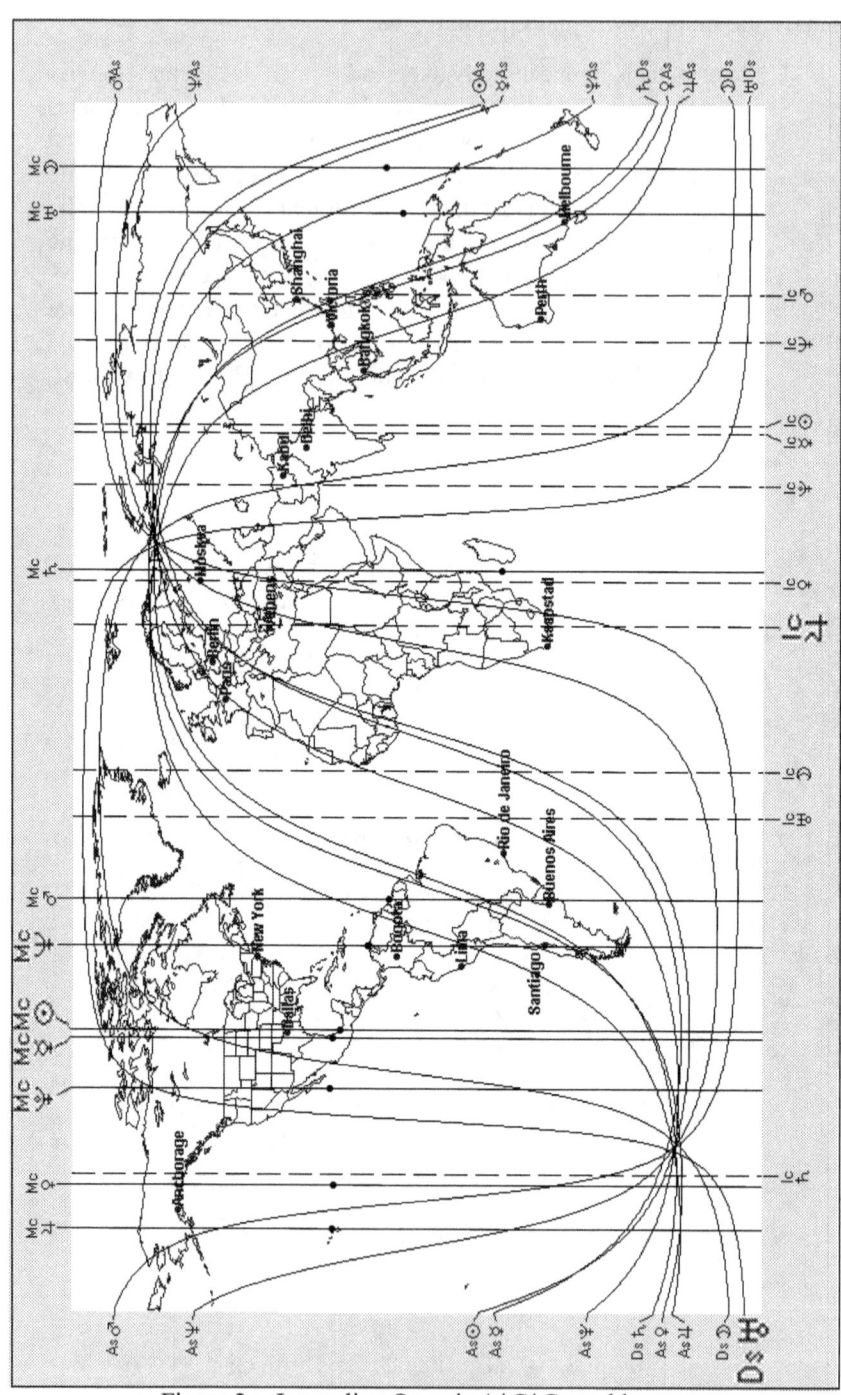

Figure 2 – Jacqueline Onassis A*C*G world map

From what has since been revealed about her relationship to JFK (her NE-MH goes exactly through his birthplace), the events in Dallas (the SU-MH and ME-MH) may have been a self-realization, freeing her from a rigid role unsuited to her true self. It did not, however, free her from publicity maniacs. The press pursued her as mercilessly as any Hollywood celebrity, and even running off to her sister in Europe where the SU and ME are again angular on the DSC did not help. Los Angeles, where JFK reputedly had extramarital affairs, is identified by UR-DSC and PL-MH on her map.

Meanwhile, over in the Mediterranean several Greek Isles were not only home to Greek shipping tycoon Aristotle Onassis, her second husband, but also Jacqueline's JU on the IC. NE-DSC crosses JU-IC nearby, and these two planets of good fortune and surrender of ego provided her with a secure financial future in an isolated and probably confining milieu.

After Onassis' death, Jacqueline returned to New York as a publishing executive (NE-MH) where it can be presumed she still deals with collective fantasies."[3]

© Arielle Guttman, material from her article, 1989.

The above was written by Lewis and Guttman in 1988. Since then, we can add that Jacqueline was diagnosed with lymphoma cancer in January 1994, and began chemotherapy. The end came quickly for her, as she died some four months later, in May of that year. She was buried at Arlington cemetery next to John F. Kennedy.

Arielle Guttman began her formal astrology studies in 1974 in San Diego, California. In 1980 she founded Astro Originals, a consulting firm utilizing astrological teaching tools. Based in Santa Fe since 1986, her work primarily focuses on private one-to-one client sessions, group seminars and writing books on astrological subjects.[4] Conversant in the many fields of astrology, her specialty areas are listed on the Astro originals pages.[5]

Guttman is well known for her work with relocation techniques, both as a teacher and active practitioner. She has written about Astro*Carto*Graphy, Parans, Local Space, and Geodetics, used individually or in combination to obtain a better understanding of a situation.

Guttman offers seminars, testing and certification in relocation techniques. She is currently teaching a correspondence course through Astro Originals, which includes Mythic astrology, Relocation astrology, Geodetics, relationship compatibility and transits/progressions. She also offers local classes in the Santa Fe area. For further information or personal consultations, contact her at:

Arielle Guttman
P.O.Box 31116
SantaFe, NM 87594
USA
001 (505) 984 8330
sophiasantafe@earthlink.net

NOTES

1. Llewellyn Publications, 1989, MN, USA.
2. The birth time used, of 2:30pm, is still widely preferred today. Quoting from AstroDatabank, it has an "A" rating of "moderate confidence". The source is Frances McEvoy, quoted from Jacqueline's friends and not released until after her death. Note that the Midheaven degree of her birth chart is 28 degrees, 54 minutes of Virgo. This within just a degree orb of the fixed star Regulus, often called the Royal star and the Lion's Heart. Properties attributed to Regulus include nobility, ambition and status. This effect holds true for Jacqueline as she was often referred to as "America's Princess" and, when married to JFK, she was called "Queen of Camelot".
3. Also on her NE MH line, in approximately 1977, she began a long term, "discreet" relationship with financier Maurice Tempelsman. They lived together in her opulent apartment overlooking Central Park.
4. For information on Guttman's books, see:
http://www.sophiasantafe.org/arielleguttman.html
5. http://www.sophiasantafe.org/astrooriginals.html

3

The Uses of Astromapping in Astrology
Martin Davis

In the previous chapter, we have seen how Jim Lewis and Arielle Guttman got everything moving in 1988-9 with their groundbreaking work, The Astro*Carto*Graphy Book of Maps. *Here, in Chapter 3, I have reprinted excerpts from my article in The Mountain Astrologer magazine,[1] adding some new material as well. This article takes us forward to the present, showing what we can do with the locality tools currently available on our home computers.*

When I include astromapping techniques in my studies, I find that they are useful for various types of investigations:

Relocation
This is the most obvious and perhaps the most popular use of Astrolocality today. A*C*G[2] maps display simultaneously where every planet would be angular over the Earth and on or near an angle of a corresponding relocated chart.[3] Angularity is important because it shows where on Earth the energies are most likely to manifest as events. In some instances, Local Space (LS)[4] direction, when combined with A*C*G location, makes our stories even more meaningful. Though LS is less well known than A*C*G, I will include LS information in the examples that follow, to illustrate its usefulness.

Lindbergh Flies to Paris
Let's first tell the story of pioneering aviator Charles A. Lindbergh 'relocating' to Paris; this can help us to better understand what happened to him there. Lindbergh captured the imagination and admiration of the Western world when he took off from Roosevelt Field, New York on

May 20, 1927 and flew solo nonstop across the Atlantic for 33 hours and 29 minutes, reaching Le Bourget airport, near Paris, the next day. This event was considered a milestone for human courage as well as aviation at that time.

There were no maps at all for an Atlantic crossing, so Lindbergh had to seek weather and directional information from fishermen who worked off the Newfoundland coast. Even more astounding was that no one knew the exact location of his destination, Le Bourget airport! He was advised to search north of Paris and not to worry, as the airport would be well lighted. In fact, it wasn't. Airport authorities had turned off most of the lights so that the crowd could catch sight of his approaching aircraft, *The Spirit of St. Louis.* As we know, he managed to locate the airport and landed to great acclaim. Lindbergh then became an instant celebrity; tumultuous and triumphant parades were given in his honour

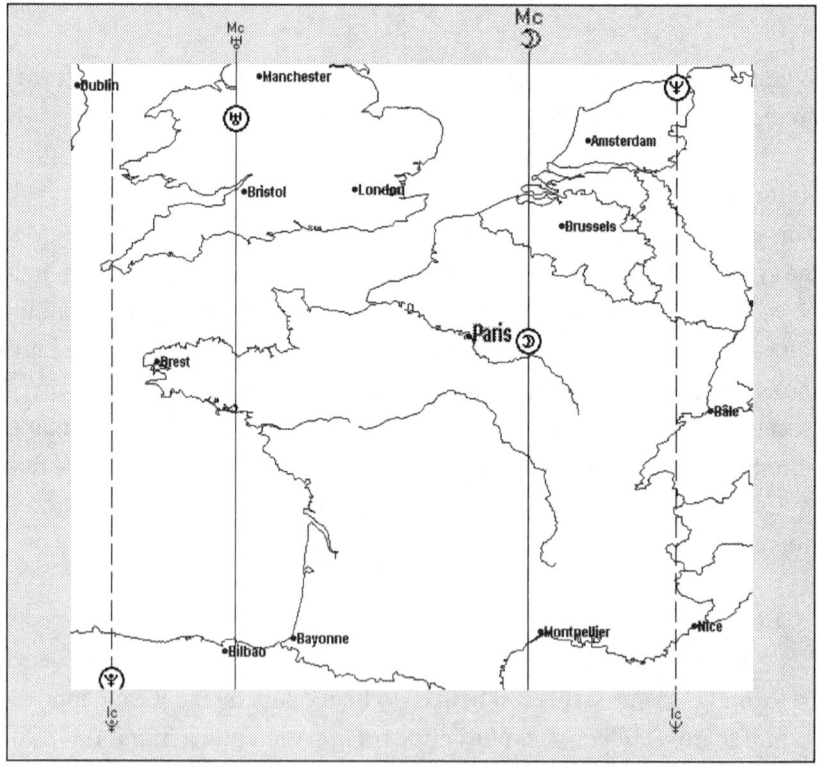

Figure 1 – Lindbergh A*C*G map, European detail

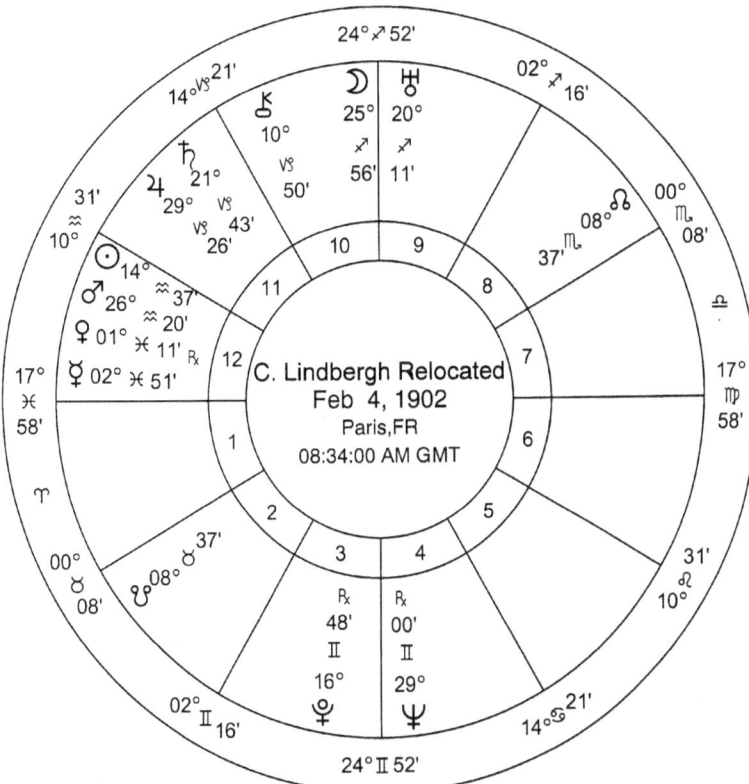

Figure 2 – Lindbergh, chart relocated to Paris

in Paris, London, and especially in New York, where he received a hero's welcome with a ticker-tape parade.[5] This was the pinnacle of his public life, however, for his later years were marred by personal tragedy and his unpopular political views.

Figure 1 is the European detail of Lindbergh's A*C*G map. This will help us to see how the location of Paris played out in the story of his historic flight. Paris is 58 miles west of his Moon-MC line. This means that the Moon will be near the Midheaven of his relocated chart there, and in the 10th house (see Figure 2), so our story includes the possibility for him to become a focus of public attention at that location. This lunar quality may also explain the emotional but ultimately ephemeral nature of the adoration that he received. John Townley[6] writes of an A*C*G Moon-MC location, "This may not be the best place for a quiet getaway, even if its location is fairly out of the way, as you'll tend to become the

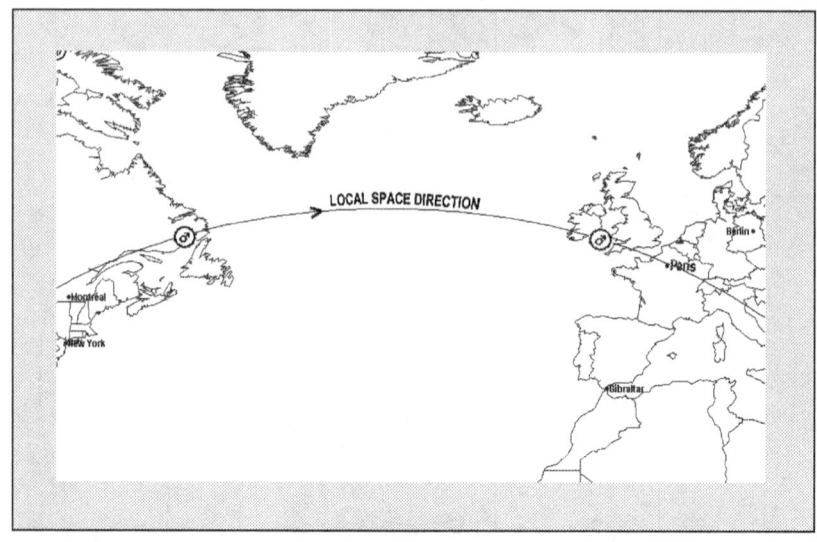

Figure 3 – Lindbergh Local Space (LS) map, Atlantic/European detail

talk of the town and folks will seek you out even when you'd just as soon they didn't …Obscurity probably isn't an option, but fame may well be."

Figure 3 is the Atlantic/European detail of Lindbergh's natal Local Space map. What we discover here is quite startling. His LS Mars line runs across the eastern Atlantic, over southern England, and right on to Paris, almost perfectly duplicating the actual flight path of his bold, pioneering journey! Might it be a surprise that his journey was planned on the path and in the direction that would give him the very Martian qualities he would need to complete it? This is, in fact, a substantiation of one of the principles that Erlewine identified when he developed Local Space: *We are drawn towards our planetary Local Space lines (directions) to fulfil the needs that require those specific energies.* Regarding one's LS Mars direction, Erlewine writes, "The Mars line and direction have to do with drive and ambition, getting things pumped up and going, and then taking action of all kinds. It is Mars and ambition that drives your career, propelling you along whatever life path you may be on. Mars places are connected to action and action events, not just sports and exercise, but adventure and adventuring of all kinds – what motivates you…"[7]

Let's now go back to the Lindbergh saga, using this astrological information to further develop and deepen our story with the help of a bi-

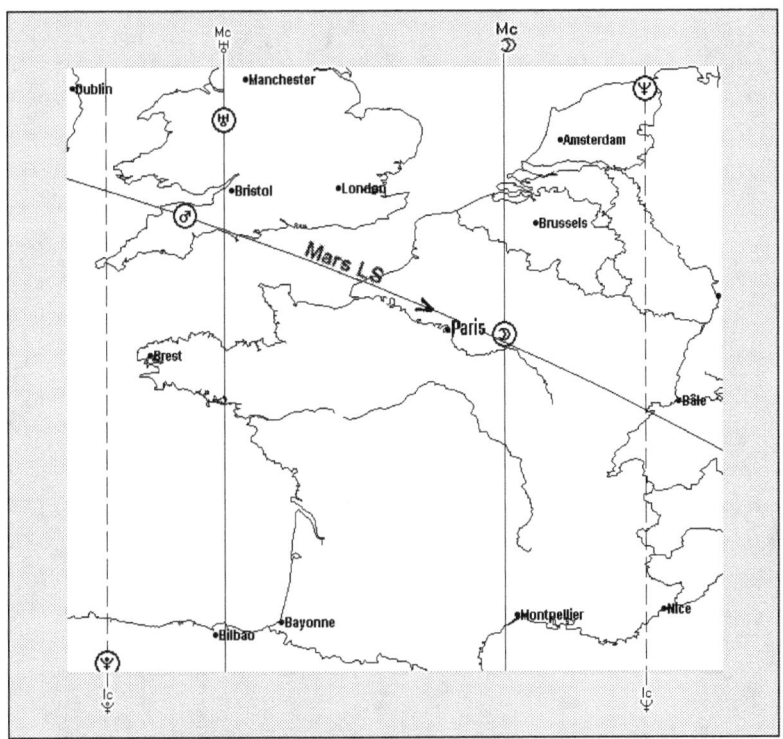

Figure 4 – Lindbergh A*C*G and LS lines shown together

paran (destiny crossing).[8] In Figure 4 we have both Lindbergh's A*C*G and LS lines shown together. The LS direction of Mars and the A*C*G location of the Moon-MC energy merge about 62 miles from Paris, France. This, therefore, is Lindbergh's LS Mars and Moon-MC bi-paran, or destiny crossing! His pioneering Mars directional line brought him (10th-house, lunar) fame at the latitude and longitude of the lines' crossing, near Paris.

Martin Goes to the Olympics

Our own experiences are, naturally, very poignant for us. They form the narratives we construct as our history, our personal life stories. One such story for me is about my 'relocation' to Munich, Germany. In late August 1972, I participated in the Olympic Games in Munich as a member of the United States foil fencing team. I had been reasonably successful in my sport, having participated in world championships and the 1963 Pan

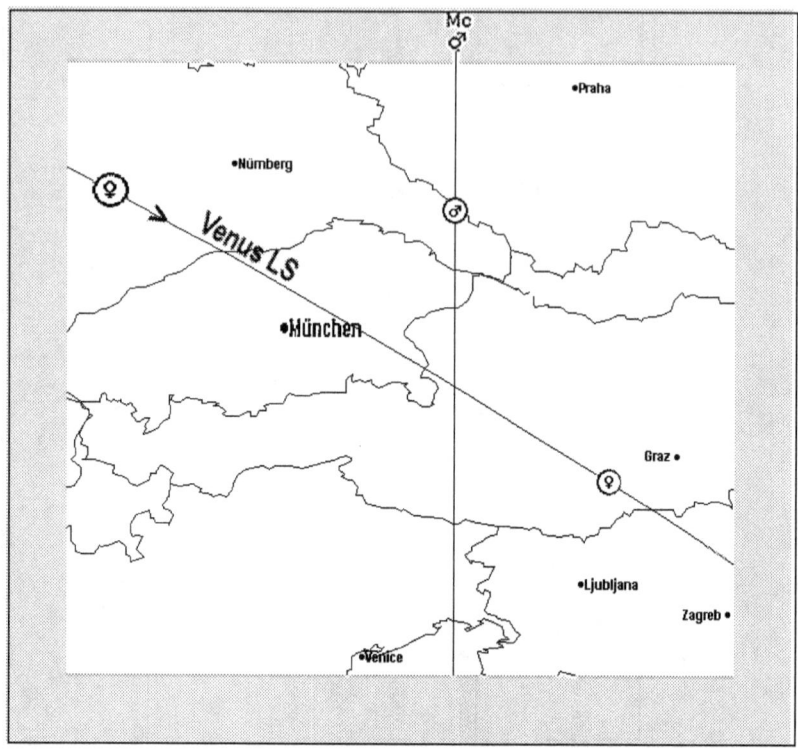

Figure 5 – M.Davis A*C*G and LS lines, European detail

American games, but I had always missed selection to Olympic teams: I fell just short as a non-participating first alternate for the Games in 1960, '64, and '68. In 1972, however, at the ripe old age of 35, I was as good as I had ever been, and I finally made the team with a number two national ranking. Why then and why there? Let's see what astromapping might add to this story.

Figure 5 is a detail of my natal A*C*G map with LS included. That map detail shows my natal Mars-MC line (vertical) and the curved LS Venus line/direction. Munich (München) is about 78 miles from the Mars line and less than 10 miles from the Venus line. The intersection of lines, a destiny crossing, is about 90 miles from Munich (I consider distances up to about 150 miles from destiny crossings as strong in influence; however, as in other astrological matters, the setting of orbs is really up to the user). A destiny location it was: many millions around the world saw me on TV, marching into the Olympic stadium, although of course I was a faceless part of a large group and a very minor figure in the spectacle at that. No matter, my Mars (combat sport) was being brought to public attention (MC or Midheaven meridian), in a pleasant scenario of enthusiasm and adulation by the spectators (Venus LS).

More on Mars-MC: In spite of my ripe old age for an Olympian (at 35, I was the oldest man on the US team), I had never felt better or stronger in my life. Near my Mars line and with my natal Mars in Sagittarius, my legs were moving as if I were ten years younger. And the world remembers the terrorist attack during those games; Israeli athletes, officials, and German police officers were killed. These tragic events happened just a few doors away from me, expressing the dangerous side of my Sagittarius Mars-MC (international terrorism?) for me at that location.

More on LS Venus: Because of my 'advanced' age, I looked forward to the trip as an interesting and growth-oriented experience rather than with the nervousness and concern of a younger man. Perhaps it was the Venus energy that protected me from the Martian danger of terrorism so close to me there. Venus energy also most likely explains the happy times I had going to a concert, visiting Munich's parks, and travelling southeast (yes, unknowingly toward the destiny crossing!) into the beautiful Austrian countryside.

Might there have been a 'resonance' between that Mars-MC location and my surge of energy and good form relatively late in my sporting career? After years of failure, did my nearby geographic destiny lines draw me to Munich for that Olympiad?

Shivdasani Founds His Business in Thailand
Sonu Shivdasani was born in London on 23 November 1965, into a family with extensive international business interests. After his education at Eton College and Oxford University, he worked in his family's various businesses, gaining an international perspective for both business and world markets. Starting moderately in 1991 he began to create Six Senses Resorts & Spas, which today is a growing chain of environmentally sensitive, high-end (five star) resorts and spas in many beautiful locations around the world.[9] Though a global business, the hub of Six Senses' operations and main office is in Bangkok, Thailand.

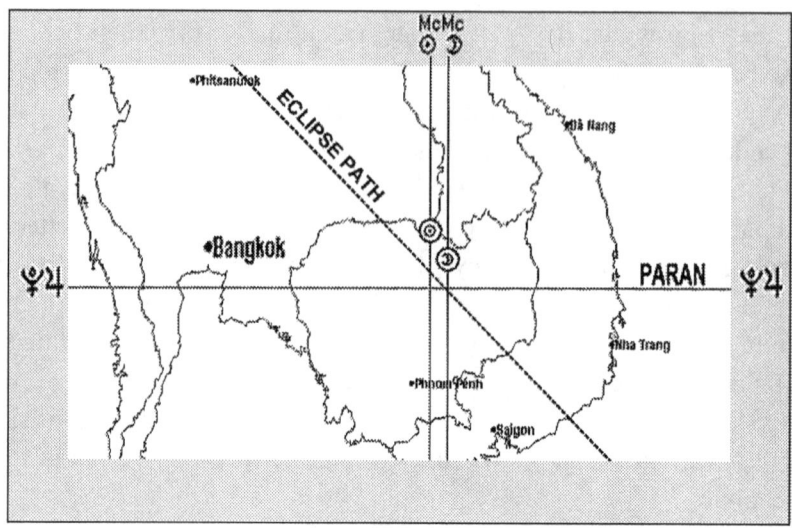

Figure 6 – S.Shivdasani A*C*G map with eclipse path

Of interest here is that Shivdasani was born about 30 minutes after a New Moon (Annular) Eclipse, giving him a pre-natal eclipse path transpiring just moments before his birth. Pre-natal eclipse paths over the Earth can be valuable tools for studies of individuals as well as for mundane events, showing us where significant events may transpire.[10] Computer programs today can plot these paths on maps which also have A*C*G and/or Local Space lines. Figure 6 is a detail of Shivdasani's A*C*G map with his pre-natal eclipse path drawn on it. With this map we can begin to see why he eventually moved to Bangkok, centring his business (and bringing most of his management staff) there. Note how Bangkok is in proximity to his eclipse path – as well as his conjoined SU-MH and MO-MH A*C*G lines. The SU and MO A*C*G lines-eclipse-path crossing is a very strong indicator of both power and destiny for Shivdasani in that region. Furthermore, a PL-JU Paran line goes right through the crossing (making it a triple crossing!) and the Paran line is only about 30 miles south of Bangkok itself. Jim Lewis spoke of combined PL-JU planetary energy as indicating places where business can go well, where miracles can happen and where setbacks can be overcome with new forms arising from the old.

Mundane Mapping

The word 'mundane' comes from the Latin *mundus,* meaning 'world'. Therefore, we use the term *mundane astrology* to refer to the study of charts and maps of countries, regions, world leaders, and various geocosmic event moments (e.g., eclipse paths, lunations, ingress moments). No other field of astrology has so immediately and directly benefited from astromapping techniques. It is hard to imagine any mundane study today that doesn't gain from them. Technically, the A*C*G (and Local Space) mapping procedures are exactly the same as in the relocation work of the previous examples. The important difference for mundane mapping is that we don't have relocation in mind when we read the map; rather, we use them to discern global hot spots where important events either have or most likely will manifest.

A political revolution in Washington DC

For example, in the issue of *The Mountain Astrologer* where this article was first published, you can find a mundane A*C*G map for the then coming moment of the Full Moon on 5 November 2006,[11] two days before the mid-term elections in the USA. See Figure 7 for this map. Looking at it from the perspective of possible locational hot spots, we see the Uranus-IC line less than 20 miles from Washington DC. Jim Lewis said of this line, "...houses may self-destruct in some fashion."[12] This, to me, prior to the election, was another indication that the Republican controlled houses of congress would 'self-destruct' for the incumbents and move into Democratic control.

Hugo Chavez talks tough

Another example of a possible hot spot from this Full Moon A*C*G map can be seen in the Pluto-Ascendant line of Figure 7, about 200 miles from the Venezuelan oil port of Puerto La Cruz. Pluto rising can indicate places where power is imposed – individuals wanting to take control of everything around them, with little patience for others' wishes. From the mundane perspective we can expect the force of the Plutonian influence to be expressed either by the government and/or the people en mass. The Associated Press reported on 4 November[13] (the day before the Full Moon), that Venezuelan president Hugo Chavez, speaking to oil workers

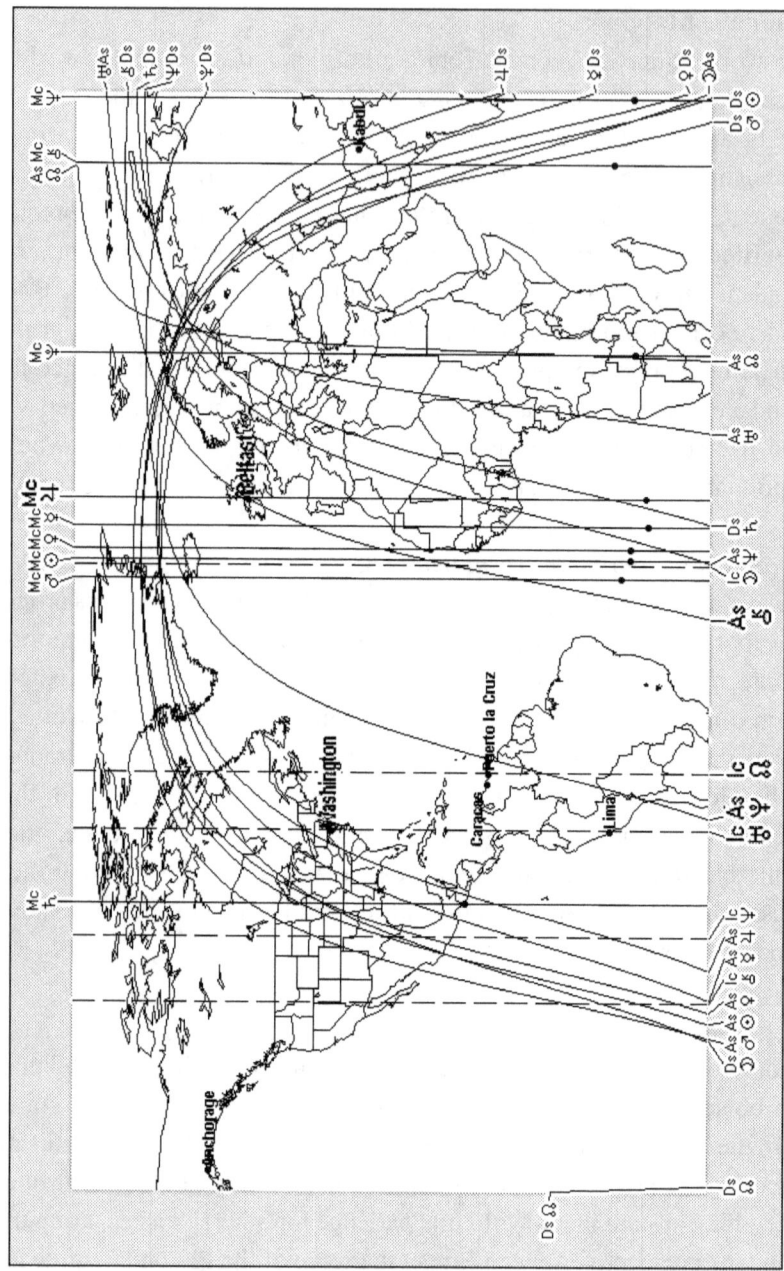

Figure 7 – A*C*G map, Full Moon, 5 November 2006

there, warned the US government that he would halt oil exports to them if there was any attempt to destabilize his leftist administration. While he was at it, he also warned any Venezuelan citizens opposing his government that they would not be welcome in either the military or the state-run oil company. The map's South Node line runs exactly over Puerto La Cruz, possibly indicating that he intends to complete his country's return to a fully nationalized oil industry.

Peace in Northern Ireland
Let's look once more at this mundane, Full Moon A*C*G map, Figure 7, to see another possible location of note for that lunar period: Jupiter-Midheaven is only about 12 miles from Belfast, NI. And, it is intersected by a nearby A*C*G Chiron rising line, making an A*C*G Paran, less than 20 miles from Belfast. Jupiter-Midheaven would indicate the possibility of some progress in the stalemated political process there, while the crossing with Chiron might offer the possibility of a healing of old wounds during this period.

On 10 November 2006 (5 days after the Full Moon), the BBC reported the following: "Signs of Movement in NI Process" and, "There are indications of movement in the Northern Ireland political process…" as both sides of the divided community had given "a cautious response" and "qualified agreement" to a possible power sharing arrangement. Considering the acrimony and previous bloodshed over these issues, this was significant in the slow healing process for that locality.

That's the gist of it in mundane astromapping: identifying significant Earth locations for national birth moments, coronations, treaty signature moments, geocosmic events (e.g., eclipse paths, lunations, ingress moments) and, as I'll show in the next example, for the maps of individuals who take on public roles.

Mrs. Thatcher Goes to War
Margaret Thatcher was British Prime Minister from 1979 to 1990. Her time in office is remembered for, among other things, the victorious 1982 Falkland Islands campaign against Argentinian forces, which made her a heroine to the British public. Let's see how mundane astromapping can deepen our understanding of this war.[14] Firstly, we should note that

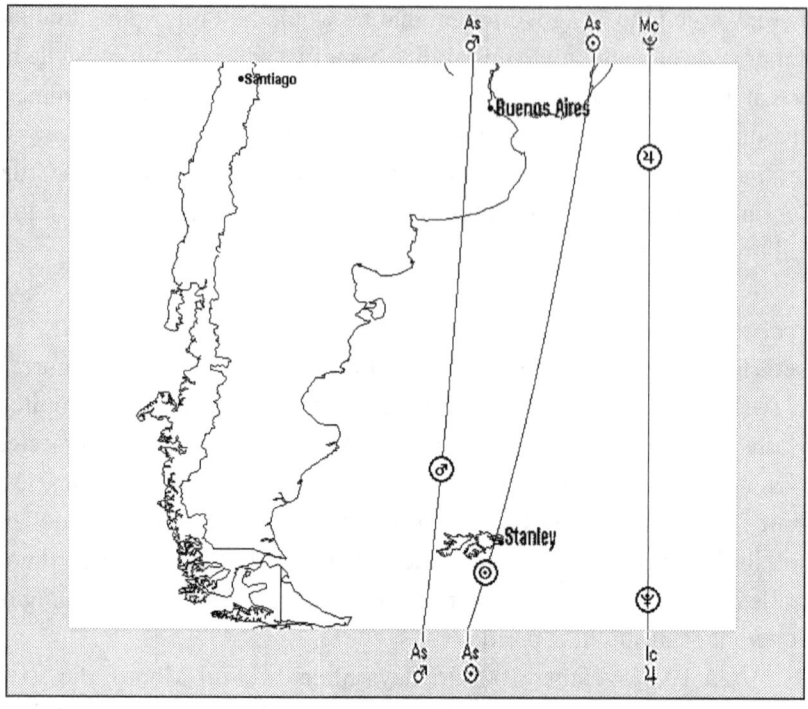

Figure 8 – Margaret Thatcher A*C*G map, Falklands detail

astromapping calculations and the planetary placements remain identical whether we map for the purpose of relocation or to identify possible mundane hot spots. What changes is how we use the information. Secondly, we note that a leader's natal chart can become pertinent to events in the country he or she governs. With this in mind, see Figure 8, the Falklands detail of Mrs. Thatcher's natal A*C*G map. We'll be looking at it for possible clues to her country's victorious campaign there.

Mars-Ascendant. It is striking that Mrs. Thatcher's Mars-Ascendant line is in the battle zone, less than eight miles from the southern tip of West Falkland. To the North that same Mars-Ascendant line is only about 60 miles from Argentina's capital city, Buenos Aires, the home of her adversary's government. What does this mean? From the mundane perspective, it indicates that courage and martial focus would easily be exercised in that region (more so than in other parts of the world). The leader or nation that 'owns' that line would be empowered and ready to act with Mars-like aggression there. Jim Lewis said about Mars-Ascendant locations, "You look for confrontation, and woe to those who affront you under a rising Mars." In other words, both Thatcher and the nation she governed were up for the fight.

Sun-Ascendant. Mrs. Thatcher's Sun-Ascendant line crosses East Falkland and is less than 15 miles from Port Stanley, the island's main city and a focus for the fighting. The force of the Sun at any of its lines will stimulate an urge to action, a desire to make things happen, and the drive to become master of one's own fate. In general, it is a positive place for an individual (or nation) where there can be strong leadership, authority, and a good plan of action. With the Sun ascending in this region, Mrs. Thatcher would embody such characteristics there to plan and lead the fight. Amongst a list of qualities, Jim Lewis said of Sun-Ascendant, "You exhibit leadership, audacity, courage, and a noble demeanour."

Pluto-MC/Jupiter-IC. Margaret Thatcher's birth chart (not shown) has a 'tight' (partile) Jupiter-Pluto opposition at 14° Capricorn and Cancer, respectively. Because these planets are in opposition, the MC meridian line of one will exactly overlap the IC line of the other. That is, wherever we find the Pluto-MC line, we will find the Jupiter-IC line conjoining it, and vice versa. Reviewing Figure 8 again, we see those conjoined lines in the battle zone, though about 300 miles east of the Falklands. This is a larger orb, but I believe that the influence of those lines on the conflict is strong and gives meaning to the story. Mrs. Thatcher was, in effect, living out her planetary opposition there, responding to those opposing Jupiter-Pluto forces. Jim Lewis said of this planetary combination, "Circumstances are frequently upset violently, but through such change you usually advance in position." Historians point out that the success of the Falklands war turned Thatcher's political career around: she had become unpopular at home, but this victory assured her re-election.

Bush Meets Resistance in the Middle East
Here we have another example of a leader's personal natal astromapping information correlating with the destiny of the country that he governs. It helps us to better tell the story of unfolding world (mundane) events. Figure 9 is a Middle Eastern detail of President George W. Bush's natal A*C*G map. I have omitted a few of his planetary MC lines (Mercury and Venus[15]) in that region to simplify the map and to focus on the

44   *From Here to There*

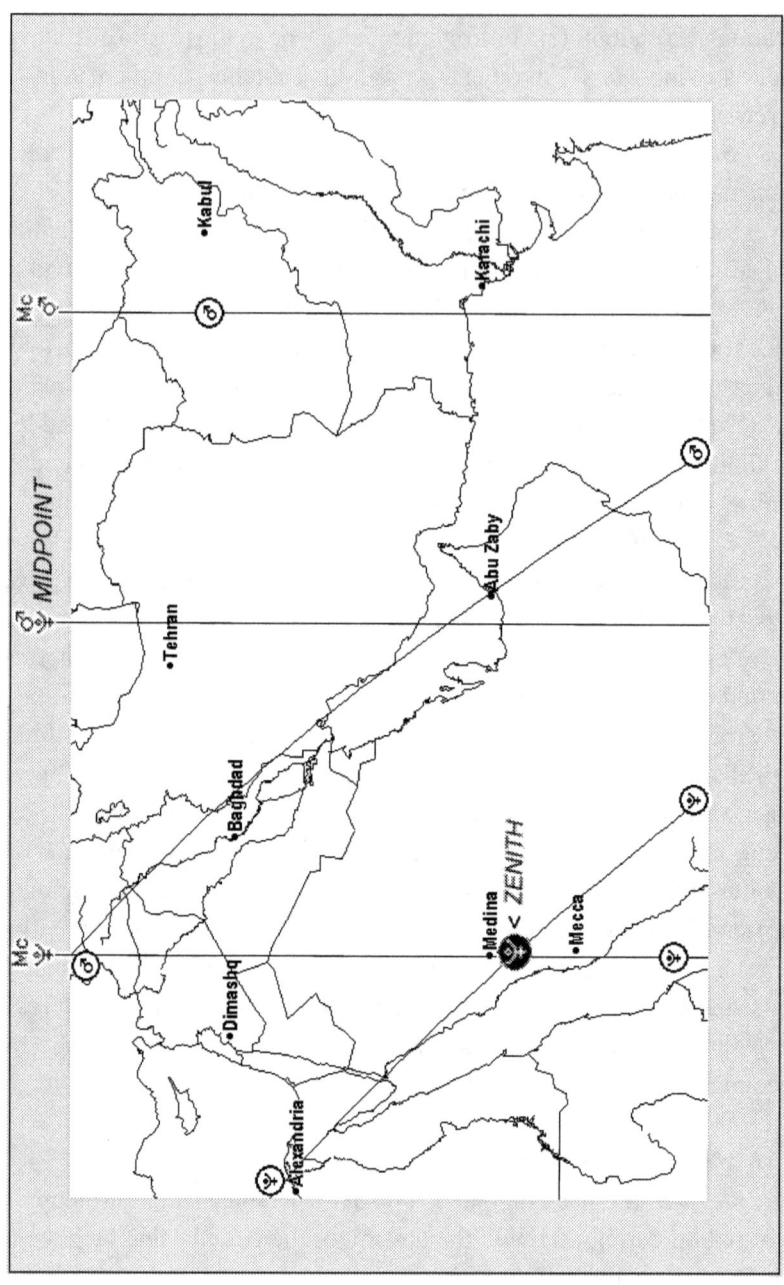

Figure 9 – G.W. Bush A*C*G map, Middle Eastern detail

dangerous, confrontational situation we find there. The vertical lines are A*C*G Midheaven lines, and the two curved lines are from Local Space. The first thing to note is Bush's Pluto-MC line on the left. At his birth moment, the planet Pluto itself was in a zenith position, almost directly over Medina in Saudi Arabia (within about 50 miles) and about 150 miles from Mecca, the centre of the Islamic world. Bush's Pluto-MC line, therefore, runs near those locations – though not shown, that same line runs further north to within 70 miles of Moscow, implying a confrontational possibility there as well. For political leaders, Pluto can represent a region or location of confrontational struggle where they desire to be an agent of change. Jim Lewis tells us that Pluto-MC locations "can be about going it alone, having a great hunger for power, and grasping it at any price – where all contesting parties risk descending into tyranny."

If we were to look at this map from a relocational standpoint – for, say, a client wanting to visit that area – this same Pluto-MC line could also speak of locations offering intense but transformational situations, where there is a possibility of change and where miracles might happen. I myself have a Pluto-MC line near Las Vegas, Nevada in the US. Years ago, I was invited to participate in a fencing competition there. I enjoyed Vegas and won that competition (perhaps by imposing my will in a confrontational situation?). However, it was the only time and place in my sports career of 17 years where I witnessed two fencers getting into a real fight with their weapons, flailing away, both trying to hurt one another. At first, I stepped in, trying to break it up, but then was forced back, sensing the danger of the steel flying about me. The altercation finally ended when a passing casino guard intervened by drawing his pistol. Pluto!

Also in Figure 9, we have Bush's Mars-MC line. This line represents an active location where the native can dominate and be courageous. This line runs through the centre of Afghanistan, some 185 miles from its capital, Kabul. (We should note that GW Bush, like Mrs. Thatcher, actually won the fighting war in Afghanistan, on his personal Mars line. The problem was that he really didn't finish it, turning his attention to Iraq before the Taliban were neutralized). Further south, the Mars line is less than 70 miles from Karachi, Pakistan, linking these countries into the Martian political theme.

The vertical MC line in the middle of the diagram is the Midheaven-Mars/Pluto midpoint line. Here, we have an example of the value of midpoints in our studies. Only with the help of modern computer programs can we can get this kind of information. Note that this line runs right through Tehran, Iran, making this potentially a very dangerous place for both President Bush, personally, and the US by association. Jim Lewis said of this Mars-Pluto planetary combination, "Violence is thought to be the answer to everything" and "Passion here can be explosive and dangerous." The curved Local Space Mars line runs about 70 miles from Baghdad, Iraq, which ties that location into the combustible mix.

Synastry (Relationship) Mapping

Synastry mapping evaluates the combined data of two individuals to tell the story of how they, as a single entity, would respond to Earth influences at various places in the world. For many years, I described the search to bring this into astromapping as the holy grail of the field. Nowadays, we can do it by using the Davison Relationship charting technique,[16] giving us another valuable tool. The Relationship chart is a proper chart in its own right, using the average in space and time of the two participants as the couple's 'birth' moment. From this information, we obtain the useful corresponding maps relevant to the story of the relationship.

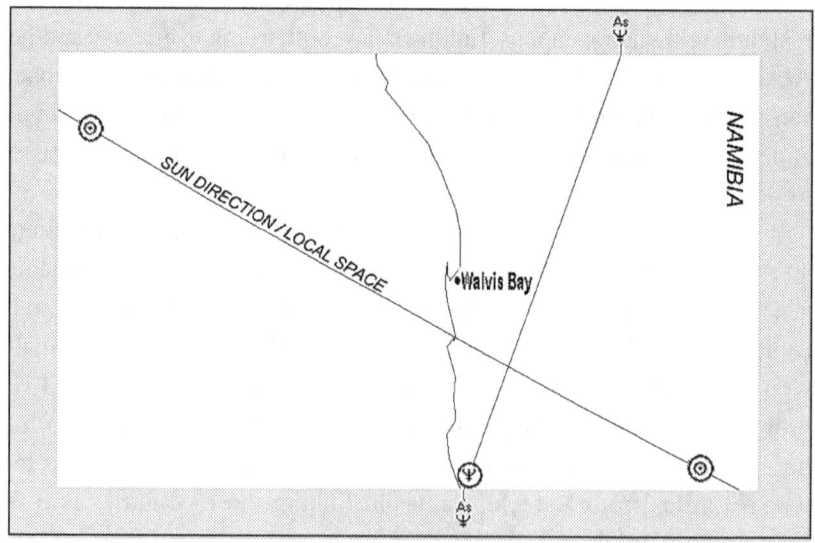

Figure 10 – A. Jolie A*C*G and LS line, Walvis Bay detail

Angelina and Brad have their baby in Namibia
Celebrities Angelina Jolie and Brad Pitt had their first child together, Shiloh Nouvel Jolie-Pitt,[17] on 27 May 2006. The child was born in Walvis Bay, Namibia. The government there went to extraordinary lengths to protect the privacy of Jolie and Pitt, who wanted to avoid photographers in the weeks leading up to the birth. Namibia refused to grant entry to reporters seeking to cover the birth without the actors' written permission. Photographers were arrested, film confiscated, the couple's hotel was ringed with heavy security and large green barriers were set up on the beach to shield the family.

As might be expected, both Jolie and Pitt, individually, have significant locality markers near Walvis Bay:

Jolie has a Local Space Sun and Neptune rising (A*C*G), destiny crossing within 45 miles (see Figure 10). Relocating there on her LS Sun line (direction) indicates that she felt energized and confident about having the child at that location. Intersecting her A*C*G Neptune rising line there at Walvis Bay, the vibrant Sun line would offset the sometimes weakening effect of Neptune, possibly leaving her with an experience much like a beautiful movie. Jim Lewis called this planetary pair "a potent combination" and on the positive side, a location that can be "intensely inspirational".

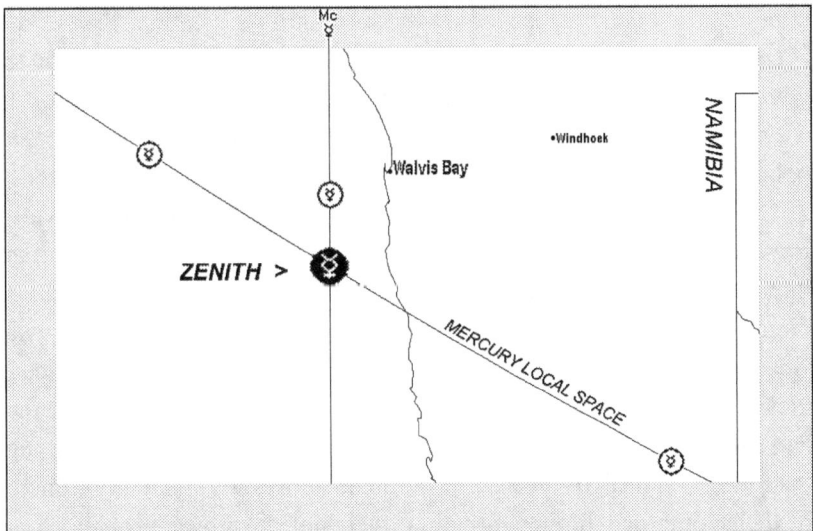

Figure 11 – B. Pitt A*C*G and LS Mercury Lines, Walvis Bay detail

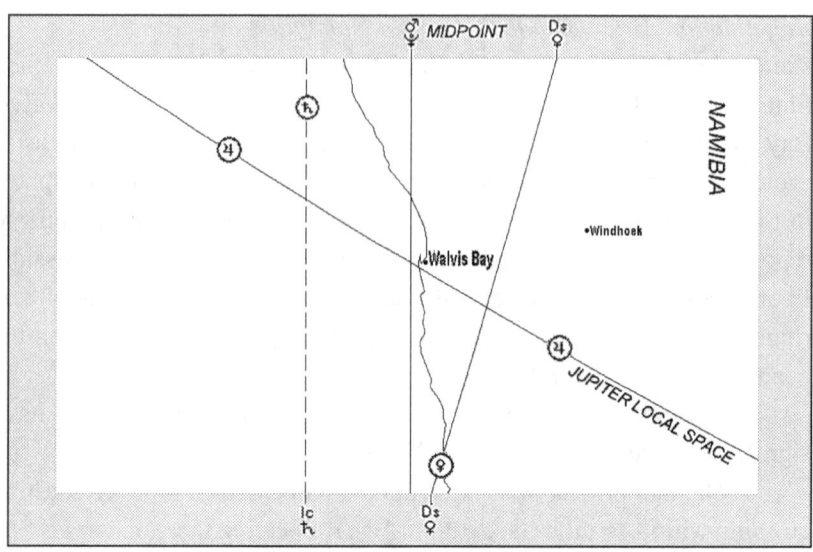

Figure 12 – Jolie and Pitt, Relationship A*C*G and LS, Walvis Bay detail

For Pitt, Walvis Bay is less than 60 miles from his A*C*G Mercury-Midheaven line (see Figure 11). In fact, the planet Mercury was at its zenith position (directly overhead the earth) only 100 miles from the bay at his birth moment. With such strong Mercurial energy, his name was brought to global public attention there, with much media attention and public consciousness focused on the birth and its location. From Pitt's Mercury placement, we can surmise his communication with the government was excellent, receiving all the help and co-operation he wished. Pitt would experience this location as a natural command centre or headquarters from which to successfully maintain his family's privacy.

As a couple, Jolie and Pitt have a strong relationship map for Walvis Bay. See Figure 12, which is a detail of the area. There are three important, interwoven patterns to review on this map. Firstly, they have an almost direct hit from their LS Jupiter line, which is only about 8 miles away (see the diagonal line labelled with Jupiter's glyph: ♃). This indicates they travelled there in an optimistic frame of mind, satisfied that they had everything in place for an expansion (Jupiter) of their family through the successful birth of their child. With the boosting – and lucky – energy of their combined Jupiter direction, their optimism was probably fully justified. Upon their arrival, they reached their joint A*C*G Venus

Descending line, making the location a Jupiter-Venus destiny crossing. This crossing is less than 75 miles from the bay where they resided. From the Venus descending energy, we can surmise that they found Walvis Bay beautiful from the first moment they saw it. And, we can further surmise that the birth was a new bonding for them, reinforcing their marriage commitments to each other. Jim Lewis said of Venus Descending lines, "This is probably the best place to get married, especially for women". Of Venus and Jupiter planetary energies working together, Lewis said, "This location is marked by good fortune, success, beauty and laughter in almost too great measure".

Was there anything there to keep them grounded for the birth? Yes! In Figure 12, we can also see the A*C*G Saturn-IC line about 120 miles west of them. Saturn on the IC at a location can bring hardship, but in this case I think we can see it as the wall built up to protect the couple's

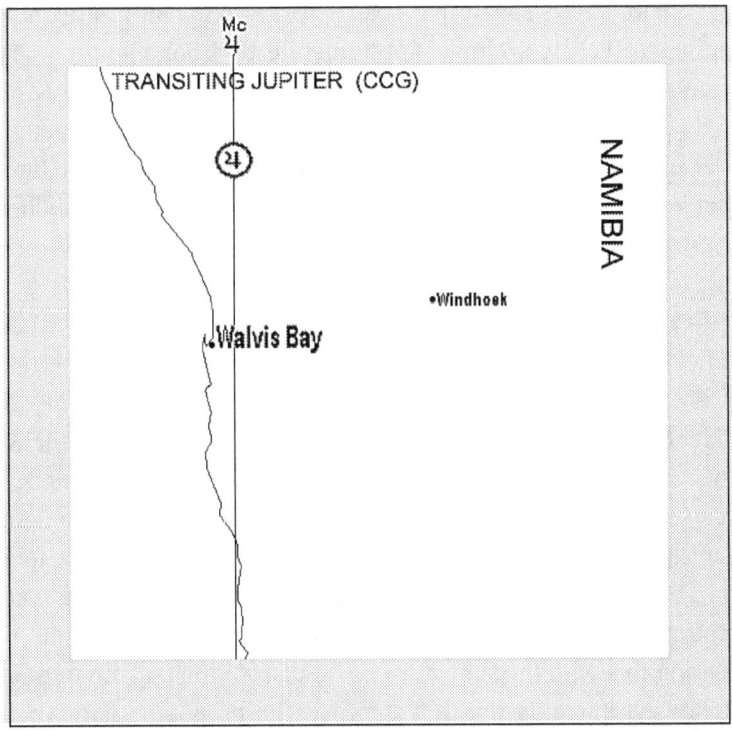

Figure 13 – Jolie and Pitt, Relationship C*C*G, daughter's birth, Walvis Bay detail

living space from the public eye. Saturn is about boundaries and their joint Saturn-IC separates them from most of Western Europe and the USA (to the North, not shown), all of which are on the other side (west) of the line.

One unexpected line in Figure 12 is their A*C*G Mars-Pluto Midheaven midpoint line, less than 10 miles from the bay. John Townley says of this midpoint line, "When you hit, you hit hard, or at least that can easily be what they say about you here".[18] I see this as the forceful measures taken to keep gatecrashers out of their living territory.[19] Another correlation with this midpoint could be the nature of the birth itself, which required surgery (Mars). *People.aol.com* reported that their daughter was "delivered via scheduled C-section (she was feet first, or in breech position, inside the womb)".

More: Cyclo*Carto*Graphy (C*C*G) is the mapping of one's moving transits, progressions and directions on or over a 'fixed' line A*C*G map. Lewis stated that C*C*G lines can "point to times when potentials of the life are most apt to manifest". Looking at the C*C*G lines on the couple's map, for the birth date of their daughter (27 May 2006), we find transiting Jupiter on the Midheaven, almost directly over Walvis Bay (see Figure 13). In other words, they were under Jupiter's protective energy, then and there! Jim Lewis said of a Jupiter-Midheaven location, "here is one of the best places to be".

Rectification
Rectification is the process of creating a birth chart when the time of birth is essentially unknown or uncertain. Charles Jayne (1911–1985), the father of modern technical astrology, called rectification the Royal Art of astrology, because it requires much from its practitioners, who must use all of their astrological knowledge, intuition, and sound judgement to complete the process. Studies will often begin by moving a chart in time through the day of birth, observing the shifting chart angles and the planets travelling through the changing houses, all the while comparing this with the subject's known disposition and circumstances. That, however, is only the first step. Next, a proposed chart would be tested for 'hits' from Transits, Progressions, and Solar Arc Directions, to see whether the proposed timing actually worked well with the subject's

known history. There are other approaches to rectification, which can be used independently or in combination with the method above. Of note, but not inclusive, are the Prenatal Epoch, the Age Harmonic and the use of directions for timing with major life events.

I suggest that we add astromapping to the mix of rectification techniques.[20] In general, the idea is to consider *where* things happened to us on Earth. Using a computer mapping program, we note the movement of planetary lines over the subject's astromap for that day, watching for the time when planetary lines might best match known event locations. We then consider this time as a possible rectified birth time. With this approach, we are no longer looking at chart angles or at planets moving through houses; rather, we are working with earth maps themselves, observing the timing of planetary lines over specific earth locations for the subject's birthday. To accomplish this, we would enter the birth date into an astromapping computer program that has an animation or stepping function.[21] Focusing on the entire world map and/or specific detailed areas of it, we watch the planetary lines move past us (right to left, or westward, if we go forward in time during that day).

What a sight to see the great dance of planetary energies parading by! Vertical MC and IC lines, curved rising/setting lines, and arching Local Space lines: all have imprinted the world that day in a unique sequence, one after the other.

Martin Seeks His Birth Time
My birth time of 10:58am is known from my birth certificate. For the sake of this example, let's pretend that I don't know my birth time at all, and my quest in astrology is to discover a good birth time for myself.

I could start by entering 00 hours (midnight) for my birth date (September 7, 1937) in my astromapping program, then stepping through it in time for the next 24 hours. Now, I admit this is a big task that requires concentration, patience, and perhaps a bit of good luck too. Doing this, I note that at about 11:00am that day transiting Mars-MC approaches Munich, Germany. As I described in a previous example, I had a Mars-MC kind of experience there years ago as a member of the US fencing team in the 1972 Munich Olympics. Because of this, I could easily be

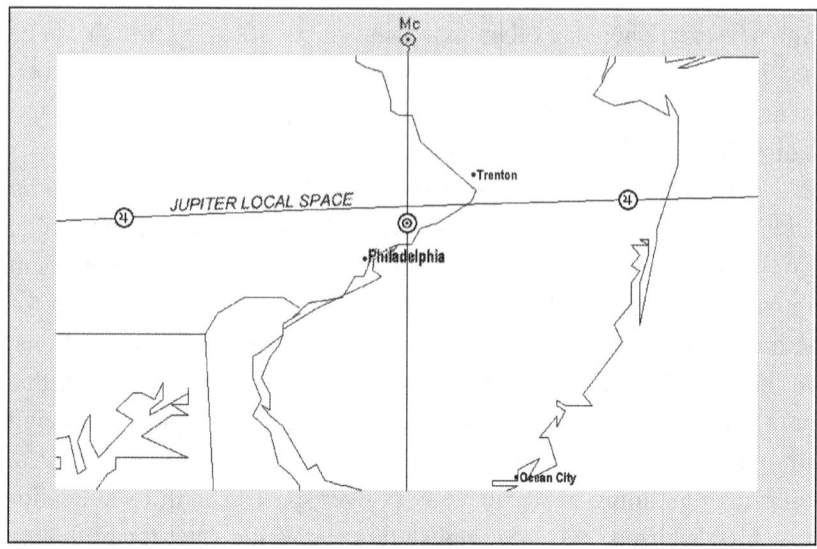

Figure 14 – M.Davis, SU and JU Destiny Crossing, Philadelphia, PA

alerted to stop the animation at that point and look more closely at other regions of the map.

Another important public event for me was the Pan American games of 1963 in São Paulo, Brazil. I had done well there, but the experience was notable because I had been carried on the shoulders of an adoring Brazilian crowd after the opening ceremonies. And guess what? Looking at the 11:00am map, I might also notice that the Moon on the MC (public, emotional acclaim) runs close to that location! It's looking good, so I zoom in on another location of interest: Philadelphia, Pennsylvania. I spent 13 years of my career as an industrial engineer there, and that's where I trained for my sport. So, still at 11:00am, I zoom in on Philadelphia and find my Sun-MC line (shining forth, career) only about 8 miles away – and it is being crossed by Jupiter's Local Space direction (vocation, honours) even more closely (see Figure 14). That 11:00am map describes the quality of my happy 13 years of residence in Philadelphia. I had been living on a very favourable Sun-Jupiter destiny crossing!

Keeping the 11:00am map on screen, I carefully move it back and forth in time, a minute here and a minute there, to get the very best fit for Munich, São Paulo, and Philadelphia. I settle on 10:59am and begin to test the chart for this time with its corresponding C*C*G Transits, Progressions, and Directions. My rectification investigation is under way.

I admit this example is simplified: The lines fit nicely, and I do in fact know that my birth time was recorded for one minute earlier, at 10:58am. However, even for more difficult studies, this technique may yield some good starting possibilities, which can then be tested by other standard rectification techniques.

Captain Edward John Smith Goes Down With the Ship
Here's another example to help us see how this works. If I were looking for a rectification *starting point* on the birth chart for, say, the captain of the *Titanic,* Edward John Smith, I might generate a map for his birthday (January 27, 1850; Stoke-on-Trent, UK). Then I'd step it through time that day, all the while noting the times when a significant cluster of planetary crossings might have formed over the location where the *Titanic* ultimately sank (41°N46', 50°W14'). Then I would look for lines over Belfast, where the great ship was built, and, perhaps, Southampton, her port of embarkation. Any such time or times would be a starting point for a possible birth chart for Smith. Get it? A good birth A*C*G map – and, therefore, birth chart – might resonate with the locations that ultimately defined his fate. Furthermore, in this case, where we have only one real defining event for Captain Smith, I would check out the corresponding C*C*G map for the night the Titanic sank, expecting to see a 'difficult'

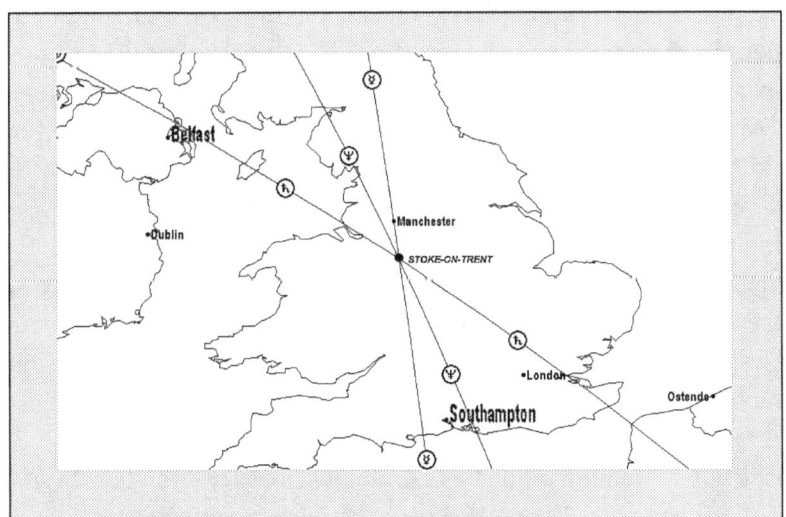

Figure 15 – Captain Smith, LS map, UK detail

array of lines for him, there and then (this would be the equivalent to checking transits and progressions for his relocated chart that night).

One interesting possibility (starting point) for Captain Smith's birth time is about 1:14am. His natal Local Space map for that moment (see Figure 15) has his LS Saturn line (direction) going right to Belfast where the great steel vessel was built. Southampton, the ship's port of embarkation, sits between his LS Neptune line on one side and his LS Mercury on the other, each within 17 miles of the city. Mercury and Neptune are the perfect symbols for a sea journey. The area of the Atlantic where the ship sank is less than 150 miles from a difficult destiny crossing on his 1:14am birth A*C*G map: Saturn Descending and Mars Local Space direction (not shown). Jim Lewis wrote of this planetary combination, "One of the least desirable of places… that leaves you open to victimization and violence" and, "Here is where physical concerns are dominant". In terms of Local Space lines only, the sinking was exactly on his Chiron line (direction) and only 50 miles from his Mars LS line. Captain Smith's Local Space Pluto line (direction) falls about 80 miles from New York City pier 59, the Titanic's planned destination. Pluto is associated with death and transformation and the kind of *force majeure* – unforeseeable circumstances preventing an act from happening – which meant the ship never arrived.

Captain Smith's C*C*G transits for the date and time of the sinking[22] are harsh – as can be expected. The ship was less than 10 miles from a Mars-Midheaven line and 128 miles[23] from a triple destiny crossing of Mars-Midheaven, Jupiter LS and a Mars-Pluto Paran. Jim Lewis' text on Mars-Midheaven includes the possibility of "accident proneness" and "overestimation of oneself" at this location. His text on the Mars-Jupiter combination is also telling: "There is raw courage, ability to 'take arms against a sea of troubles', though many of these troubles may be self created". The Mars-Pluto Paran also has a dangerous edge. John Townley writes of it, "Forceful, no-holds-barred action may be your first instinct here, but it could be your last."

Thank you for joining me on this astrological journey through both space (location) and time. I hope I have shown how mapping can add to our astrological investigations, indicating where on earth events may transpire or from where they may come to us.

© Martin Davis 2006, with new material added 2007.

Martin Davis' first book, Astrolocality Astrology, *presents the techniques of A*C*G, Local Space, and Geodetics as one interconnected field. The book won the year 2000 Spica Award for excellence. Martin can be reached via his Website: www.astrologymapping.com*

Chart Data and Sources (In alphabetical order)

George W. Bush, July 6, 1946; 7:26am EDT; New Haven, CT, USA (41°N18', 72°W56'); AA: birth certificate.

Martin Davis, September 7, 1937; 10:58am CST; St. Louis, MO, USA (38°N38', 90°W12'); AA: birth certificate.

Angelina Jolie, June 4 1975; 9:09am; Los Angeles, CA, USA (34°N03', 118°W14'); AA: birth certificate.

Jolie-Pitt Relationship chart data (spherical Earth midpoint): September 10, 1969, 2:20pm GMT; (35°N09', 107°W40'); combined data, each from an AA source.

Charles Lindbergh, February 4, 1902; 2:30am CST; Detroit, MI, USA (42°N20', 83°W03'); AA: birth record, as reported by AstroDatabank; I slightly rectified the 2:30am time to 2:34am and have used that time in my studies.

Brad Pitt, December 18 1963; 6:31am, Shawnee, OK, USA (35°N19', 096°W55'); AA: birth certificate.

Captain Edward John Smith, January 27 1850; 1:14am GMT; Stoke-on-Trent, UK (53°N00', 02°W10'); DD (caution), preliminary rectification by M. Davis.

Margaret Thatcher, October 13, 1925; 9:00am GMT; Grantham, England (52°N55', 00°W39'); A: from memory; reported to Charles Harvey from Mrs. Thatcher's private secretary.

NOTES

1. *The Mountain Astrologer*, October-November 2006, Issue #129, Mercury Direct section, page 2.
2. Jim Lewis (1941-1995) was the developer of Astro*Carto*Graphy* (A*C*G) and Cyclo*Carto*Graphy (C*C*G). Both terms are trademarks registered to him. Lewis' development of the techniques and his writings about them remain unsurpassed to this day. Interested readers should visit http://continuumacg.net, a website devoted to his work.

3. For a discussion of 'angularity' and 'En Mundo' vs. Zodiacal positioning, see: *Astrolocality Astrology: A guide to what it is and how to use it*, by Martin Davis, The Wessex Astrologer Ltd., 1999, Appendix 6, page 221.
4. Michael Erlewine is the sole developer of Local Space (LS). Local Space is the registered trademark of Matrix Software, a company that he founded. Erlewine is known for his pioneering work in astrological software programming and his writings on astrology and music.
5. *A Biography of Lindbergh* (A. Scott Berg, Lindbergh, Penguin Group, 1999) makes the point that he was the 20th century's first media hero because of the newly employed 'wireless', which instantly informed the whole world of his exploits.
6. John Townley is a noted astrologer and author; his text is quoted from Horizons, Matrix Software's astromapping program. For more on Townley's work, see: www.astrococktail.com
7. This selection is from Michael Erlewine's text in the Horizons computer program.
8. See Davis, *Astrolocality Astrology*, pp.73-75, for a more detailed explanation of Destiny Crossings.
9. The chain's core purpose is 'to create innovative and enriching experiences in a sustainable environment'. See their website: http://www.sixsenses.com/
10. Astrologer and financial expert Bill Meridian lectures on eclipse paths and their use in understanding both personal and mundane situations. Meridian can be reached via his website: http://www.billmeridian.com
11. 5 November 2006, 12:59pm, GMT.
12. All quotes from Jim Lewis can be found in the Astro*Carto*Graphy official booklet, unless otherwise specified.
13. http://www.iht.com/articles/ap/2006/11/05/america/LA_GEN_Venezuela_US_Oil.php
14. For the full A*C*G analysis, see: www.skyscript.co.uk/acg.html
15. The Bush family has a very friendly and lucrative relationship with the Saudi royal family. Bush's Venus-Midheaven line is less than 150 miles from the Saudi capital city of Riyadh.
16. A post-Davison improvement to this technique employs spherical geometry in the calculation, giving spherical Earth midpoints for the couple's longitude and latitude. The spherical method is employed here.
17. CBS news reported: "Shiloh – which in one longstanding translation from the Bible has come to mean 'the peaceful one' – was born in The (nearby) Cottage Hospital in Swakopmund."
18. From the Horizons computer program, by Matrix Software.
19. Pitt had his own personal security team in addition to Namibian police.
20. I'm certainly not the first to propose this. For example, David Meadows had an article on rectification with astromapping in the first-ever 'Mercury Direct' section of *The Mountain Astrologer* magazine (June/July 2000).

21. Horizons by Matrix Software and Solar Maps by Esoteric Technologies are two mapping programs that have this feature.
22. April 13 1912: Titanic hits iceberg at 11:40pm Greenland Time. The ship sinks about 2 hours and 40 minutes later.
23. This is within the orb of up to 150 miles that I usually use. At sea, where locations are not really specific, an even greater orb could be considered, though it is not necessary here.

4

Relocation can be a Career Move

Robert Currey

In this chapter we present a personal history of George W. Bush, written by Robert Currey. Note how Currey weaves Astro*Carto*Graphy into the very fabric of his narrative. This is an excellent example of A*C*G in biographical writing, using it both from relocation and mundane perspectives.

How the extremes in the life of President George W. Bush (GWB) are mapped out by Astro*Carto*Graphy

A tale of two cities

One of most pathetic news images in recent times was a sad George W. Bush gazing helplessly out of an aeroplane window at the flooded city of New Orleans. Yet, one of the most inspiring sights was the same man addressing the rescue workers at Ground Zero, New York.

Why such a contrast? Is this as simple as the difference between a Neptune IC line and Pluto Ascending line? Under his Neptune crisis (New Orleans), Bush's popularity plummeted [36% CBS] while under Pluto (New York City), he hit his highest ratings [90% CBS]. This dramatic contrast is more concerned with the way these planets work in GWB's chart, than what some astrologers consider to be the fundamental positive or negative nature to these two outer planets. Neptune is in a challenging square to his Sun, while Pluto is in a singleton conjunction with Mercury, close by his Leo Ascendant. Under Neptune in New Orleans, Bush's fragile ego, incompetence and misplaced sensitivity surfaced. Under Pluto, his instinctive mind, leadership and persuasive powers of speech emerged.

George W. Bush's Astro*Carto*Graphy map has already provided a wealth of insight into the man and his underlying strategy. So far, his

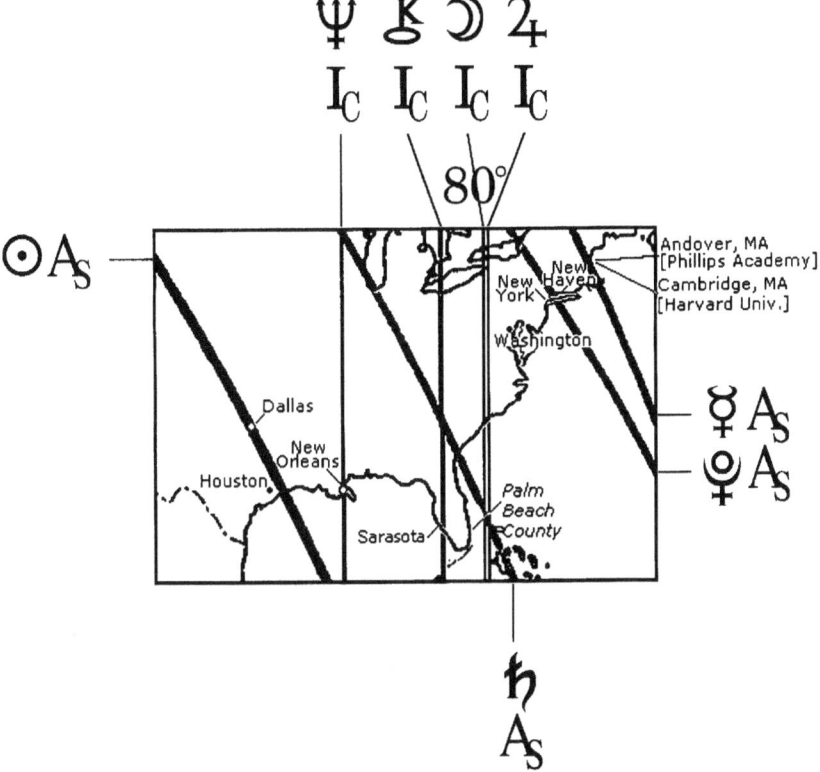

Figure 1 – Detail from George W. Bush's natal A*C*G map

presidency has become a textbook case for the technique of Astro*Carto*Graphy. Just to prove how closely it follows the text, I have included published quotes from Jim Lewis (1941-1995), the pioneer of the technique we know as Astro*Carto*Graphy.

Moving to Mercury for education
George Walker Bush's first significant relocation was in 1961. He moved from near his Sun line in Texas to Andover, MA to attend Phillips Academy. Here he landed spot onto his Mercury rising line – a fitting planet for learning his basics and ball games including basketball, American football and, his obsession, baseball. Mercury can be vocal and GWB was head cheerleader.

In 1973, Bush returned to his Mercury line for more education in the form of an MBA from Harvard Business School in Massachusetts.

> "You may be known for your mental abilities, repartee ...manual skills. Physical coordination ...may improve here."
>
> 'Mercury Ascendant'

> "These are good places for perfection of mental and verbal skills, education, a mischievous irreverence ...Lines of communication develop through involvement in public affairs." 'Mercury Lines', in *Handbook of Astro*Carto*Graphy* by Jim Lewis. *(H.A.C.G.)*

Membership of an elite secret society - Skull and Bones under Pluto

In 1964, he enrolled at Yale in the centre of New Haven, Connecticut – the city of his birth (6th July 1946 7.26am EDT). Now, he was hard back onto his Pluto rising line. Here George became head of the Delta Kappa Epsilon fraternity and a member of the exclusive Skull and Bones, a secret society whose membership included his father and grandfather. Bonesmen, as they are called, are forbidden to reveal what goes on in their inner sanctum: the windowless building on the Yale campus that is called "The Tomb". Bush included several bonesmen in his administration and his democratic presidential rival, Senator John Kerry, was also a member.

> "A tendency to hide self and personal secrets, and to live apart from others. There is hidden power within you, that often acts to change other's lives by mere contact with you."
>
> ' Pluto Rising', *H.A.C.G.*

Back to the Sun in Texas

GWB returned to his Sun rising line in 1971 when he went to work in agriculture in Houston, TX. He was also "involved in a mentoring program for children in inner-city Houston."

> "Children (of all ages) find you irresistible, and you will probably do everything you can to ensure that you have a following of some sort." 'Sun Ascendant lines', *Psychology of Astro*Carto*Graphy (P.A.C.G.)*

During this time, he flirted with the idea of running for state representative in Texas but decided against it. Along Sun lines, Jim Lewis writes about:

> "...an urge to action demand that you become master of your own fate, be your own boss ...leadership [is] accented ...ruthless in your quest for fame. Men become fathers here." *H.A.C.G.*

Being on his Sun line has been a mixed blessing for Bush. Because his Sun is square his stellium in Libra, gaining any credit or recognition in the large shadow cast by his outrageously successful father was a superhuman task. In pursuit of this quest, he drilled many dry wells as an oil man and saw the bottom of many a bottle in his private life. However, the Sun is his chart ruler and he eventually struck oil in a different form. The form this took was a share in the Texas Rangers baseball team, which he bought in 1989 and sold at a huge profit ten years later. In keeping with the location on his Sun rising line, Bush became their spokesman. Under Sun rising lines:

> "You pattern yourself after your father."

> "Work succeeds in areas that attract other's attention."

> "A profession that puts you before the public is thus likely to attract your attention, as you feel quite self-confident, impulsive and extroverted." *H.A.C.G.*

Gaining popular support by fostering the myth of the all-Texan hero
Bush's Sun rising line covers the two largest cities of Texas (comprising over half the population of the state. Source: *The Economist Diary 2006*). This solar energy enabled Bush to create his own heroic image in the eyes of Texans and win popular support. Oil interests backed him on the basis that he was his father's son, an oilman at heart. Through carefully choreographed photographic shoots on his ranch in his cowboy hat, Bush managed to look the archetypal Texan rancher. His public connection with baseball also enhanced his image as a spokesman for the people. He even managed to win support from traditional democratic voters such as the Hispanic minority. So, it was in west Texas that George Bush found his path on his heroic journey. This state proved to be an ideal foundation for his surprisingly successful bid for governorship, followed by an even greater majority in his re-election to a second term. Like his father, George H. W. Bush, Texas was his springboard into politics.

> "Your relationship with your father may lie deep beneath this personal quest for identity, as you consciously or otherwise seek to imitate the power that he exercised over you in your relationships with others." 'Sun on the Ascendant,' *P.A.C.G.*

How GWB's lines gave him the momentum to clinch his first presidential election, but only just …!

> "His (George Bush's) win in South Carolina set the stage for an eventual triumph in the final round of primaries. Through the primary season, his mother and father made appearances on his behalf." *First Son*, by Bill Minutaglio, Crown, 1999 & 2001.

His Jupiter, Moon and unaspected Saturn lines cross South Carolina.

On Moon IC lines:

> "…you are able to blend into any environment, seem to belong where you are, despite the constant change and emotionalism."
> *H.A.C.G.*

> "Family matters may take up more time and energy than you are used to. Any comfortable sense of belonging, however, is balanced by a constant fear of loss of security …unpredictable things keep happening and people keep intruding into your life unexpectedly." *P.A.C.G.*

On Moon lines:

> "you identify with your mother." *H.A.C.G.*

It was this same Jupiter/Moon IC line, that worked so well for Bush in the primaries, which helped him to pip Al Gore, who won a majority of the popular vote in the race for the presidency. With less than half a percent difference in the vote and several court rulings, it came down to shrewd lawyers, family influence and luck.

The combination of Jupiter and the Moon on the IC can, in simple terms, be described as good fortune through your family. In Bush's natal chart, this conjunction also includes Chiron. Because his Moon (and the whole stellium) is square his Sun and trine Uranus, Bush is likely to have mixed feelings about his closeness to family. Certainly, his relationship with his mother, Barbara has been up and down.

> "Bush said the Queen asked him why his mother had seated them so far apart. Bush said he told the Queen it was probably because he was the 'black sheep of the family.'"
> (Referring to a dinner at the White House in 1990, in an interview with Oprah Winfrey Sept 20, 2000).

Yet, family support has been decisive along his Jupiter/Moon line. After South Carolina, it was critical at election time in Florida, where his brother, Jeb was governor, and later in Washington, DC, all along these supportive lines.

On Jupiter IC lines (Washington, DC and Florida), according to Jim Lewis:

> "You ...become a patriarch, pillar of society, and successful though conservative politician." "You become benevolent and generous, as you contentedly pursue your own religious or family destiny."

Moon IC:

> "You react to circumstances and situations, that require you to come to terms with your family and your ancestral background."
> *H.A.C.G.*

GWB personifies the USA so his potential personal crises manifest as national disasters

George W. Bush identifies very strongly with his homeland and he takes anything that occurs to the USA extremely personally. There are two strong astrological pointers to this. First he was born on 6th July so that his Cancer sun is conjunct the chart of the USA (4th July 1776). The second factor is that his Moon and Jupiter are on the IC in Washington, DC. He feels at home in the capital city and a close connection to the mood of the nation. So, in personifying the nation, his chart comes into effect on a national scale. With Pluto rising in Leo, GWB is prone to spectacular crises in his personal life. This may account for such major national disasters occurring on sensitive zones on his A*C*G map during his presidency. We have returned to a pattern from earlier millennia, when the astrologer would use the birth chart of the king to interpret the fate of the kingdom.

"Our nation is somewhat sad, but we're angry." *GWB*

Ridiculed for the 'My Pet Goat' episode on his Chiron line

It was along his Chiron (IC) line in Sarasota, FL that George first received confirmation of the terrorist attack on the twin towers. GWB came in for stinging criticism for his stoical reaction to the news, as he remained seated in that Floridian classroom. He was ridiculed in the film *Fahrenheit 9/11*:

> "Mr. Bush just sat there and continued to read My Pet Goat. Nearly seven minutes passed with nobody doing anything."
> *Fahrenheit 9/11*

His supporters argue that his blank response was dignified in that he did not alarm the children. Cynics say he was more interested in hearing what happened to the pet goat than face the national catastrophe. Nevertheless, within a short time, Bush was on Air Force 1 heading west towards his Neptune (confusion) line where he touched down in Barksdale Air Force Base in Louisiana.

Mr. Bush says the first hours were frustrating. He watched the horrifying pictures, but the TV signal was breaking up. His calls to Cheney were cutting out. And he says he pounded his desk shouting, "This is inexcusable. Get me the vice president." "I was trying to clear the fog of war, and there is a fog of war," says the president. "Information was just flying from all directions." (*60 minutes,* CBS Broadcasting September 10, 2003.)

After landing at an underground command centre in Nebraska, Bush was back in Washington, DC within nine hours of the attacks. In the aftermath of 9/11, Bush mostly remained on his more relaxed, responsive and easy-going Libran Moon/Jupiter zone in Washington, DC. His first reaction appeared timid and uncertain (very Sun Cancer in 12th house).

> "Immediately after the assaults on the World Trade Center and the Pentagon, [the President] did not get off to a distinguished start. 'Where is the president?' people wondered, and understandably so." *The Alchemy of Leadership*, by Warren G. Bennis and Robert J. Thomas, Harvard Business School Press.

Pluto rising in New York brings crisis and transformation

Pluto, the planet associated with destruction, revenge and re-birth, runs through New York in GWB's map. There is no doubt that GWB personally felt the bitter collective pain of mass destruction caused by vengeful suicide terrorists to this wealthy and powerful metropolis.

It was not until Bush moved onto his Pluto (Rising) line in New

York on September 14th, that he reinvented himself as a warrior with a mission.

> "Even more dramatic was how President George W. Bush seemed to be transformed in the same crucible." (Also quoted from *The Alchemy of Leadership*.)

I remember witnessing his epiphany on television. The scene on Ground Zero was one of desolation and tragic debris. Smoke was still rising from what had become a pyre. Bush later described the atmosphere as ghostly. Surrounded by firemen and clearance workers chanting "USA! USA!" Bush tuned into the mood of his audience. His voice and language changed. He had rediscovered his personal power. At one point, a voice in the crowd calls "I can't hear you." Spontaneously, Bush responds, "I can hear you. (Applause.) I can hear you. The rest of the world hears you. (Applause.) And the people who knocked these buildings down will hear all of us soon." (Applause.)

"There was [sic] tears, there was anger," recalls the president. "There was a lot of bloodlust. People were, you know, pointing their big old hands at me saying, 'Don't you ever forget this, Mr. President. Don't let us down.' The scene was very powerful. Very powerful."

By the end of that day, Mr. Bush flew to Camp David, visibly drained. "He was physically exhausted, he was mentally exhausted, he was emotionally exhausted, he was spiritually exhausted," recalls president's chief of staff, Andy Card.

The next day – Saturday, Sept 15 – Mr Bush told members of his war cabinet in a last decisive meeting at the presidential retreat:

> "My message is for everybody who wears the uniform – get ready. The United States will do what it takes." *CBS News*

New York: the phoenix was born again, out of the ashes

Within a few moments on the corner of Murray and West Streets in downtown New York, President Bush metamorphosed from a verbally challenged, psychologically paralysed head of state, to an inspirational leader. The symbolism of Pluto was palpable. America (and Bush) symbolically became a phoenix rising out the ashes of the old incarnation. At the time of writing this, 9/11 had been the greatest crisis of his presidency, and, with Pluto rising in his natal chart, he picked up the gauntlet. Now he had a purpose, he felt he could fulfil his destiny. Only history will tell whether his subsequent path was of benefit to the world or simply destructive and counter-productive.

The connection between Bush, New York City and Mercury
Now the symbolism of New York goes even further. Having lived in the city in my early twenties, I have long felt that the Big Apple is ruled by Gemini. It is a city full of change, mobility, quick talkers, cops who talk as if they have just kissed the Blarney Stone, fast taxis with drivers with unpronounceable names and sharp-witted radio station disc jockeys. So, I was not surprised to find that the city was incorporated as New York (from New Amsterdam) on June 12, 1665. On that day the Sun, Moon, Mars and Pluto were in Gemini.

The twin towers symbolised the heavenly twins and the attack occurred with Saturn and the Moon in Gemini, opposite Pluto in Sagittarius. Now Bush has the ruler of Gemini, Mercury, conjunct his Pluto Rising in his natal chart, suggesting that this mercurial energy is tied up with crises. Mercury is connected with siblings and, by association with the sign of Gemini, twins. So, whenever this type of familial tie features in George's life, Pluto is also invoked, bringing potential crisis. For example, when George was seven years old, his sister tragically died of leukaemia. Years later, the birth of his twins brought George to another critical point. After trying to conceive for three years, he and Laura considered adoption. So, the eventual arrival of Barbara and Jenna, five weeks prematurely (due to toxaemia), must have felt like a miracle to George. Twenty years later, on a clear autumnal day, his Mercurial crisis arrived from the sky in the form of four Boeing 757/767 aircraft. It took three days for Bush to connect with his inner power to handle this crisis and to start to pronounce his plans for extreme and decisive retaliation.

GWB's hot spot with his Mars line through Afghanistan
For you or me, Mars lines on our Astrocartography maps show zones (about 300 miles either side of the line) where we are more oriented to sports, workouts and other activities. Here, we are more direct and at times more confrontational. This also applies to heads of state, but here

Figure 2 – Detail from George W.Bush's natal A*C*G map

Mars also manifests in their foreign policy. Mars defines areas of potential conflict, which could escalate into war.

For George Bush, Afghanistan – right on his Mars Midheaven line (see figure 2), became his first proactive battleground. With an "on-off" unaspected Mars, GWB's inner aggression found expression in his outer world. This Mars is a strong planet and we should not forget that he shares this configuration with Sylvester Stallone a.k.a. Rocky and Rambo (born on the same day as GWB). The theme in his chart with Mercury conjunct Pluto and his unaspected Mars may explain why GWB tends to "fluff his lines" when he talks about emotional issues, but becomes articulate and single-minded when making hostile statements. Mars MC lines:

> "Here, you strive for success and position in society, often through military work …there is a definite identification of self as somewhat 'macho'. Success comes through initiative, courage

and confidence in self, and through the overcoming of antagonisms and competition." *H.A.C.G.*.

"… conflicts with authorities that lead to violent confrontations …you learn your true power to exist and prosper in a hostile environment that demands taming." *P.A.C.G.*

On Mars lines:

"Pain and danger are dealt with frequently …the world is seen as a hostile place where one does battle with others for selfish ends. You take actions that commit you to the struggle for survival." *H.A.C.G.*

Mars lines have a history of prescribing war zones, but there's always an exception

The Mars line is a good indicator of potential war zones for world leaders. For example, Margaret Thatcher's Mars line goes through the Falkland Islands and Jimmy Carter's through Tehran, Iran. JFK's Mars line does not go through the Bay of Pigs as one might expect, but through Moscow. While for Bill Clinton, his Mars line joined Venus and Neptune (in Libra) over the UK, where the slogan "Make Love, Not War" took on a special meaning. As a student in the 1960s he marched with the peace rallies demonstrating against the Vietnam War outside the US Embassy in Grosvenor Square, London. And it was as a student in Oxford University that he famously smoked cannabis but he claims did not inhale. However, a friend who was a contemporary at University College disputes this. The sporting potential of Mars came out as Clinton played rugby while at Oxford. Later as President, he took key initiatives in setting off the peace process in Northern Ireland close to his Mars/Neptune (pushing compassion) lines. So, Mars doesn't always point to aggression or war. On Mars and Neptune combined:

"In unusual cases, there may be non-violent victory, implementation of ideals."

On Neptune MC:

"You come to stand for certain ideals, especially non-violent ones."

Drugs are mentioned under Mars/Neptune and Venus/Neptune. *H.A.C.G.*

Besides Afghanistan, GWB's Mars line goes through southern California, within orb of GWB's third major presidential crisis, where over half a million acres were destroyed by wildfires in October 2007, the Azores where he met Tony Blair and the Spanish Prime Minister in preparation for war, and Canberra, Australia (see figure 3). In October 2003, Bush addressed the Australian parliament thanking them for their support in "his war on terror". During the speech, two Australian Green party senators heckled him. For Bush, Mars was setting exactly in Canberra when he was born. War in Afghanistan was his first major action as President. He acted in his professional capacity as leader of his nation and it furthered his career by gaining popular support. All this is in keeping with Mars being at his MC over Afghanistan. However, in Canberra, Mars on the descendant took the form of a personal attack. In keeping with the symbolism, here he was confronted by aggression within his personal presence.

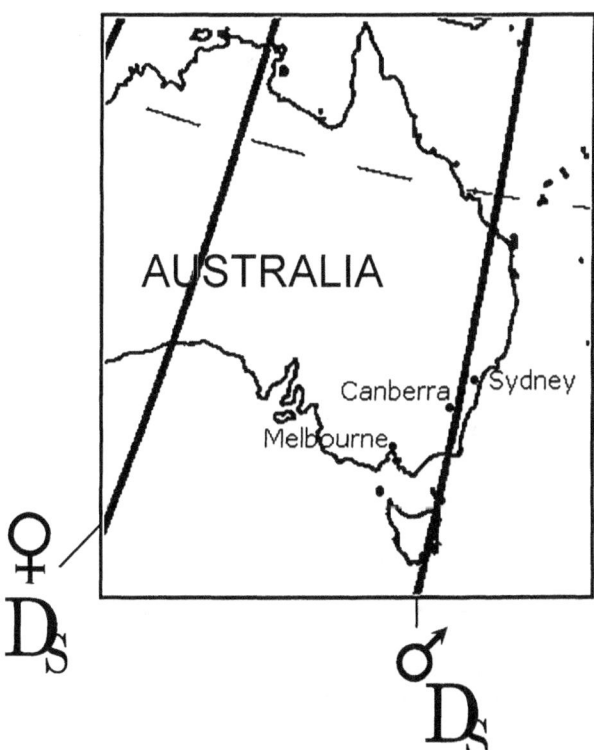

Figure 3 – Detail from George W. Bush's natal A*C*G map

Middle East: a complex love/hate zone for GWB

For Bush, the Middle East is a 'love/hate' zone. This pan-Arabic region is bordered by Mars over Afghanistan to the East; Venus over Tehran, Iran and East Saudi Arabia; Pluto over Mecca, and Mercury over West Syria, Lebanon and West Jordan.

In the Sibley chart for the United States (July 4th 1776 at 5:10pm LMT Philadelphia, PA), Pluto in Capricorn is opposite personal planets in Cancer. This aspect instils into the US national psyche a congenital feeling of threat to security from outside. Historically, this has taken the form of an intense aversion to any controlling dictatorial leadership. It started with George III and British imperial power, but continued with Hitler, pre-perestroika Soviet leaders, and Fidel Castro, Saddam Hussein, Osama bin Laden, to name a few. This almost paranoid fear was bound to become a reality around the Millennium when transiting Pluto crossed the US

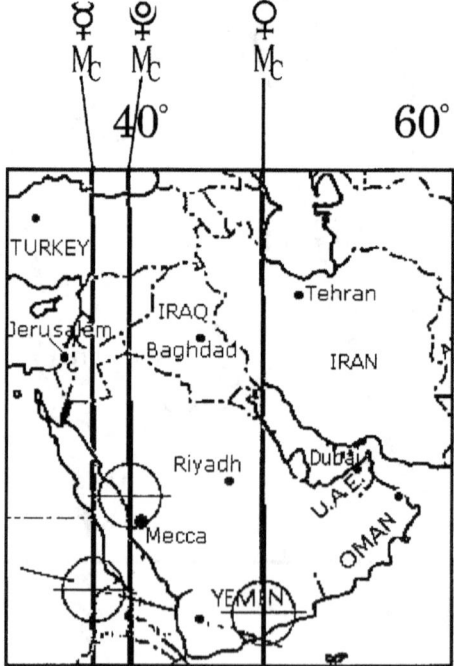

Figure 4 – Detail from George W. Bush's natal A*C*G map

Ascendant. With Baghdad on the US A*C*G Pluto line, Saddam became a natural scapegoat and a dangerous threat, with his supposed weapons of mass destruction.

To add to this dangerous line-up, GWB's Pluto MC line also goes over Mecca, the symbolic heart of the Muslim region. It is as if GWB and the USA are meeting their projected demons out there. In true Plutonic form, the encounter between Bush and the Muslim nations has been, and will be, intense and neither will ever be the same again. The more Bush tries to control Islamic fundamentalism, the greater the backlash for US interests and for future generations. In this clash, Pluto is primarily about oil and control under the banner of democracy.

> "Here, a basic alienation from society causes great power hunger, and it is grasped for at any price, with danger of tyranny existing. You resent authority, yet crave it for yourself and seek to become number one at any price, so there is alternate hero-worship and desire for power. In this location, you could become famous, murdered, notorious, a fugitive or great leader. Your image, perhaps in the press, comes to stand for some popular ideal, or its antithesis, and the ultimate battle of life is fought …with mortally high stakes." 'Pluto MC line', *H.A.C.G.* (GWB's line over Mecca, Saudi Arabia.)

It is worth remembering that Saudi Arabia may be a US/Bush ally (with Venus), the Pluto influence (as described above) surfaces in that the majority of the 9/11 terrorists including Osama bin Laden were of Saudi origin.

The presence of Bush's Venus, a planet connected with love, in this potential war zone seems inappropriate. It hints that Bush is not simply locked into a crusade against the Muslim faith; the Middle East is for him a bazaar filled with treasures. Venus is also connected with alliances and finances. Well before 9/11, the Bush family were 'in bed' with Saudis through the Carlyle Group – primarily a defence consortium.

While George's Venus line crosses allies, like Saudi Arabia and Kuwait, who supported both Desert Storm wars, it also goes over Tehran, capital of his current adversary, Iran. Though this clash has yet to run its course (at the time of writing), reports suggest that there have been behind-the-scenes requests by the US for Iran to exert its influence on the Iraqi Shi'ite Muslims.

Tony and George – like Swan Lake: a love affair across a pond based on myth, fantasy and misapprehension

In the UK, GWB's Neptune ascending line is within 50 miles (80 kilometres) of London and Tony Blair's Neptune (and Saturn) Midheaven line crosses George Bush's ranch in Midland, Texas. Even though their two countries have been close allies since 1812, an American Republican and a British Socialist are not natural allies. However, with Neptune so strong, it appears that they saw in the other what they wanted to see. For Blair, the combination of Saturn and Neptune may have prompted a sense of social and spiritual obligation, possibly followed by disillusion when Bush failed to get a UN mandate for his Iraq war.

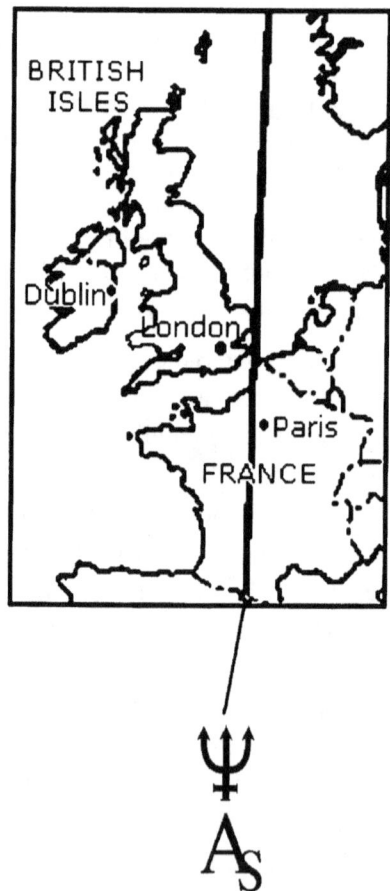

Figure 5 – Detail from George W. Bush's natal A*C*G map

It is interesting that while there are no clear or strong Neptunian aspects in the Bush/Blair synastry, this astrocartographical theme of Neptune does appear to colour their alliance. Both leaders have revealed that God was behind their decision to go to war. They each promoted what now appears to be the myth of Saddam's weapons of mass destruction. So while Bush benefited from Great Britain as a leading country in "the coalition of the willing", the shared intelligence and joint planning has revealed a pattern of confusion and delusion. For both Bush and Blair, Neptune is a difficult planet in their natal chart. For Bush, as we will see, it points to a vulnerable blind spot.

This type of locational synastry is similar to the Lennon/Ono A*C*G synastry. John Lennon's Venus rising line ran through southern Japan and Yoko Ono's Venus MC ran through Liverpool.

What happens when Poseidon lies at the bottom of the chart?

In September 2005, I was looking at a giant image of George W. Bush's world A*C*G map on display on our booth at the New Living Expo in Fort Lauderdale, Florida. No matter how closely GWB's life follows his map, it took my breath away to see his Neptune IC line fall right on the then recently flooded city of New Orleans. Neptune (or Poseidon to the Greeks) was the god of the sea and placed on the zone of the home (IC), we can expect an encounter between water and homes. In most charts, it might describe an urge to live near water, though it can also manifest as rising damp or a liability to flooding. Well this last potential became a reality for the citizens of New Orleans, one day after the category 4 hurricane, Katrina, made landfall. The resultant storm surge broke the levees and soon 80% of the city was flooded. What did Jim Lewis write about the Neptune IC line?

> "Real estate and home matters usually don't go too well, and you begin to become dependent on others for sustenance..."
>
> "Community living may be best ...So that the past can be left behind here." [The Louisiana Superdome provided shelter for 9,000 refugees.]
>
> "Whatever is built has foundations of sand ...and it too is subject to self deception and illusions. Isolation and non-attachment make feeling rooted here impossible, except where you depend on others." *H.A.C.G.*

When it rains at home, it pours!

Was GWB's natal Neptune activated on August 29, 2005 when Katrina made landfall? Yes – Neptune, in his natal chart is widely conjunct his Moon and Jupiter in Libra – so when it rains at home, it pours! At the time, Jupiter, Venus and the South Node were conjunct GWB's Moon in the middle of his Libran stellium.

There's another take on transiting Jupiter and Venus in Libra (indulgent pleasure) going over his natal Moon (at home). This may explain why George was slow to end his extended holiday and why his mood (Moon) was so optimistic (Jupiter) about the impact of the hurricane!

> "Leaked video footage and transcripts of top-level briefings in the six days before the storm showed federal officials telling Mr Bush the storm could breach levees and overwhelm rescuers. ...He did not ask a single question in the final briefing on August 29 last year, the day before Katrina made landfall. But he told officials in Louisiana: 'We are fully prepared'. ...The footage, obtained by the Associated Press, appears to contradict Mr Bush's announcement four days after the storm that he did not think 'anyone anticipated the breach of the levees'. The inept initial handling of the disaster shattered Mr Bush's reputation as a strong and decisive leader." Alec Russell, *Daily Telegraph*, 2nd March 2006.

At this time, Saturn was crossing his Leo ascendant (exact on 13 September 2005) and in typical style, the Katrina disaster brought him down to earth with a bump. Being Leo rising, his only option was to respond with a humiliating public apology. In the event, he shouldered his responsibilities (Saturn) and publicly (Leo) accepted blame as the commander in chief.

George Bush and his advisers initially misread the scale of this massive disaster. In an antediluvian moment, even newscasters were announcing that New Orleans "had dodged a bullet". This misreading of the threat along with the ensuing chaos and disorder, are symbolic of Neptune – the key planet directly under New Orleans when GWB was born. However, Neptune can also bring guilt and GWB's uncharacteristic comments afterwards suggest that he might have been moved by the plight of the victims of the disaster. According to the BBC, on 16 September GWB said:

> "The task of rebuilding after Hurricane Katrina is a chance to wipe out poverty and remnants of racial injustice."

Was the flood part of George Bush's karma?
There's a strange irony that the extreme nature of the two big 2005 hurricanes, Rita and Katrina were a result of rising temperatures in the Caribbean. While some climatologists argue that this is part of a natural cycle, a larger number point to increasing fuel emissions as the cause of global warming. In the USA, the principal fossil fuel is oil. The path of both hurricanes went through USA's primary petroleum processing centres. During his first term George W. Bush was notorious for his refusal to cooperate with world initiatives to limit fuel emissions and fierce in his protection of oil companies. Is this the Earth 'making a statement' or karma or just an unfortunate coincidence?

© Robert Currey 2006.

Robert Currey trained in Astro*Carto*Graphy under Jim Lewis and is a certified Astro*Carto*Graphy consultant. He has practised astrology since 1981. His company, Equinox, prepares a range of chart analyses written and programmed by himself, plus authorised Astro*Carto*Graphy world maps and analyses by Jim Lewis. He has added an interpretation for Chiron to Lewis' original Astro*Carto*Graphy handbook. In 1989, he founded the Astrology Shop in central London. He now runs Equinox as an international mail order service – see www.astrology.co.uk for more information about written analyses and www.astrolivelink.com for Astro*Carto*Graphy and other astrological consultants.

NOTES

1. Sometimes I have put keywords next to a planet. This is to help people unfamiliar with astrology understand one dimension to the energy of the planet. However, it is important to note that the planet will not always manifest in this way and that the nature of the planetary energy is much greater than a few keywords.

2. When I write that New York is ruled by Gemini, I am saying that the sign of Gemini is very strong in the chart for the founding of the city and in the life of the city.
3. Astro*Carto*Graphy® is a registered trademark. See: http://continuumacg.net/ for more information about licensed users and certified consultants.
4. Thanks to Donna Cunningham for bringing to my attention that George Bush is a twin of Sylvester Stallone, Adrian Duncan for pointing out that Baghdad is on a Pluto line in the US chart and to my wife, Karen, for various ideas including noticing GWB's Mars Descendant line on Canberra.

5

My Summer Vacation

Maya White

Locality astrology is useful to everyone who wishes to tell a story. Here we have a fine example from Maya White. White has been an astrologer for over 25 years. She specialises in Astro*Carto*Graphy, having earned her certification in 1992 from Jim Lewis. Over the years she has become one of the most experienced practitioners in the US. White set off on a dream holiday with the highest of expectations. Things don't quite turn out for her as she nearly loses her life!

> That which does not kill us makes us stronger……
> Friedrich Nietzsche

Astro*Carto*Graphy has long been my passion. I ordered my first A*C*G map in 1979, and earned certification from Jim Lewis in 1992. The synchronistic nature of A*C*G has been a driving force in my life, and it continues to fascinate me. There is no palette which better illustrates the accuracy and strength of Astrolocality than my own experiences.

I left my brother's house under the best of circumstances – a crisp, clear, late summer morning. Never had I seen Colorado looking so beautiful. The land was lush with overgrown prairie grasses and rich green cottonwood trees. I'll never forget the date: August 15, 2004. I began my journey in Denver at 8am, full of hope and anticipation, and I ended it in Billings, Montana, at 8pm, with parts of my body shattered, in fear of losing my life, and being held in the arms of an angel.

My entire trip to Colorado had been planned with an eye to current astrological transits. As Saturn entered my 4th house, I purposefully chose to visit my childhood home and my aging father. You know, burn the karma; get it before it gets you. I did indeed get a chance to say a last farewell to my father, but the rest of my chart also sprang into action. I

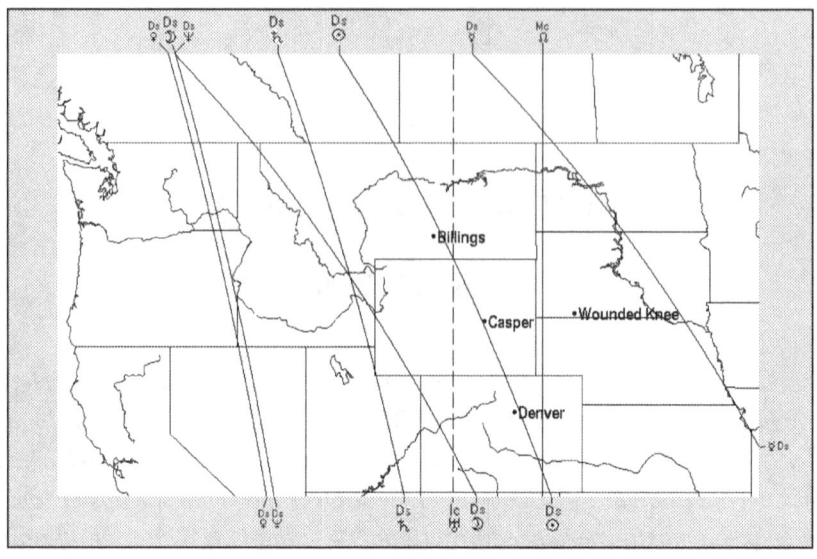

Figure 1 – Detail of natal A*C*G map, Maya White, Nov 6, 1953, 4:47 PM, Longmont, Colorado.

am one of the fortunate survivors of an incident which is played out in a drama that has shattered many lives: an automobile accident caused by an intoxicated driver. The road to recovery has been a long and twisted journey which rocked my foundations. Every step of the way, the A*C*G maps illustrate my story.

A*C*G is a synchronistic interface between one's natal chart and resonant Earth locations. Planetary influence lines pinpoint the geographic places where each luminary is shifted into a point of activation. The heart of A*C*G is the power of angularity conveyed by each planet's Midheaven (MC), Imum Coeli (IC), Ascendant (ASC), and Descendant (DSC) locations. These four points of activation are where and when things happen, both in natal chart astrology and on the A*C*G maps. While software options in mapping programs make it possible to create maps with dozens of other lines, such as house cusps, major and minor aspects, coordinate system reference planes, etc., I think the strength of planetary angularity reigns as the primary brilliance of A*C*G.

See Figure 1. Billings Montana sits on the 45th parallel, only 67 miles from the direct crossing of my Uranus IC and Sun DSC. I also have a Saturn DSC and Moon DSC crossing only 200 miles further west. Both

My Summer Vacation 79

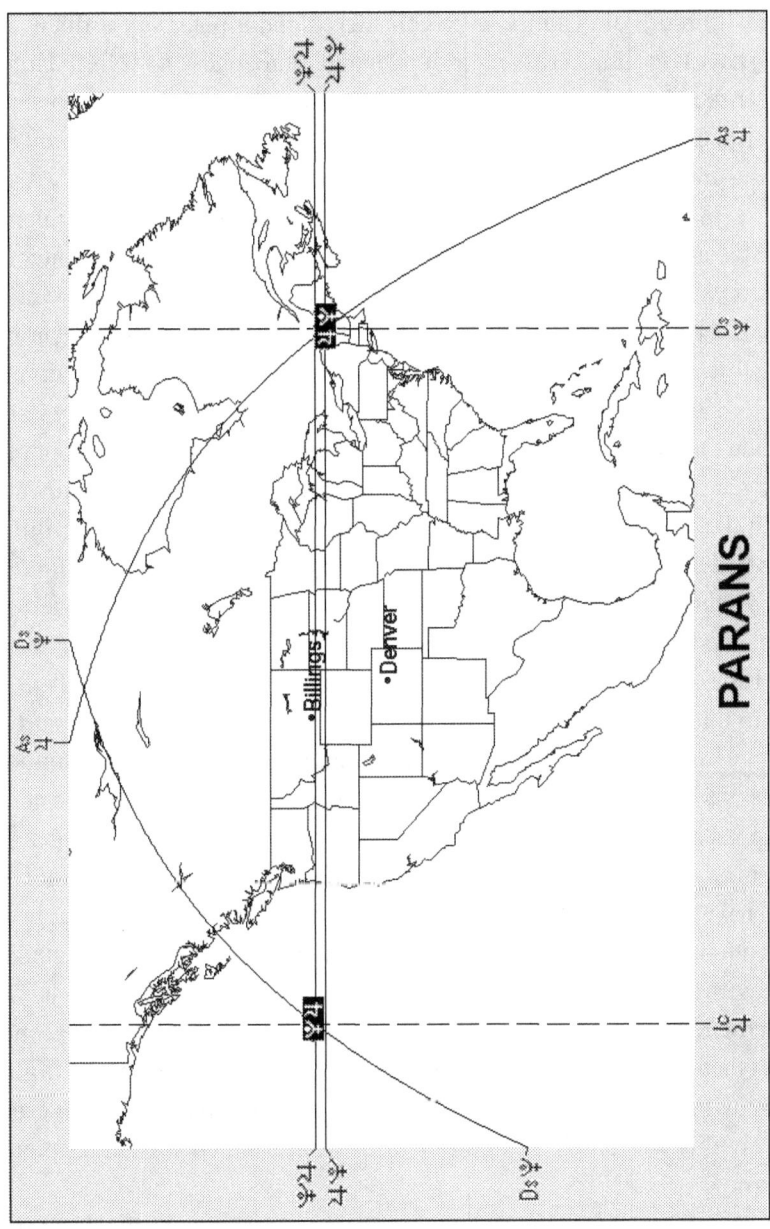

Figure 2 – Jupiter-Pluto parans.

are within orb of distance to be considered major planetary influences. I also have two paran[1] crossing of Jupiter and Pluto, one at 44° North latitude (over the North Eastern US), and another at 45° North latitude (over the Pacific Ocean, 660 miles West of Oregon); both played a significant role in this event. See Figure 2 for those parans.

In my natal A*C*G map, Billings invokes the locational influences of Sun and Uranus, as well as Moon and Saturn and parans of Jupiter and Pluto. With a loose trine between the Sun and Uranus in my natal chart, I was expecting the more positive manifestations of Sun and Uranus: once-in-a-lifetime events, creativity and increased personal freedom.

I eagerly looked forward to my visit in this astrologically exotic locale on the 45th parallel. In my innermost being, I had visions of past-life reconciliation with known and unknown ancestors. My plan was to visit the new home of a dear friend who had recently moved to Billings. We had also planned a short trip into the South Dakota Native American lands, the place where my father was born and raised. I had long felt that I retained a connection with another disaster, the Wounded Knee Massacre of 1862. This journey was initiated with an intention to ritually heal my tie to this ancient wound; I just had no idea how much it would hurt.

I took the long way out of Colorado that summer day, into the Rocky Mountains and up over the Continental Divide. Just before noon I stopped in Allenspark to revisit another childhood memory, 'Charlie Eagle Plumes', a well-known Native American store in Allenspark, Colorado. As I was leaving Charlie's store, a strand of prayer beads caught my attention, begging to make the journey with me. I continued my excursion, pleased to have threads from a distant past hanging on the rear view mirror of my red rental car. The weather was perfect, the scenery spectacular and the wildlife abundant. As I drove over the highest mountain pass, my car was accompanied by a low flying Golden Eagle; surely this was another good omen for what I hoped was an auspicious journey.

Perhaps it is because the planetary gods were with me that I lived to tell the story of that day. Just minutes before arriving at my destination in Billings, I witnessed the unthinkable: ahead, a car was speeding the wrong way out of an exit ramp, coming headlong towards me! It seemed to have me in its sights, as if guided by a demon. I had only a split second in which to make a critical choice of which way to swerve, but no matter, it seemed locked in on my path, and I suffered its head-on assault. Next I heard and felt a deadly thud and crunch, which I knew would change my life forever. As time passed, I never lost consciousness, even while being cut out of the car by technicians using power tools. The safety airbags diligently saved my life, and yes, I was wearing my seatbelt! In addition to various cuts and bruises, I experienced the most intense pain in my right foot – a pain beyond anything I had ever imagined possible.

My excursion to the highly charged A*C*G zone of Sun/Uranus, Moon/Saturn and Jupiter/Pluto had suddenly turned deadly. Without warning I experienced the influence of the Imum Coeli (IC) aspects of Uranus on my core being (Sun). And, I had suddenly drawn into my life a manifestation of the most troubling Moon and Saturn aspects in A*C*G: health concerns, poor treatment, and seeming activation of an ancestral or karmic curse. One of the questions posed by use of A*C*G maps is 'how long does it take until one feels the effects of planetary influences?' My answer regarding this location has to be that the effects manifested almost immediately. My life was dramatically changed in an instant.

Dismally, the accident was only the beginning of my change in fortune on that fated day. Because of the high-speed impact, my car was spun around and left facing the oncoming interstate traffic. Beside terror, my only thought was how ironic it would be to have survived such an accident, only to be cut down again by oncoming cars. Thank God for my angel, the woman who stopped to comfort me before the ambulances arrived. I was trapped inside my vehicle, but she cradled my head and reassured me that those blazing headlights from oncoming high speed traffic would stop in time. Simultaneously, two ambulances arrived and my angel disappeared into the night. As she walked away, so did my only connection to hope and sanity in the hours which followed.

The first clue that I was in for a bad spell could have been that the driver who had obviously caused this accident was transported to the hospital before me. Although his injuries were far less than those I sustained, the onsite medical personnel could not evaluate his condition because he was passed out, drunk. I had to wait, all the while in torturous physical and emotional pain. Once inside the hospital, I felt like a stranger in an even stranger land.

My right foot, the one I had unconsciously gripped onto the brake in a desperate attempt to avoid impact, was severely damaged from the head-on collision. My hospital stay was a bizarre nightmare of pain and nausea. Morphine made me violently ill, but other drugs barely touched my agony. For the first two days I laid in bed with bits of auto glass still stuck to my body! To make matters worse, the physician assigned to my case was barely civil. I could not understand why this doctor was so incredibly rude, and I was in too much pain to really care. (Months later, I considered that perhaps he wrongly thought it was I who was the intoxicated driver). More painful days passed there. After the swelling subsided I had a four-hour operation to rebuild the heel of my right foot, requiring a steel plate and twelve metal screws.

Drunk driving is a tragedy which has affected far too many lives. In that area I am just another statistic, yet a fortunate one, because I lived to tell my story. The man who ran into me pled guilty to his offense. He received a $600 fine, one day in jail (suspended), and restricted driving privileges for six months. This was his second intoxication crime involving personal injury of another driver, yet he did not really even lose his legal right to drive – or go to jail! Montana seems to be peculiarly behind the times in both judicial attitudes and laws. At the time of this tragedy (August of 2004), it was actually legal for a person to drive with an open alcoholic beverage! I understand that statute has since been changed; however, in addition to a lifelong physical injury, I suffered a gross denial of justice from the state of Montana legal system.

Not only did my natal A*C*G map point to the possibility for danger, my personal transits were also active and illustrated in the Cyclo*Carto*Graphy maps. C*C*G is an auxiliary technique which displays progressed and transiting planets as an overlay to the natal Astro*Carto*Graphy map. The C*C*G map is a quick and accurate locality visualization of one's progressed Sun, Moon, Venus, Mercury and Mars. The outer planets, Jupiter, Saturn, Uranus, Neptune, and Pluto are displayed by transit position on the C*C*G map. The next map reveals more relevant detail to this drama. Transiting Saturn IC on the C*C*G map is approaching Billings (36 miles) at the moment of the accident, as is progressed Mars DSC, less than 200 miles away. See Figure 3.

Thankfully, this story has a happy ending, and there are numerous

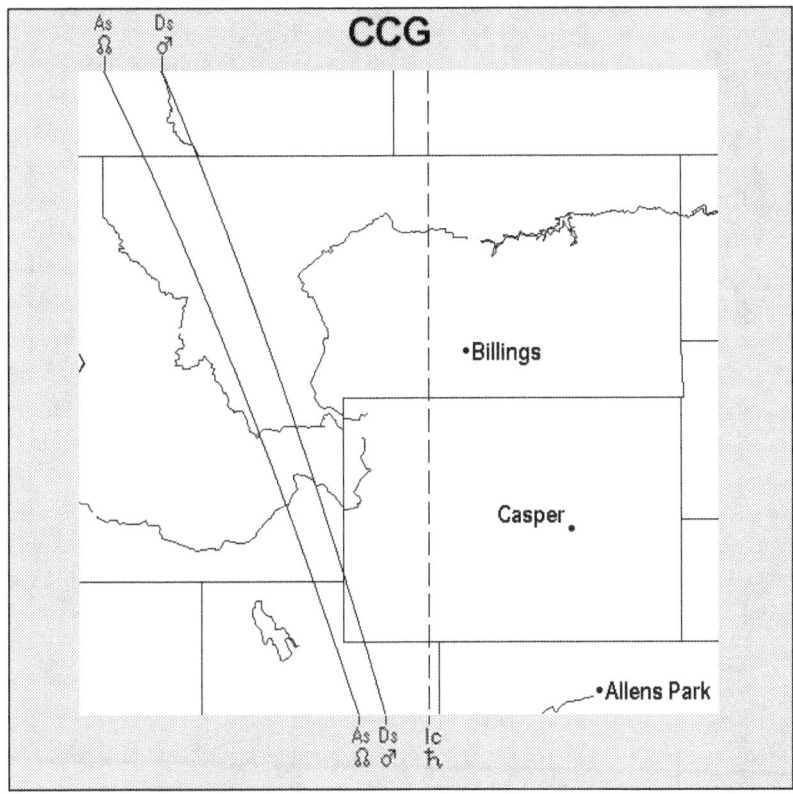

Figure 3 – Montana detail. C*C*G for Maya White, August 15, 2004, 8:00pm

angels included in my tale. The first one was the mysterious lady who appeared only minutes after the accident and comforted me during the darkest moments of my life. As the ambulance arrived that horrifying night, she disappeared from the scene, never to be seen again. I shall always thank God for this helper who gave me hope when I had none.

The next angel was my dear friend whose house was only minutes away from the scene of the accident – yet a far distant light. She stood by me every step of the way and for two months graciously nursed me back to health in her home. I shall be forever grateful to my spiritual sister who fed me nutritious food, gave me healing herbs, and shared so much love. She also went with me to retrieve the prayer beads out of the wrecked vehicle from which I so miraculously emerged. Those prayer beads from Charlie Eagle Plumes' store had surely served their purpose.

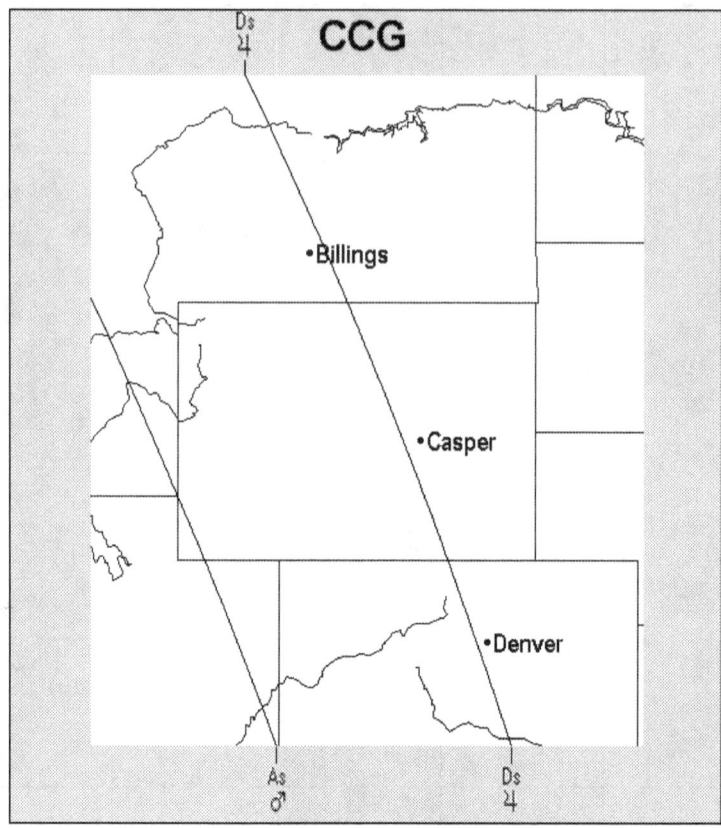

Figure 4 – Billings MT. Detail, C*C*G transits. December 22, 2005.

Amazingly, my adventure also brought a welcome face from the past that I had not seen since my early teens. I was reunited with a long-lost cousin during my unexpected stay in Billings! In this strange and distant town, I found a true paternal blood relative. One of my cousin's hobbies is genealogy, and she showed me pictures of ancestors whom I had no idea ever existed. Together we examined our common blood line in photos of gypsy-like European immigrants who camped and lived on the great plains of America. More leaves and branches of my family tree were brought into focus.

One more angel who had crossed my path previously was a competent automobile insurance agent. Thank Jupiter I had adequate uninsured motorist coverage in my policy! It came as no surprise that the drunken driver who assaulted me carried only a bare minimum of insurance – nothing near what was needed to cover even the first 24 hours of my hospitalization. But, I was armed with the blessing of my 44th parallel crossing of Jupiter and Pluto in the Northeast, which materialized as financial abundance backed by integrity. "Money business and inheritance are the areas of life that go well under these planets, and to some few people, miracles may happen. You can become rich, find, win, or inherit wealth, and seem to be protected by guardian angels in times of trial".[2] Finally a positive manifestation of Pluto: a large sum of money! My insurance company located in Maine (less than 120 miles from my Jupiter ASC- Pluto IC paran) came through for me with a decent settlement; certainly a life changing contribution towards my recovery. I received my settlement check on the day Jupiter transited my natal Sun (therefore, also conjoining my natal SU DSC line through Billings MT, the scene of the accident)! See Figure 4, transiting Jupiter DSC line through Billings on the day I received my settlement check.

Even armed with astrological knowledge, one faces endless doubts when the worst possible outcome of a challenging transit manifests. As Saturn continued its transit of my natal 4th house, I worked diligently to build my new foundation, literally one step at a time. The accident happened in seconds, but my long journey towards healing was measured in years as I daily confronted uncomfortable body changes which brought issues of mortality into crystal clear focus.

In addition to the physical trauma, I also faced psychological ramifications from an accident of this proportion. Current New Age philosophy would advise me to explore why I created such an event. That is a good question, and I have done so, but the reality denies a simplistic answer. How does my peaceful state of mind on that particular day reconcile with the last hours? Did I indeed attract this? Was I relentlessly pursued by a negative force, or a victim of my own hungry ghost? Maybe I was just in the wrong place at the wrong time. Perhaps I encountered a devilish pocket of energy whirling around on the Earth. What can explain the fact that 24 hours after my accident – at the same location – a woman my age was killed in another head-on collision?

There are unanswerable questions which still spiral around this event. Sadly, my father took his life a few short months after I almost lost mine. My visit with him in August, on the day before my journey to

Billings, was our final goodbye – for this lifetime. The single answer I can provide is that the only thing I could control about this entire situation was my attitude. I learned to affirm life. What I could command was how well I went about my daily routines on the road to recovery, and finally, embracing a lightening of my heart and soul.

Thanks to the grace of blessings housed within this personal tragedy, I harvested a much needed psychological reconciliation as well as financial sustenance. But it's not about the money. It's about healing a sacred wound. Much of the work was simply in regaining a sense of normalcy about life. Transformation comes as a necessary expression of rising from the ashes of tragedy, and I choose to fly with the Golden Eagle who accompanied me over the highest mountains. I have journeyed with Inanna into the underworld, then returned. And, with my sisters I raise a toast to the blood of the Phoenix: that precious elixir which brings back life, passion, and joy.

© Maya White 2007.

Maya White's astrology columns have been found as far afield as in the 'Korat Post' in Korat, Thailand, and 'Being' magazine, in Hollywood, Florida. She is the creator of Easy Astrology Oracle Cards, *scheduled for release by Hay House, Intl. in September of 2008. White can be reached via her website: www.WhiteStarAstrology.com or directly by email at: maya@mayawhite.com*

NOTES

1. In A*C*G theory, the term 'paran' is used to convey the concept that the energy of any planetary crossing has a secondary effect at that given latitude anywhere around the entire Earth. So, at any place on the planet where I am on the 45° North latitude, I am affected by my direct Sun/Uranus and Moon/Saturn crossings in the western United States. I also have the activation of my Jupiter/Pluto paran crossings, which are located in the Northeastern US and the Pacific Ocean. Paran influences are not as strong as primary planetary lines, but they do have a role in A*C*G interpretation.
2. Astro*Carto*Graphy interpretation booklet, Jim Lewis, 1976, Pages 41-42.

6

Between Heaven and Earth
The Influence of Astrology on Earth

Angel Z. Thompson

Angel Z. Thompson is a noted participant in the Astrolocality field. She writes on the subject, teaches, and develops new material as well. In this chapter Thompson gives us a helpful overview of locality.

> "The world was given to us in motion and the forces of natural evolution keep it in motion. It is the responsibility of the stellar geographer, or astrologer, to keep an eye on that motion, to call our attention to that motion. And to give shape to that motion with maps and charts."
>
> *Sister William & Angel Thompson*

A traditional horoscope is a study of movement through time. It is a symbolic representation of the planets, as they are arranged in the heavens at a specific time, and is connected to the Earth by the longitude and latitude of a specific place.

Placement colors the phenomena of time and space because where you are determines what you are able to see. Change the place and the time will change. Change the time, and the horoscope changes. For example: at 9:00am in California the Sun appears to be rising and a horoscope cast for this time and place will have the Sun in the twelfth house. At the very same moment in New York it is 12 noon. The same Sun that was rising in California is now high in the New York sky, and a horoscope cast here will position the Sun in the tenth house. When the longitude and latitude change, the connection to the Earth changes and the chart reflects these differences.

Astrology gives meaning to time. It is an abstract discipline of the mind that conceptualizes the complexities of the human spirit, and objectifies cyclical patterns of behavior. However, life is organic, the human experience subjective, and the chart is subject to modifications based on placement. As a result, astrology doesn't always work the way we think it should. Even as we struggle to fit the concept to the individual, symbols on paper distance us from planetary energy. With our head in the stars, we miss the power of the planets at our feet.

Spatial astrology gives shape and meaning to planetary power as it is expressed on the Earth. It offers us the opportunity to experience directly the forces that give shape to destiny. And since the most profound wisdom is learned without teaching, this experience shows us how to accentuate or diminish planetary energy at will, making us co-creators of fate, and astrology a moveable feast.

No matter where you go, there you are. Yes, the birth chart is set for a specific time and place and will always be the primary vibration of one's life. Yet, when the location changes, the vibration changes, shifting our perception and stimulating latent potential. We experience life a bit differently in New York, we get that 'New York state of mind'; in Los Angeles, the sun and sea help us to relax and unwind. One place may be luckier for the individual while the other place is not: tragedy happens to a tourist on holiday, wedding bells ring for another; the conservative librarian dances on a table, while the party girl is down with the flu. Is it the place or is it the planets? It is both.

The astrological technique of relocation offers us the opportunity to see what our life might be like in a location different from that of our birthplace. 'Change your latitude, change your attitude'; a relocated chart modifies the radical chart, it does not replace it. To calculate it, use the longitude and latitude of the alternate location and adjust the time to compensate for any differences (PST at 9am is 12pm EST). This does not change the sign or degree of the planets but it can change the signs and degrees of the house cusps. Because the angles change, planets can gain or lose power and influence over the chart. Some astrologers use this technique to find the 'perfect' place to experience their solar return; others use it to understand the influences surrounding the life in the new location. However, there are times when we just don't know what place would best serve our needs. When that happens, an Astro*Carto*Graphy map can help one discover where in the world is best for them.

Astro*Carto*Graphy is an ancient technique perfected in the twentieth century by Jim Lewis. Instead of a wheel with signs, planets and houses, an A*C*G map is a flat map of the world, with vertical and curvilinear lines drawn through it. The lines mark the places on Earth where each planet reaches maximum angularity, or where each planet is on the first, fourth, seventh or tenth house cusp. The angles are the most powerful spots in the chart and planets positioned on them have maximum expression, and manifest in the world of physical phenomena. Their expression is strong, active and visible. However, a complete and comprehensive understanding of the natal chart is essential in order to determine what will happen when a planet comes to an angle. Activate a strong planet and many good things can happen. Activate a poorly placed or severely stressed planet, and the problems of that planet are magnified. For example, a woman with heart problems, born in Chicago at Central Standard Time, had Mars placed in the physically weak twelfth house. She relocated to Pacific Standard Time, in Portland Oregon, where Mars was conjunct the physically strong ascendant, and her heart condition disappeared. Sometimes, however, it is better for a planet to be off the angle. For example, President John Kennedy had a fortunate and safe chart in Boston. In Dallas, Texas, a potentially dangerous planet came to the Midheaven angle and he was assassinated while visiting there. And yet, an individual born in San Diego had the Sun and Jupiter in the angular fourth house and was completely dominated by his mother. When he relocated to Boston, the Sun and Jupiter moved into the third house, here he was able to reclaim the powerful energy previously projected onto his mother and become a world famous psychic.

If there is no possibility of relocating, or if a planetary line goes through an undesirable or inaccessible place, you can use the law of correspondences to bring a more positive place to you. Say your Venus line runs right through Siberia, but you have no desire to go to Siberia. You can activate that Venus line by listening to Russian music, eating caviar, drinking vodka and watching Doctor Zhivago and in this way bring Siberia to wherever you are.

Another technique that places planets on the Earth is Local Space Astrology. Local Space Astrology gives meaning to space and helps maximize the potential of your planets. Created by Michael Erlewine, a

Local Space chart has no signs, houses or aspects. Using azimuth and altitude to calculate their location, the planets are placed around a 360 degree compass. This gives a map of the horizon surrounding a birth time or event: a circle in which all the planets are arranged around a compass and North, Northeast, East, Southeast, South, Southwest, West and Northwest become the arenas where planetary energy is expressed. To activate or access a planet, position yourself, your furniture, equipment or objects on the line. For example, placing a telephone on a Pluto line assures you peace and quiet, because the telephone never rings. On a Mercury line, the telephone may never stop ringing. If a planetary line is not accessible, or is in an inappropriate place (for instance, if the Sun line runs through your closet) do not panic. The directions hold for 45 degrees, so exactitude can be sacrificed for effect. And, you may be able to extend the planetary influence to a more suitable location.

In addition, directions extend along a continuum – North eventually becomes South, Northeast becomes Southwest and so on. Rather than sitting on a planetary line, facing the direction of the line also activates it. For example, say you want to place your dining table on a Venus line, but the Venus line is in the North and the dining area is in the South. Place the table in such a way that the head chair faces North and you have Venus energy 'in your face'.

Also, by using the law of correspondences, as we did in A*C*G, we can bring any planet to us by using the appropriate colors and objects. If the dining room table is on the Saturn line and cannot be moved, using copper accessories, silvery-blue colored linens or other 'Venus' items in the table decorations will emphasize Venus qualities and create a more harmonious dining experience. A word of caution: each horoscope is unique. In some charts, Venus can be light-hearted and cheerful, while in other charts it may be indulgent and lazy. Study the horoscope carefully to determine the strengths and weaknesses of each planet.

To try this technique, you must use a Local Space chart, not the natal chart. A computer generated Local Space chart is the most accurate, though you can draw one yourself, using the 'eye-ball' method. Divide a 360-degree circle into eight segments, each with 45 degrees. Then, using your natal chart as a reference, start with the Midheaven, which is due South and the only point in the horoscope aligned to space. This will give you a compass-like circle. Now, using your horoscope as a reference, place the planets in their approximate directions. This is about 70 per cent accurate, but since each direction spans 45 degrees, it is close enough for 'field work' or when a computer report is not available.

Perhaps you want to live in a state where the Sun line is prominent, or to find a gym in your hometown located on your Mars line, or to go to a school near your Mercury line. You can use your Local Space chart to discover the places where your planetary lines are most active. To do this, place your Local Space chart over a map of the world, or over a specific country, state or town.

To discover the effect of your planetary lines in your home or office, place your Local Space chart over a diagram of the entire building or house, aligning the Local Space chart with the direction of the entry. To determine the direction of the entry, stand in the main doorway, looking out. Use a compass for accuracy and check the direction your nose is pointing towards. This is called the 'facing direction' and from it you can determine all the other directions. For example, if the entry door faces South, place the Local Space map within the interior and align the South of the map to the South of the entry door. If the entry faces West, align the West point of the Local Space map with the entry door. Now, discover the rooms or spaces within the rooms where each planetary line finds expression.

A Mars line through the bedroom can account for a noisy neighbor or barking dogs. A Venus line through the refrigerator can portend weight gain, while a Saturn line running through a reproduction of an antique armoire will add to the illusion of genuine antiquity. When the alignment is inappropriate, use the law of correspondences to reduce the negative and accentuate the positive.

To refine these techniques, Feng Shui, the ancient Chinese art of placement, offers some help. Feng Shui is the study of energy and how it affects the spaces we occupy. The eight directions are used to define eight specific areas of life. Each direction is associated with an element, a planet, a color, a shape and many other correspondences. All eight directions must be included in every space, otherwise certain areas of the life will be lacking. When this occurs, objects, colors, images and shapes can be used to imply or compensate for the missing directions. In addition, functions and forms work best when they are placed according to their directional correspondence. For example, the South is ruled by Fire and represents fame and popularity. To activate the South, and your potential for fame, place pictures of yourself in this direction and use Fire colors and flame-like shapes and objects (such as lights and candles) in this area of the home or office. Placing watercolors, shapes and objects on a South wall can diminish your popularity in the same way that storm clouds shroud the Sun. Of course, if you desire privacy, adding Water to the South can hide your light.

Poised between Heaven and Earth, we can be conduits of planetary energy. No longer victims of our horoscope, the techniques of spatial astrology enrich our understanding of the power of the place and enable us to harness the planetary energies. Planets on the Earth assist us in enhancing every area of life and offer us the opportunity to change our destiny and make astrology a moveable feast.

© Angel Thompson 1992.

Angel Thompson is a well-known astrologer and feng shui practitioner who for the past twenty years has been building the bridge between Western astrology and Chinese philosophy. Her approach and her interpretation is humanistic yet practical. She combines the location techniques of astrology with the solutions and cures of compass school feng shui, to create harmonious spaces for her clients.

She is the author of "Feng Shui, How to Achieve the Most Harmonious Arrangement of Your Home and Office," published by St. Martin's Press in 1996, which is now in its sixth printing! Thompson was a founder of www.ContinuumACG.net, which is the center of A*C*G information on the web.

7

Reincarnation in Local Space & A*C*G Maps

A T Mann

Tad Mann's work is unique. It is known for its embracing of the ancient arts along with the mystical and mystery traditions. In this chapter Mann describes his system for determining previous incarnations from natal astrological parameters.

Thirty-five years ago I developed a system for determining one's previous incarnations based on the position by sign of the planets in the horoscope.[1] One of my starting points was a statement by Sigmund Freud that "ontogeny recapitulates phylogeny," which is a scientific way of saying that in our individual life we relive the developmental stages of human history. When we learn language at the age of three (during the 3rd House/Gemini time in my Life Time Astrology system), we are at a similar developmental stage to that humanity was in when language evolved in about 14,000-7,000 BC. Another influence is Jung's theory of the collective unconscious, which posits that we all contain a repository of the common archetypal religious, spiritual, and mythological symbols and experiences of humanity.

I believe that the sequence of zodiacal signs (and houses) is a metaphor for the developmental stages in individual human life, and echoes our collective historical development. To portray this, we grade history logarithmically over two precessional cycles (about 50,000 years), making a (logarithmic) time line. This time line is then correlated with zodiacal signs, creating what we call the Reincarnation Time Scale (see diagram 1 from *The Divine Plot: Astrology and Reincarnation*, HarperCollins, 1986). In the Reincarnation Time Scale each developmental stage is about half as long as the previous stage, reflecting the increased density and population through history, and its subsequent compaction of time as we approach the present time. Early stages take thousands of years, while later stages, more toward the present, take mere decades. The positions of the planets and personal points in the horoscope indicate our twelve primary incarnations and their equivalent historical times. The mechanism ties us to historical ages and the cast of characters that influence future generations with their work, ideas, creations or personalities. It shows the specific influence we derive from previous generations. One needn't be Shakespeare (Venus in Sagittarius) or Walter Raleigh (Mars in Sagittarius) to be influenced by Elizabethan England; if you have planets registering at this time, you will be naturally drawn to the appropriate place and time. This is often verified by one's interest in certain foreign places, periods of historical time, particular religious beliefs or customs, taste in art history, where you live and even where you choose to take your holidays. In such cases, we are recapturing the essence and feel of parts of ourselves that are embedded in history.

The metaphor is powerful, especially when one sees the correlations of signs to the sequence of historical eras. The first four signs are the *Mythic Era* before there were specific historical individuals in 3000BC, and this correlates with the deepest archetypal or mythic layers of the psyche that are often the focus of Jungian depth psychology. Aries is nomadic; Taurus is the time of agriculture, Earth Mother cults and domestication of animals; Gemini is tribal and the creation of language and diversity of crafts; and Cancer is the first cities and hearth and grain goddesses. The *Era of Consciousness* begins when the first legendary individuals appear around 3000 BC, with Leo being Babylonia, Chaldea and Egypt and the age of kings like the legendary first Emperor of China and the first pharaoh; Virgo is the Classic civilizations of Greece and Rome and the major religions founded by Confucius, Lao Tse, Buddha and Jesus Christ; Libra is the East-West cross-fertilization after the fall of Rome, the Arthurian mysteries and also the origin of Islam; Scorpio is the Middle Ages, the Crusades, cathedrals and the Black Death. The Era of Individuality begins in 1500AD with Sagittarian world voyages of discovery and the profound philosophy and art of the Renaissance; Capricorn is the industrial revolution, the world states in revolution (France, the US and Russia), Protestantism and the ascendancy of science; Aquarius is the Victorian era, Socialism, Darwin's Origin of Species and

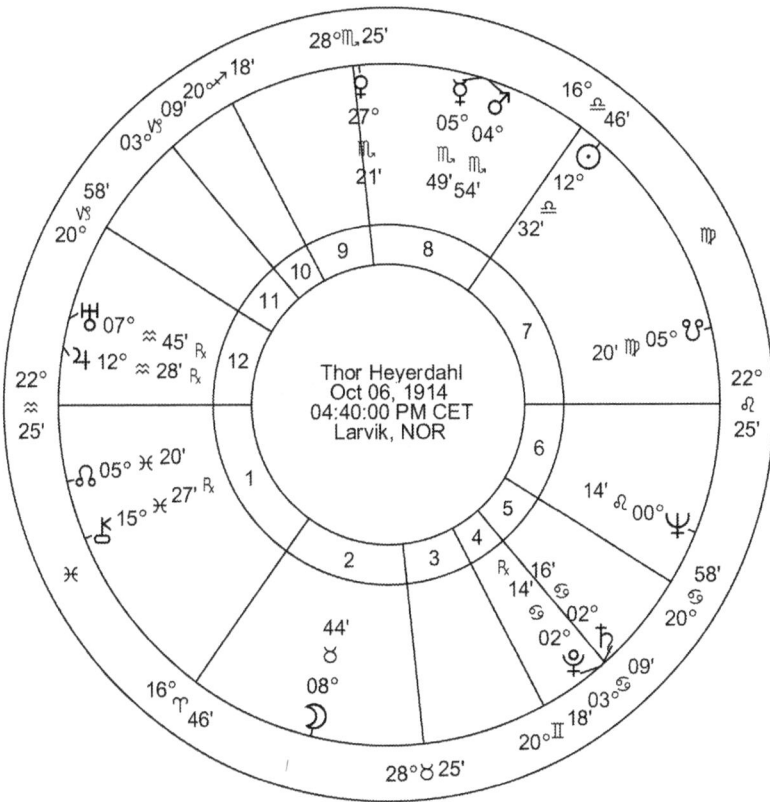

Figure 1 – Thor Heyerdahl birth chart

the United States Civil War; Pisces is the dissolution of classical science, mathematics, music and the two World Wars.

The idea is that the positions of our planets place us in certain historical ages and carry the quality of the planets into the present, which we then interpret by studying it or writing about it, attracting sympathetic energies. For example, it would be logical that historians are drawn to the time periods in which they have planets, particularly those related to their studies. What is even more interesting is that the Local Space (LS) or A*C*G map may show the places of their interest.

The Norwegian explorer and historian Thor Heyerdahl was of Viking origin (his Sun in Libra dates at 750AD, the height of Viking civilization. He postulated that the Polynesian peoples were populated

96   *From Here to There*

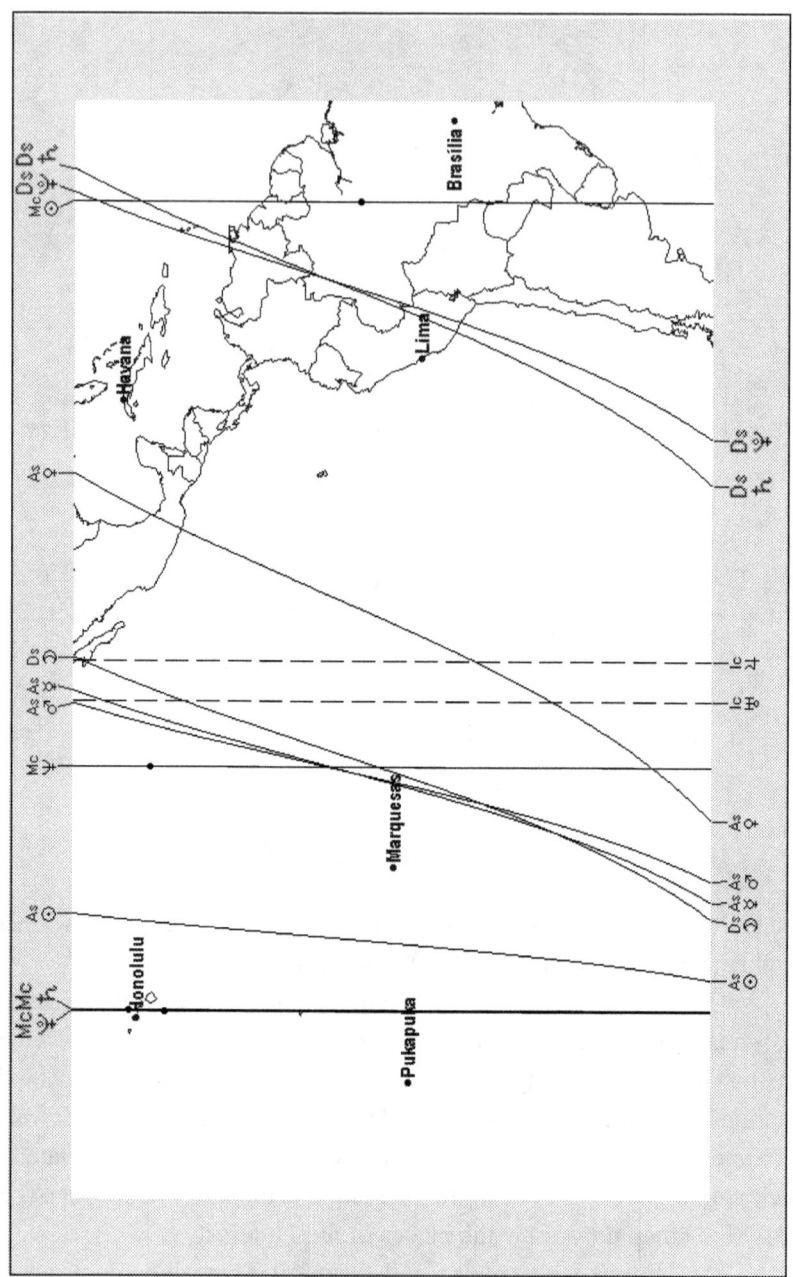

Figure 2 – Thor Heyerdahl, detail of A*C*G map

Reincarnation in Local Space and A*C*G Maps   97

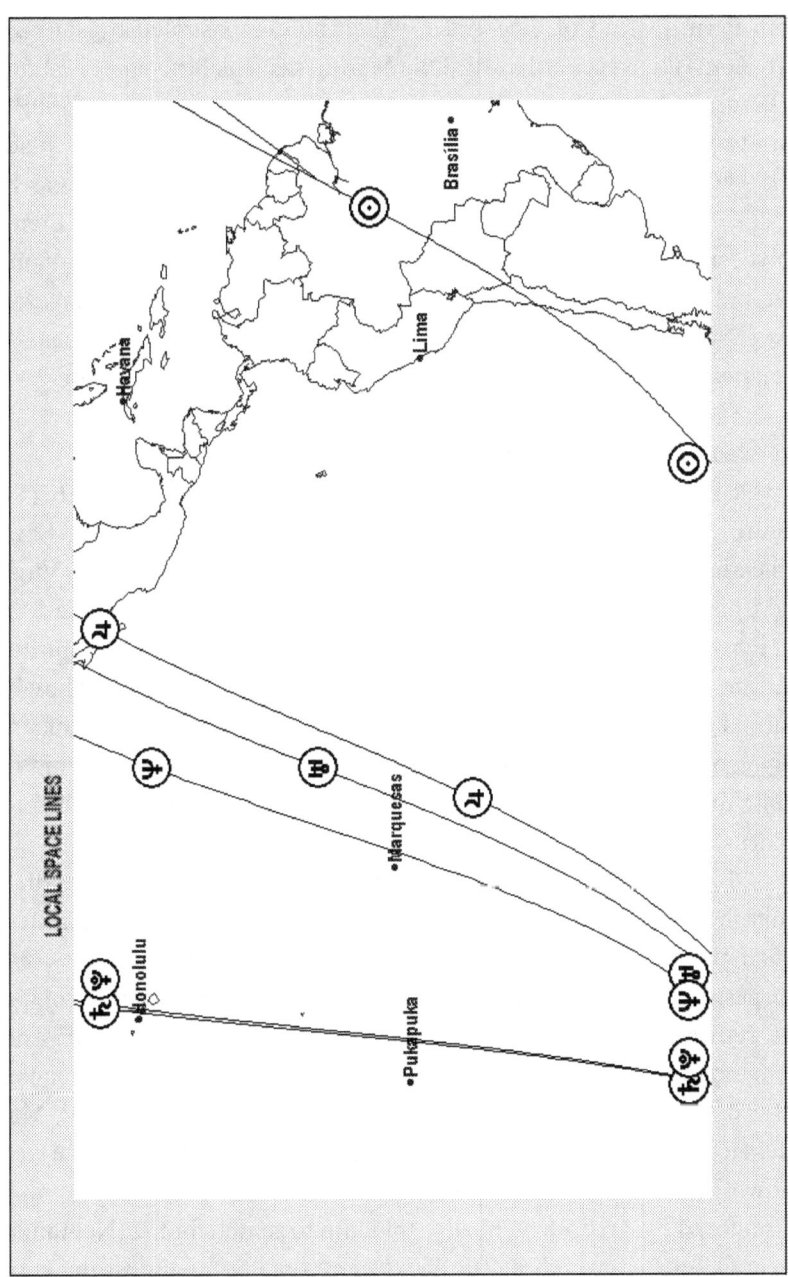

Figure 2A – Thor Heyerdahl, detail of Local Space map

from Peru, instead of vice-versa, which he demonstrated by sailing a raft, Kon Tiki, westward toward the Marquesas. His birth chart is shown in Figure 1. Note that his PL-SA conjunction registers around 6500BC, the Stone Age time when this original voyage supposedly took place. His A*C*G SA-DSC and PL-DSC lines pass through Peru, and his A*C*G PL-MH and SA-MH lines pass west of the Marquesas in French Polynesia, the ultimate destination of his voyage. See Figure 2. Not only that, but his Local Space SA and Local Space PL lines also pass west of this area, as well as through Hawaii. Pluto shows major movements of societies and SA with PL is toughness and endurance. See Figure 2A.

Napoleon Bonaparte

A well-known case of reincarnation is that of Napoleon Bonaparte (See Figure 3: Horoscope of Napoleon), who believed himself to be a reincarnation of Alexander the Great (356-323 BC is 9° to 10° Virgo) and Charlemagne (AD 742-812 is 12° to 15° Libra). His Neptune-Mars conjunction is in early Virgo, corresponding to Alexander as the spiritual warrior. The Ascendant in Napoleon's horoscope is 10° Libra, showing that his personality is within two degrees of the time of Charlemagne. Napoleon's Sun in 22° Leo, which is equivalent to 1280BC, during the prime of Egypt and just after the time of the Sun-worshipping Pharaoh Akhenaten.

Figure 4 is an A*C*G and Local Space map detail for Napoleon (Note that some lines have been omitted for clarity). What is extraordinary is that his Local Space SU line passes through Cairo and his A*C*G ME line passes along the Nile River valley where he sent his armies to conquer and retrieve the secrets of the pharaohs (1798-1801). His Mars and Neptune Local Space lines pass through Athens and the heart of ancient Greece. As these refer to his incarnation as Alexander the Great, Mars refers to the legacy of his skill in battle, and Neptune represents the well-known interest of Alexander in spiritual matters and philosophy, as he was tutored by Aristotle, who also told him to search for the (Neptunian) Great Outer Sea, which led to Alexander conquering almost the entire known world east of Greece. These lines show *where* his incarnations are, just as the degree points show *when* they happen.

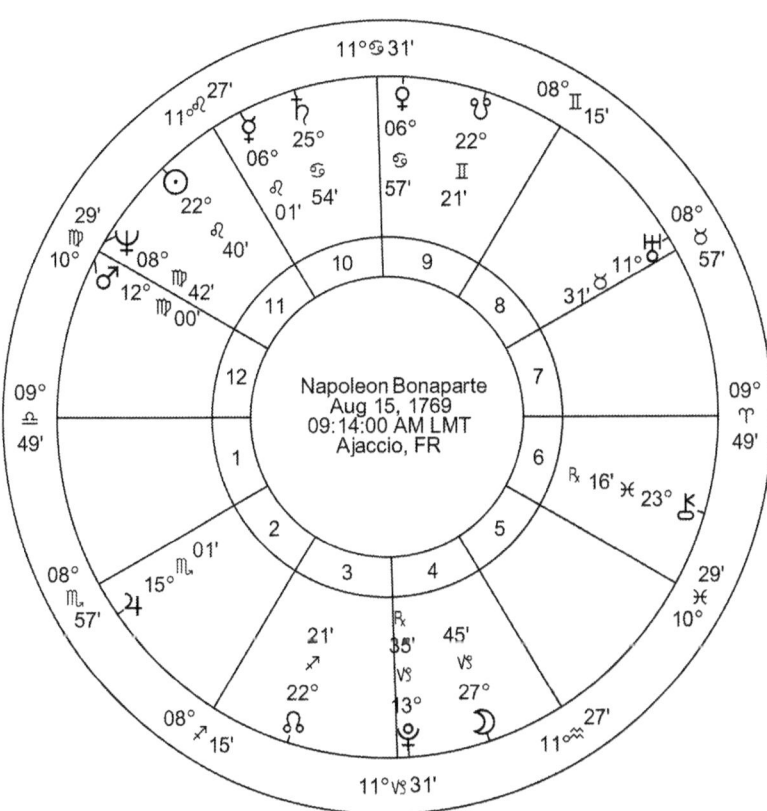

Figure 3 – Napoleon Bonaparte birth chart

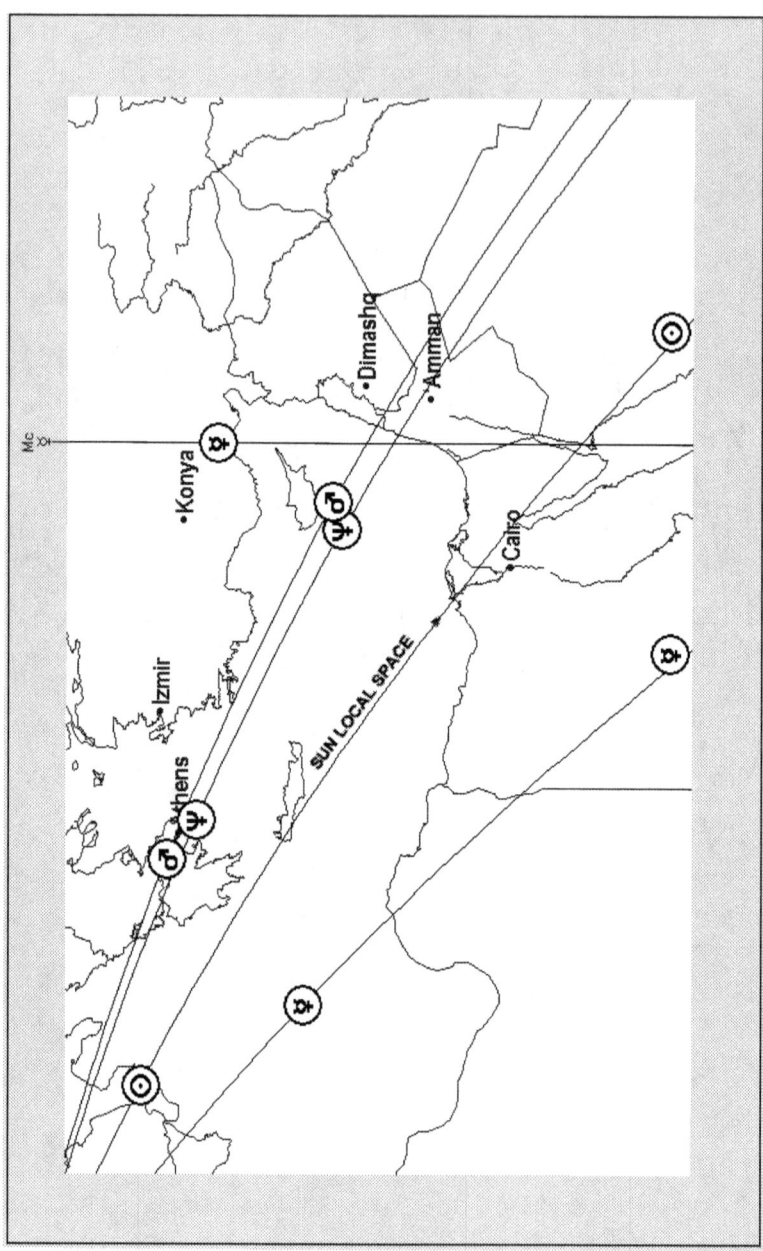

Figure 4 – Napoleon Bonaparte, detail of A*C*G and Local Space map

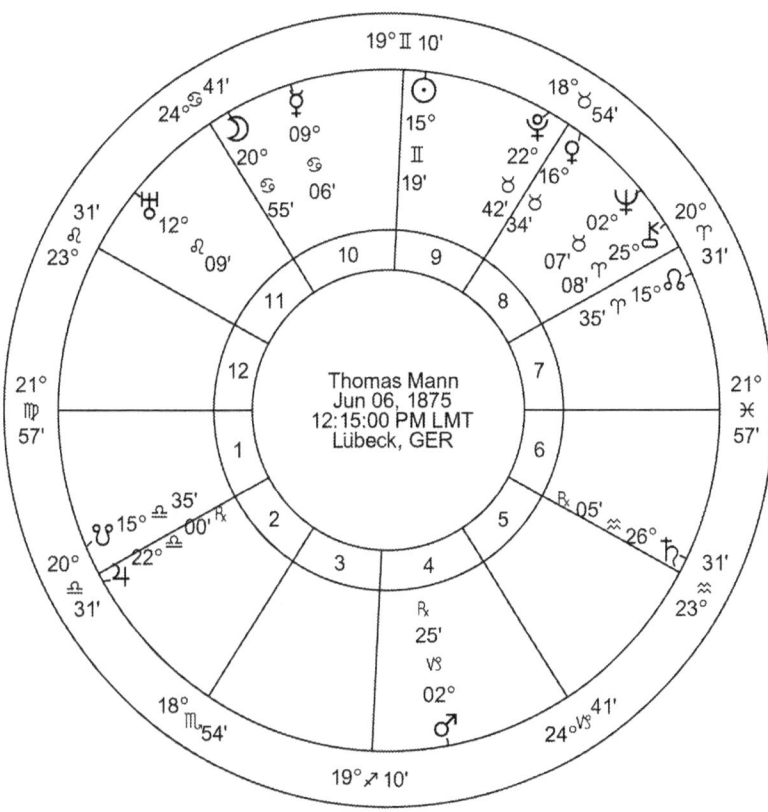

Figure 5 – Thomas Mann birth chart

Thomas Mann

A fascinating example of reincarnation theory is the great German novelist Thomas Mann (1875-1955) (see Figure 5: Horoscope of Thomas Mann). His masterwork *Joseph and His Brothers* was started in 1927 and not finished until 1944. In the first of the four volumes, *Tales of Jacob*, Mann refers to the astrological mythology of Joseph's time and specifically describes the personal points in the horoscope at Joseph's birth. Perhaps not surprisingly, Joseph and Thomas Mann have the same angles in their horoscopes. In both horoscopes, the Gemini Sun is conjunct the Midheaven, indicating noon births, Virgo is on the Ascendant and the Moon is in Cancer.[2]

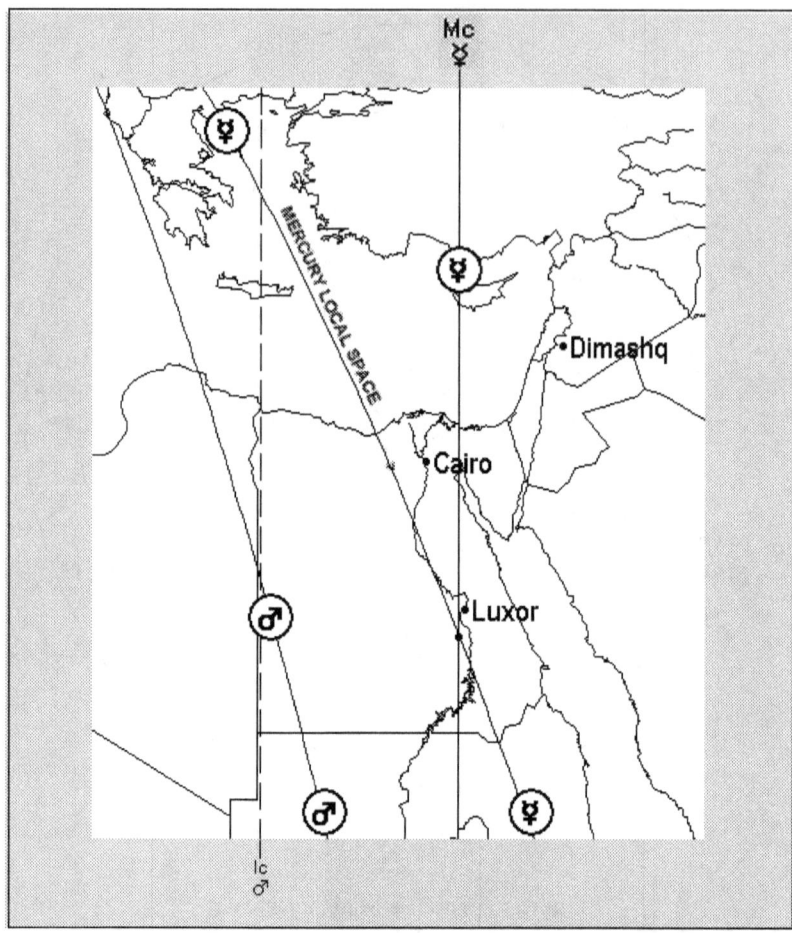

Figure 6 – Thomas Mann, detail of A*C*G and Local Space map

As there is no evidence that Thomas Mann knew astrology, it would be natural for him to instinctively use his own horoscope as that of Joseph, and the agreement between the two lives is striking. It would seem obvious that Mann felt a sympathy and strong connection to Joseph, but the life parallels are beyond chance because the Bible records the plot of the Joseph story. What is amazing is that the life of Joseph is prophetic of Thomas Mann's life during the years when he wrote the novel. Many of the events in Mann's life happened after he had written about them in Joseph's story. One example is the parallel between Joseph receiving the Coat of Many Colours over his ten older brothers and Thomas Mann winning the Nobel Prize over his more famous brother Heinrich. Another is that Joseph famously interpreted the Pharaoh's dream of the coming of war and Thomas Mann's prediction to Franklin Delano Roosevelt (FDR) that America would eventually have to enter the Second World War.[3] In addition, both Thomas Mann's A*C*G ME-MH and ME-LS lines pass through Egypt near Cairo, showing a communication and writing connection. See Figure 6, a detail of Mann's locality A*C*G and Local Space lines.

Robert Graves
The English poet and author Robert Graves wrote a novel, *I, Claudius*, that spawned a very successful television series and is based on the life of the Roman Emperor Claudius (10BC-54AD). What could the

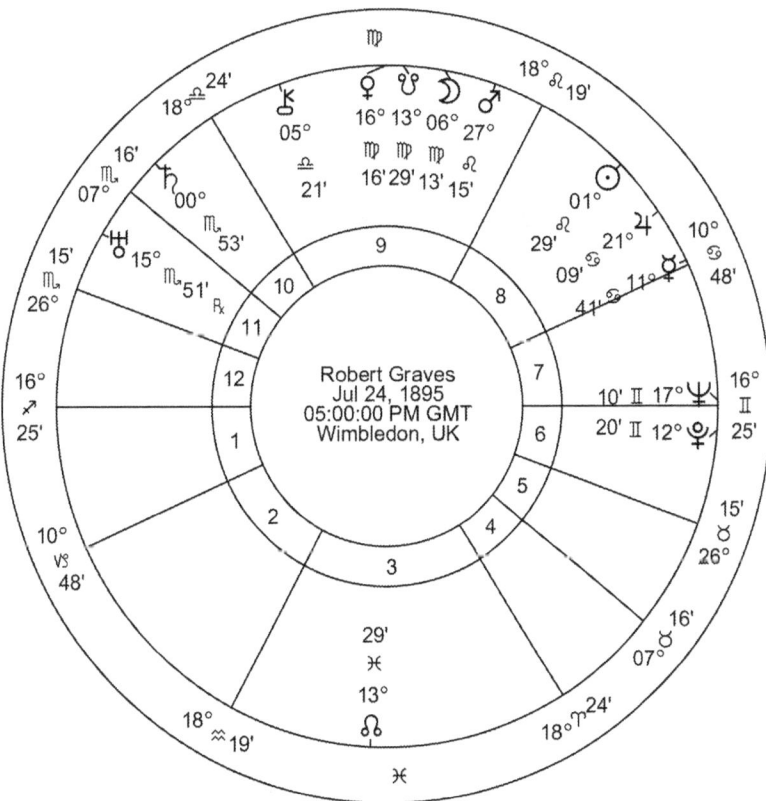

Figure 7 – Robert Graves birth chart

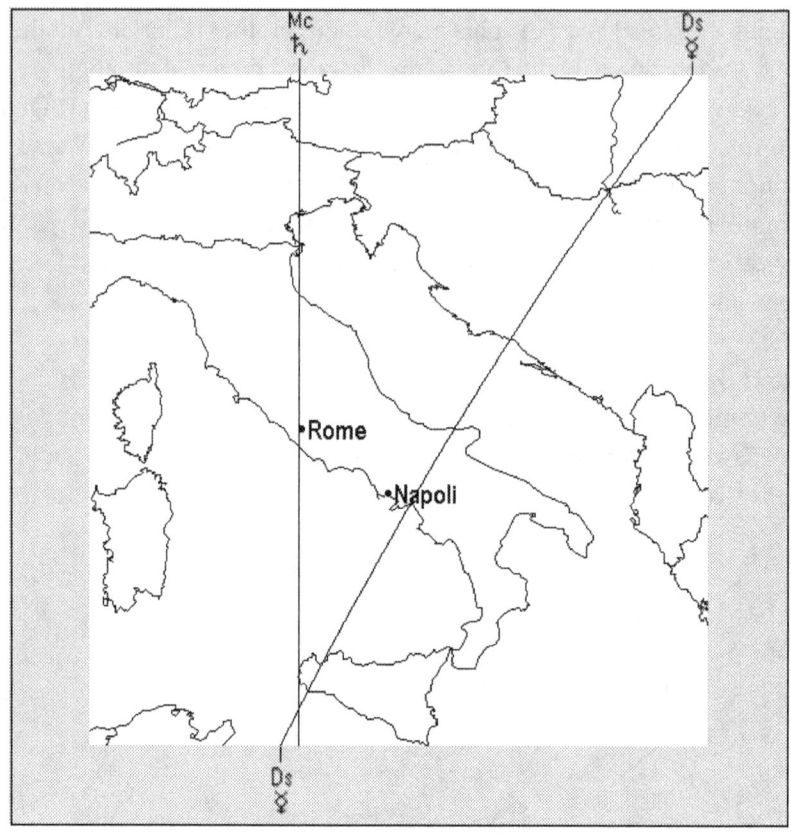

Figure 8 – Robert Graves, detail of A*C*G map

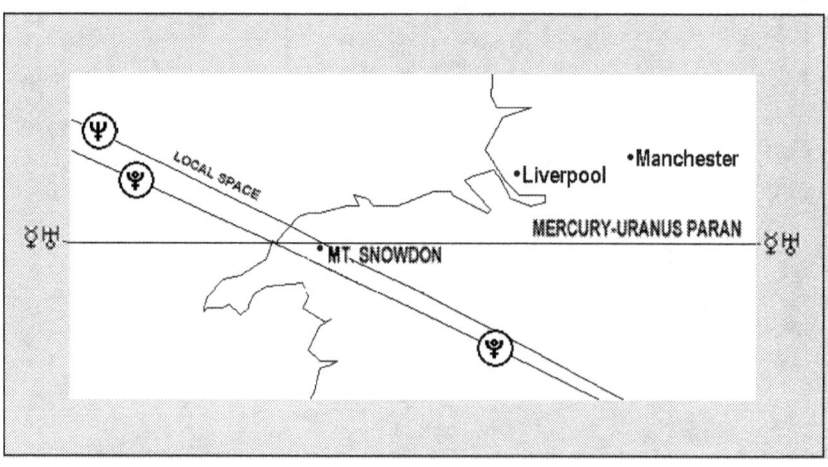

Figure 9 – Robert Graves, detail of A*C*G and Local Space map

connection be? Graves has Venus in the 17th degree of Virgo, which is just one degree away from a perfect correlation with Claudius' birth year. See Figure 7: Graves' birth chart.

He also has his A*C*G SA-MH line going right through Rome, and his ME-DSC only about 115 miles away, which would seem to be appropriate, considering this series in some ways 'defined' him (ME-SA). See Figure 8.

We also see that Graves' PL-LS and NE-LS lines run through North Wales, near the Druidic sacred mountain where his *White Goddess*, about early Celtic goddess and tree cults, is set. Neptune and Pluto in Gemini are in the time when language was developed and they are in a close square to Venus, possibly linking these two great interests of his life. Figure 9 shows those Local Space lines through Wales with the ME-UR paran line from his A*C*G map. Note the crossing of all of those lines is exactly at the Druid's initiation center, Mt Snowdon. The Mercury-Uranus paran intersecting the LS lines (in North Wales) shows a powerful connection, as Mercury is the ruler and depositor of both Venus and his Neptune-Pluto conjunction. Furthermore, the ME-UR paran at that crossing indicates his great talent for speaking and writing about it, possibly emanating from his early historical influences.

Pablo Picasso
The work of the cubist painter Pablo Picasso is very instructive. It is often remarked that many of his paintings, drawings and other imagery evokes African art: amorphous female bodies, unusual proportions, strange patterning and other stylistic qualities. All this makes sense when we see that Picasso has a stellium in Taurus, (see birth chart, Figure 10), the sign historically of the Earth Mother cults throughout Europe and Africa twenty thousand years ago, and that in LS the same stellium of SU, SA, NE, PL, JU and ME passes through the heart of Africa. See Figure 11, the Local Space map for Picasso. In Figure 12 we see that Picasso's Saturn, Neptune, Chiron, Jupiter and Pluto were all at their zenith positions over Africa at his birth moment. This powerful Earth-aligned stellium is bounded by the Sun on the IC to the west, and Moon on the IC to the east, both also over Africa.

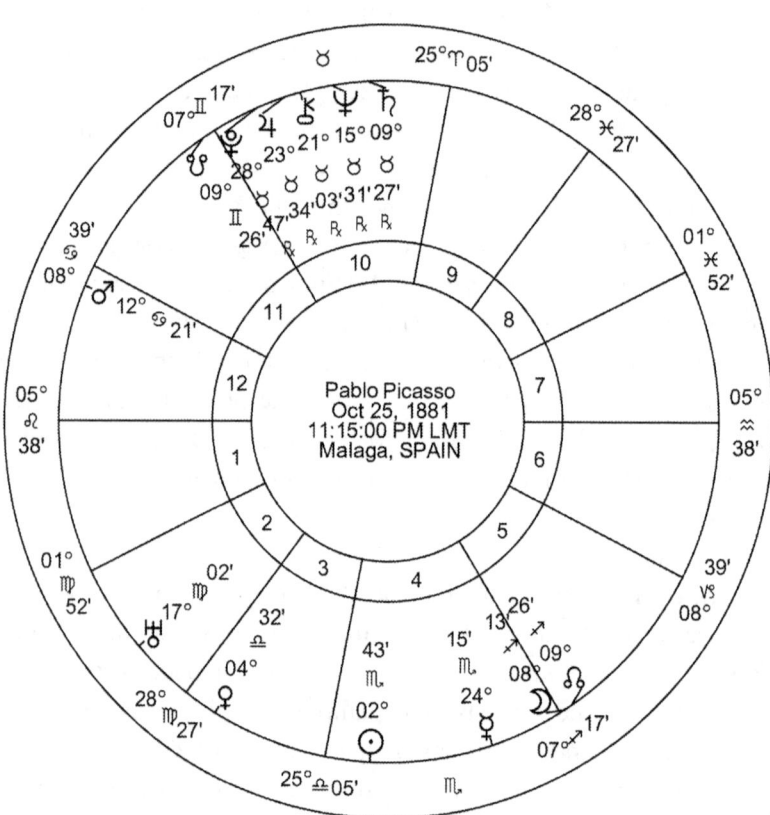

Figure 10 – Pablo Picasso birth chart

Reincarnation in Local Space and A*C*G Maps 107

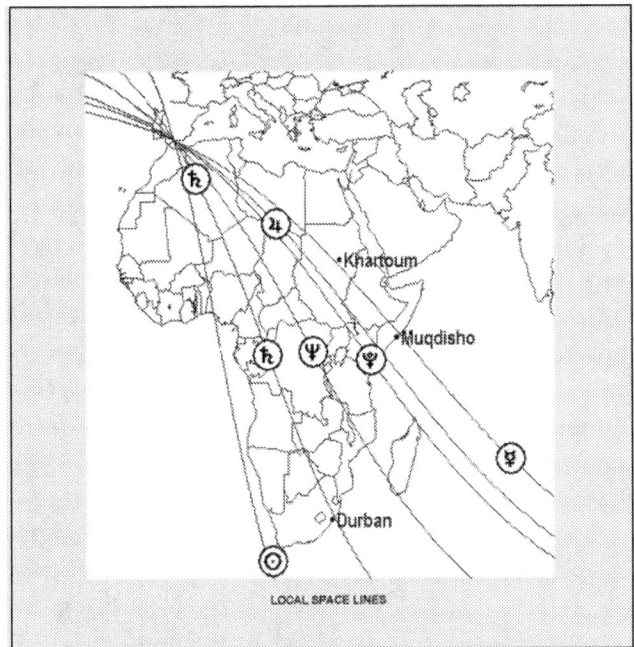

Figure 11 – Pablo Picasso, detail of Local Space map

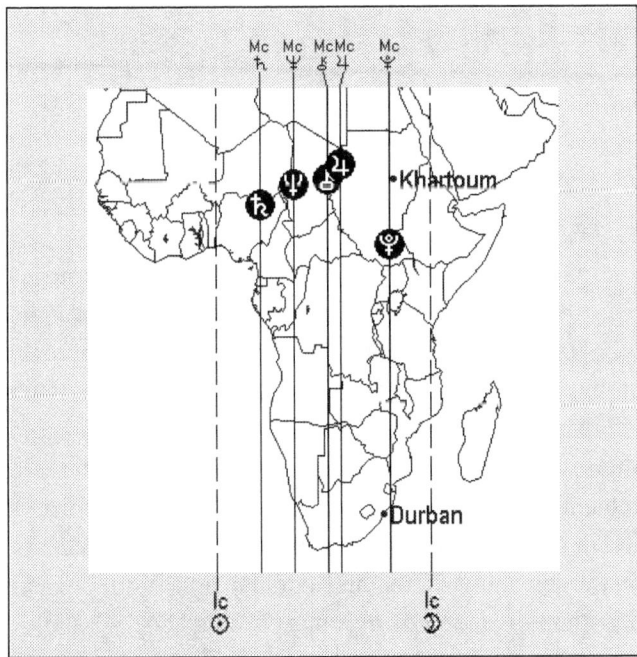

Figure 12 – Pablo Picasso, detail of A*C*G map, Zenith positions

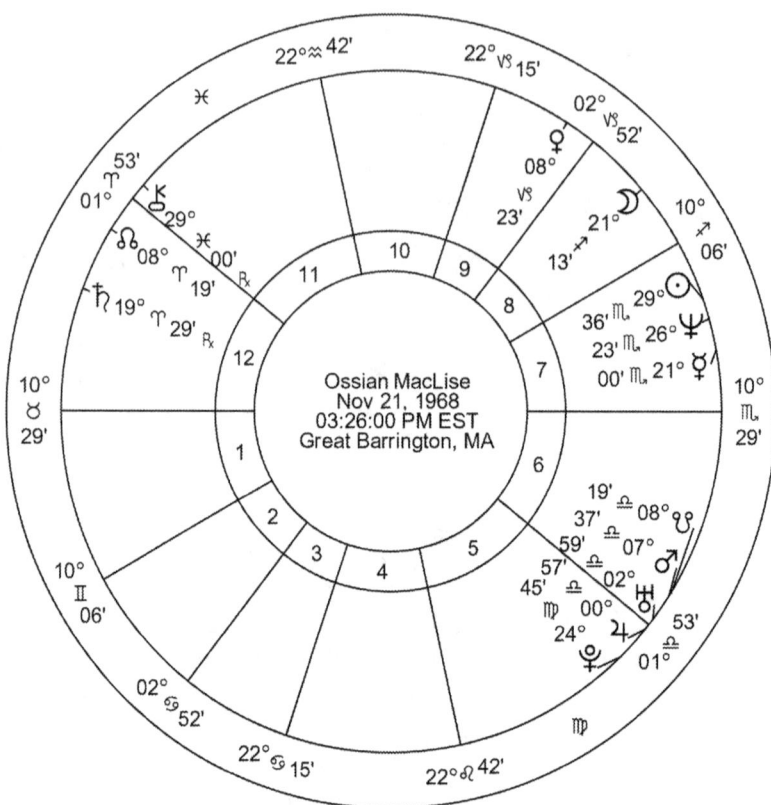

Figure 13 – Ossian MacLise birth chart

Ossian MacLise

An aware individual has primary consciousness only of the stage in which he/she lives in the present time, with partial access to the octave immediately before or after. During our gestation, many previous lives may be simultaneously recalled, and in childhood, the gestation octave of previous lives is still sensed, although such memories begin to fade and are often suppressed as unnatural. There are many cases of young children remembering past lives so vividly that objects, words and ideas totally alien to their new life are recognized instantly. Such a process is in action in the selection of Tibetan Buddhist lama or tulku incarnations. Figure 13 is the horoscope of a young Western boy, Ossian MacLise, who was recognized as the incarnation of a high Tibetan Buddhist lama at the age of seven, in Kathmandu. MacLise was born in Massachusetts,

Reincarnation in Local Space and A*C*G Maps 109

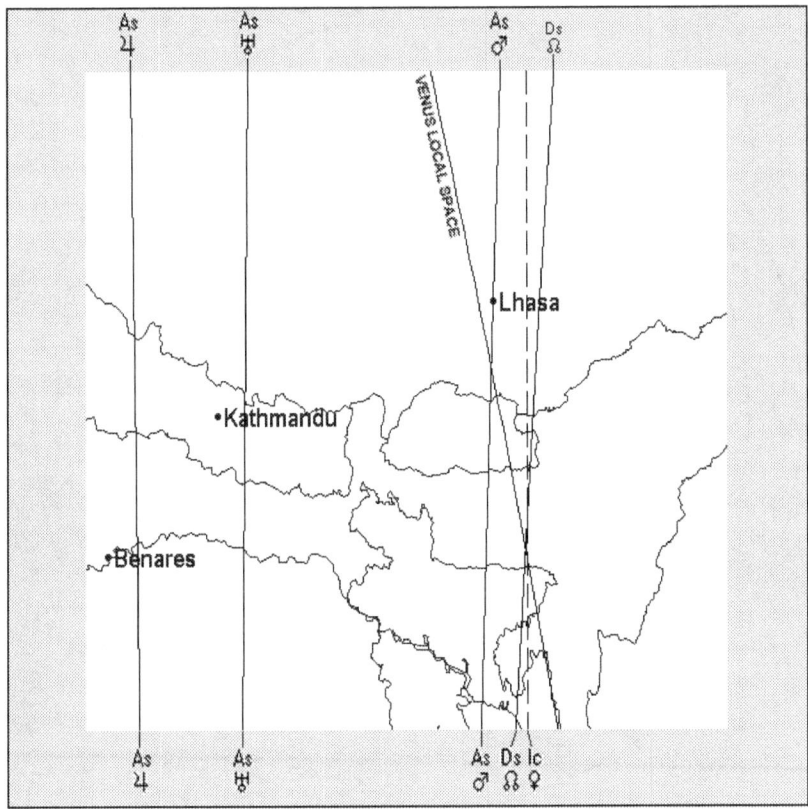

Figure 14 – Ossian MacLise, detail of A*C*G and Local Space map

of Western parents who were interested in Tibetan Buddhism. Shortly after his birth the whole family had moved to Kathmandu in Nepal. While walking past a monastery, the young child ran into the courtyard and began speaking Tibetan with the other young monks. Shortly afterwards, elder monks were dispatched to find him in Western Massachusetts, but he was already in their monastery!

We see that his Venus is at 8° Capricorn (dated 1758 AD) and that his LS-VE[4] and A*C*G VE-IC both pass through Lhasa, the capital of Tibet, as does his action-packed A*C*G MA-AS. He also has JU-AS and UR-AS A*C*G lines (dated 1639 AD) passing through Kathmandu, where he spent much of his early life and where he was 'discovered' (See Figure 14). I have a suspicion that this is when and where his Tibetan Buddhist lineage was established.

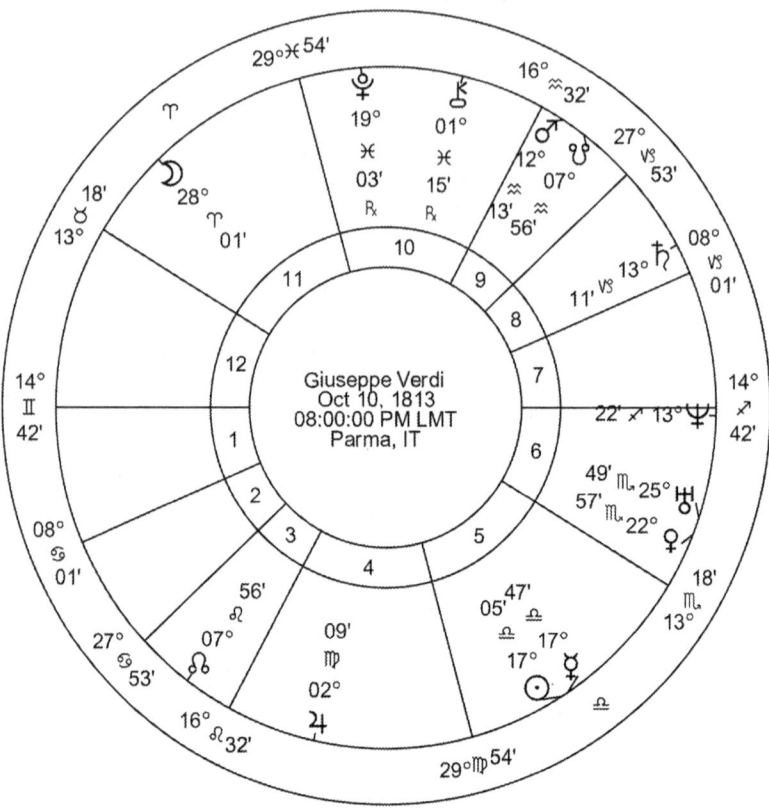

Figure 15 – Guiseppe Verdi birth chart

Giuseppe Verdi

The great opera composer Giuseppe Verdi's (1813-1901) most famous opera is *Aida*, which tells a tale of an Ethiopian princess during the Ethiopian Wars with Egypt. JU at 2° Virgo in his horoscope registers around 700BC and A*C*G JU/IC aligns with the western deserts of Egypt. See Figure 15, Verdi's birth chart and also Figure 16, which shows a Moon-Saturn paran in orb (less than one degree in latitude) from *Mit Ruhaynah*, the site of the ancient city of Memphis. It was here where Aida was enslaved, hiding both her true royal identity and her love for the Egyptian warrior Radames. Moon-Saturn paran latitudes have been associated with the 'cautious heart', where a reluctance to show true feelings may be necessary for one's survival.[5]

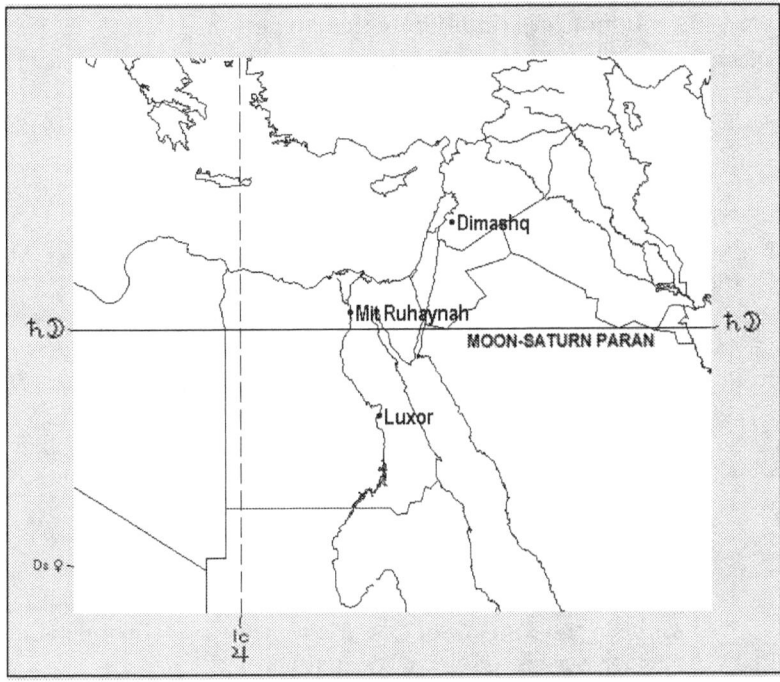

Figure 16 – Guiseppe Verdi, detail of A*C*G map

There are many more examples of the correspondences between historical individuals who felt previous incarnations that guided them through their lives, but test them and see where and when your historical roots lie.

© A T Mann 2007.

A T Mann is an architect, astrologer, artist, teacher, designer and author. His twenty books explore time, astrology, calendar systems, symbolism, tarot, dowsing, healing, reincarnation, sacred architecture and sacred sexuality. Tad practices many arts: astrology and tarot; Feng Shui and sacred architecture; the sacred arts and design education. He worked with Mystic Fire Video on the DVD of the Dalai Lama's Kalachakra Tantra Teachings *and is a founder/partner of UniversalQuest.com. His website is: http://www.atmann.net*

Chart Data and Sources (in alphabetical order)

Napoleon Buonaparte, 15 August 1769, 09:14 AM LMT, Ajaccio, Corsica. Italy (Source: Cirkels, Jan Kampherbeek, Schors, Amsterdam, 1980.)

Robert Graves, 24 July 1895, 17:00PM GMT, Wimbledon, England (Source: *The American Book of Charts*, Lois Rodden, 1980.)

Thor Heyerdahl, 6 October 1914, 16:40 PM MET, Larvik, Norway. (Source: *The American Book of Charts*, Lois Rodden, 1980.)

Ossian MacLise, 21 November 1968, 15:26 PM EST, Great Barrington, MA (Source: Birth Certificate from his parents.)

Thomas Mann, 6 June 1875, 12:15 PM LMT, Lubeck, Germany (Source: *Thomas Mann Diaries*, Andre Deutsch, London, 1984.)

Pablo Picasso, 25 Oct 1881, 23:15 PM LMT, Malaga, Spain (Source: *The American Book of Charts*, Lois Rodden, 1980.)

Giuseppe Verdi, 10 October 1813, 08:00 PM LMT, Parma Italy (Source: Cirkels, Jan Kampherbeek, Schors, Amsterdam, 1980.)

NOTES

1. *The Divine Life: Astrology and Reincarnation* is a combination of *Life Time Astrology* and *The Divine Plot* and is available as an eBook published by the author. See his website: www.atmann.net.
2. Mann, Thomas, *Joseph and His Brothers*, Knopf, 1944, New York, p.231.
3. See Mann's book: *The Divine Plot: Astrology and Reincarnation*, pp.235-7.
4. It is noted that his Local Space VE line directly connects his birth location with Lhasa, the capital of Tibet. MacLise's natal VE is in his 9th house of religious and philosophical study and long-distance travel. In Capricorn, it speaks of the love of tradition and ceremony.
5. See John Townley's MO-SA paran text in the Horizons computer program by Matrix software.

8

Looking at the World Geodetically
Chris McRae

Chris McRae's book, The Geodetic World Map, *brought the geodetic technique to the attention of the astrological community in 1988. Developed from the Geodetic Equivalent Theory of Sepharial, it was another unique and innovative contribution to locality astrology popping up at that time, supported by advances in computer technology. McRae lectures widely on this subject and is considered the leading light in the field.*

The Geodetic Equivalent (GE) concept is an effective way of systematically assigning the zodiac to locations on Earth for use in making political or geophysical predictions, as well as for ascertaining how a person feels or functions in a given location. For that purpose we essentially have a specific and unique house cusp structure for each and every geographic location, into which we can insert natal planetary positions, current transits, lunations and/or eclipses. As shown below, the Midheaven and ascending angles, at any location, can be plotted on a map for a quick analysis.

To determine the specific Midheaven for any geographic location, the zodiac is stretched eastward from Greenwich, each longitude degree representing a corresponding zodiacal degree commencing at 0 degrees Aries. In other words, 0 degrees Greenwich translates to a GE Midheaven of 0 degrees Aries. Berlin, with a geographic longitude of 02°E20', would have a Geodetic Midheaven of 02°20' Aries. Likewise, Moscow, with a geographic longitude of 37°E35' would have a Midheaven of 7°35' Taurus. New York is situated at 73°W57'. We could move forward from Greenwich or backwards in the zodiac to determine New York's Midheaven at 16°03' Capricorn. You can see that fairly closely even on a small map. (See

114   *From Here to There*

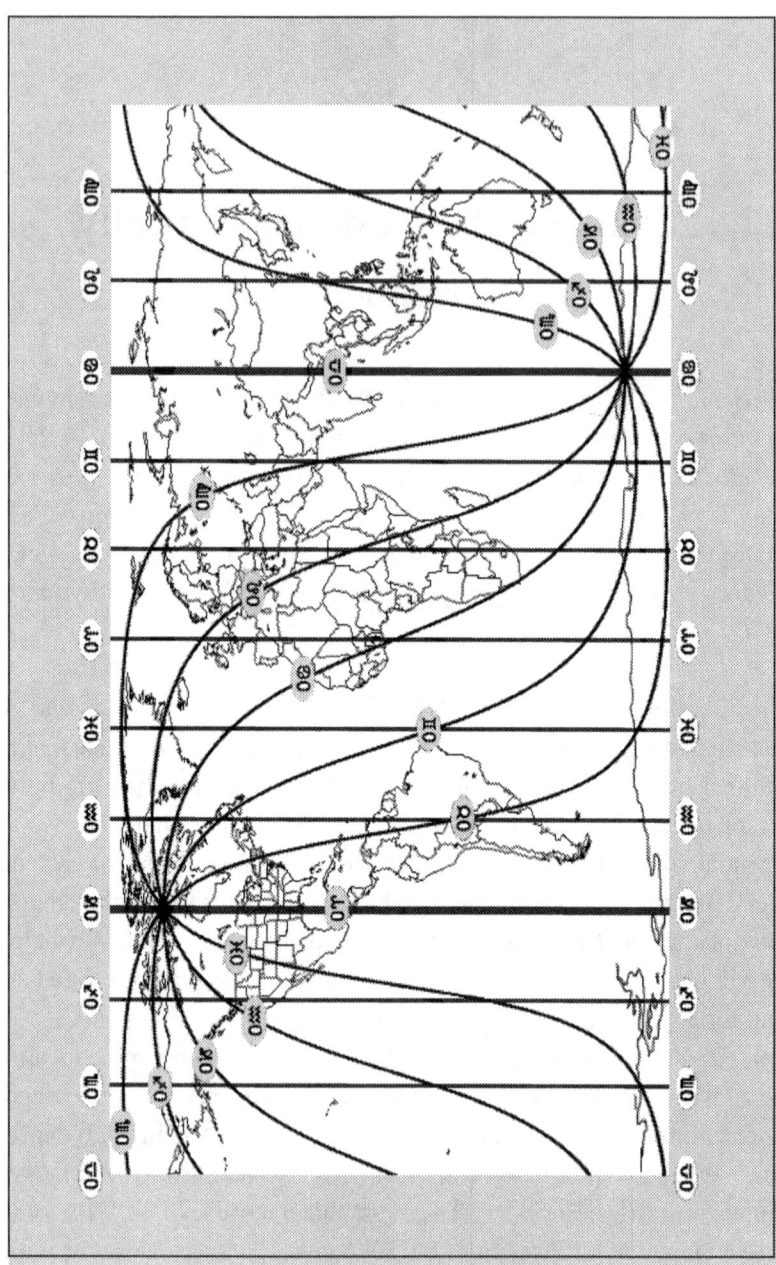

Figure 1 – Geodetic World Map. The Midheavens run north and south on the map and you can observe the Zodiacal signs marked across the top of the graphic.

Figure 1, Geodetic World map.) Once a Midheaven is ascertained, the Ascendant is derived from the geographic latitude of any location. This can be done manually in a Table of Houses or by computer. Note from the map that, in most instances, the Ascendant lines angle across the Midheaven lines with 0 Aries rising, beginning at 90 degrees west geographic longitude and moving through the zodiacal signs in 30 degree segments in an easterly direction. For clarification, please note that Spain is enclosed in a Cancer Ascendant, as is a segment running through Africa.

With such a map, one can easily see where transits, eclipses or other planets are geodetically effective anywhere on Earth. Coordinates for constructing a geodetic map can be found in my book, *The Geodetic World Map*.[1]

Geodetics was used by various mundane astrologers during the early 1900s, then slid from use until it was again popularized by this book, which plotted the Geodetic angles on a world map making the concept recognizable to many.[2] Since the publication of the book in 1988, I have lectured widely on the subject, bringing it to the attention of many astrologers who have found it very useful in both their personal and mundane studies.

Country Rulerships

As we look at the map, it is easy to understand why, over the ages, since the time that Ptolemy assigned signs to countries, that it has been difficult to assign a specific sign to a country as large as Russia. We can see that it has six different Midheavens, stretching across its vast region, and four different Ascendants. Canada, with the second largest landmass in the world, next only to Russia, has four Midheavens and seven Ascendants. No wonder the country has difficulty expressing its national identity. The United States has the third largest landmass, and has four Midheavens and seven Ascendants. There is little doubt that the eastern part of both Canada and the United States are much more traditional in their thinking and habits under their Capricorn Midheaven, while getting freer in expectation and habit going west with a Sagittarius Midheaven. In fact, there was a saying, "go west young man and make your fortune".[3]

The Midheaven of a nation or locality represents how the inhabitants wish others to see them, their reputation, and what they collectively deem most important. The Ascendant symbolizes their collective attitude and how they express themselves. We could use this theme to view a country from the geodetic cusps of their capital city, or we can relate other factors of a city with its distinctive characteristics. For instance, Las Vegas, the gambling capital of the world, has a Geodetic Sagittarius Midheaven (gaming) and a Geodetic Aquarius Ascendant (Las Vegas' casino architecture is eclectic, unique and eccentric; visitors there can be seen as independent, free spirits). Tokyo, with a geodetic Scorpio Midheaven and Leo Ascendant, has distinctive features in this regard. It has often been called "The Land of the Rising Sun", and the Tokyo Stock Exchange is renowned as being the most powerful money market in the world. The western seacoast of Europe with its watery Pisces geodetic Midheaven and Cancer Ascendant is reported to have the most and best seaports in the entire world. As you scan the globe from a geodetic point of view, you will be able to correlate many cities and regions with the symbolism of their geodetic angles.

Geodetics for Personal Relocation
We know important events occur when planets are in angular positions. We can use the geodetic map to see visually where planets fall into angles on it. However, it is also advantageous to set up a personal chart inserted into the geodetic cusps of a location for a fuller analysis. You will note the natal chart of Sir Edmund Hillary,[4] Figure 2.

We are more interested in observing his planets, so we can see their effect in a geodetic location, than we are in studying the placement by house in a natal chart interpretation, but this chart does, nevertheless, have relevance to his life. We can observe the energy, dedication and commitment from his Mars/Pluto conjunction with a Uranus trine, as well as the powerful transformative effect he had upon Nepal over his lifetime. This combination should also be notable for a mountain climber. Hillary's Sun/Jupiter in the 9th would certainly indicate world acclaim and his knighthood, his Mercury/Saturn conjunction, in the 10th house of this chart, ruling the 8th, 11th and 3rd, would exemplify the education he brought to the area and the transformation it created. In fact, he built over thirty schools, two hospitals, twelve medical clinics, and also built bridges and reforested. He built an airstrip so he could fly in and out

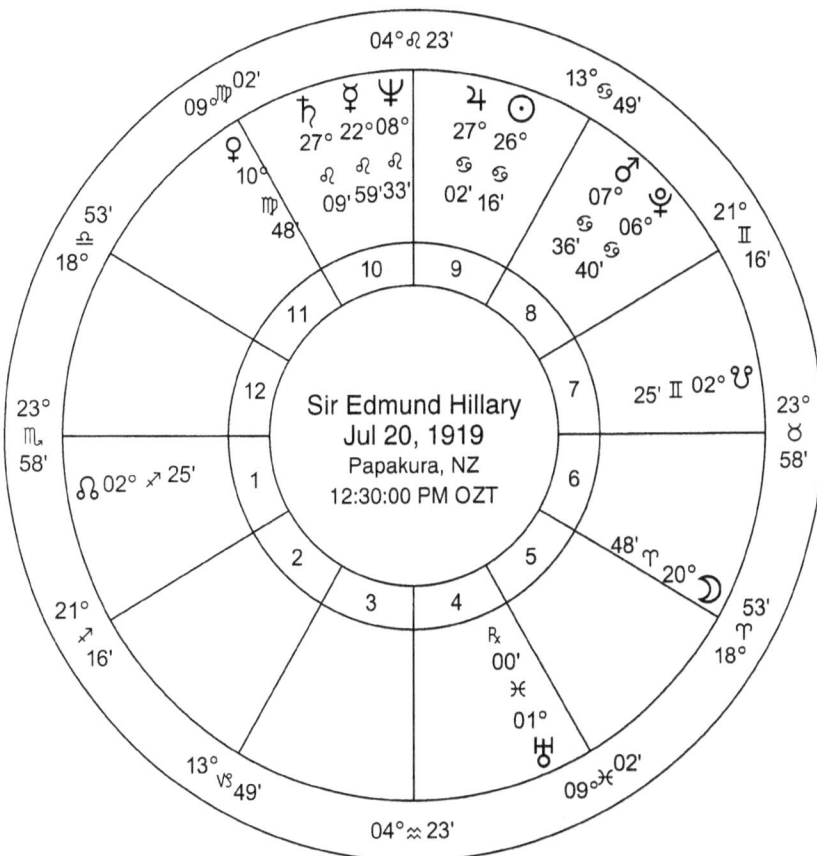

Figure 2 – Natal Chart for Sir Edmund Hillary, 20 July 1919, Papakura, NZ, 12:30pm local time. Rodden DD.

from his various fundraising expeditions, and to bring in supplies. Sadly, Hillary's wife was killed in a plane crash while landing on this field.

We will now look at his natal planets inserted into the geodetic cusps for the location of Mount Everest. See Figure 3. This tells us about his specific, personal relationship with that location. Please note that the natal Ascendant and MC are not included due to the uncertainty of his birth time. If known they could be inserted into the GE cusps as well.

Note the proximity of the powerful Mars/Pluto conjunction on the MC, as well as the angular Sun/Jupiter conjunction. The Mars/Pluto conjunction forms a trine with Uranus in the 6th house in Pisces, indicating that Hillary used his strong will to improve the living conditions of the

118   *From Here to There*

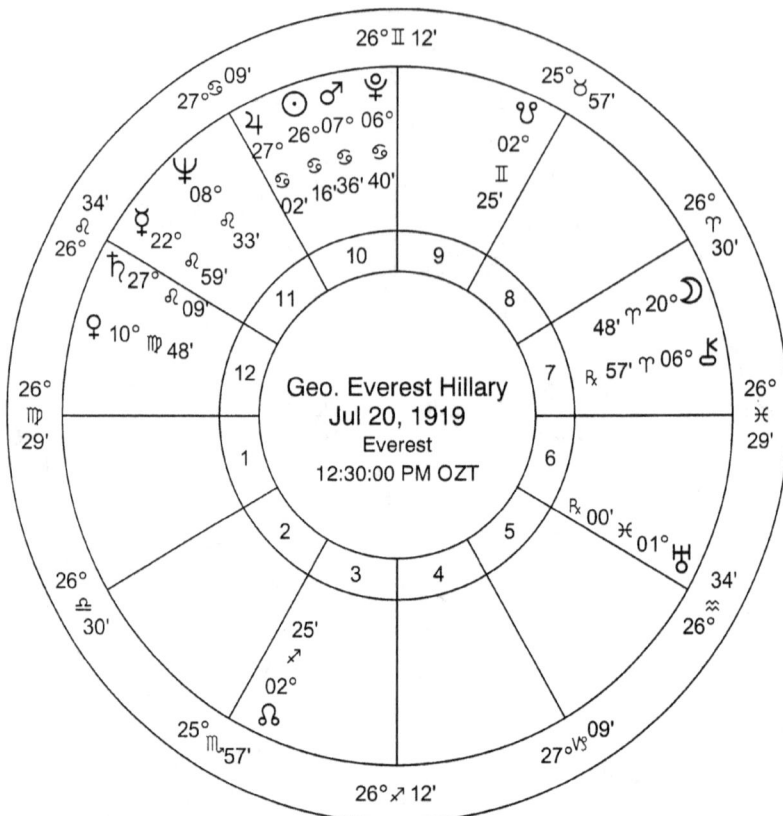

Figure 3 – Geodetic Chart of Sir Edmund at Everest

people in the region. It became his life's work, as previously indicated. In this instance we can use cusps with confidence because they are not the uncertain natal cusps but known geodetic ones.

It should now be interesting to see the whole geodetic world map using Sir Edmund Hillary's natal planets where they appear on the map angles. (See Figure 4.)

Now we can clearly see the global area of influence from his Mars/Pluto conjunction. Note, it is within proximity to his GE Midheaven at Mount Everest. The Ascendant of this planetary combination runs in the vicinity of his birthplace, as well as Sydney and Melbourne, Australia, where he often went to raise funds for the wonderful work he was doing.

Also note that the Sun/Jupiter conjunction geodetic Ascendant line runs right through England where he was honored and knighted by the Queen of England.

Looking at the World Geodetically 119

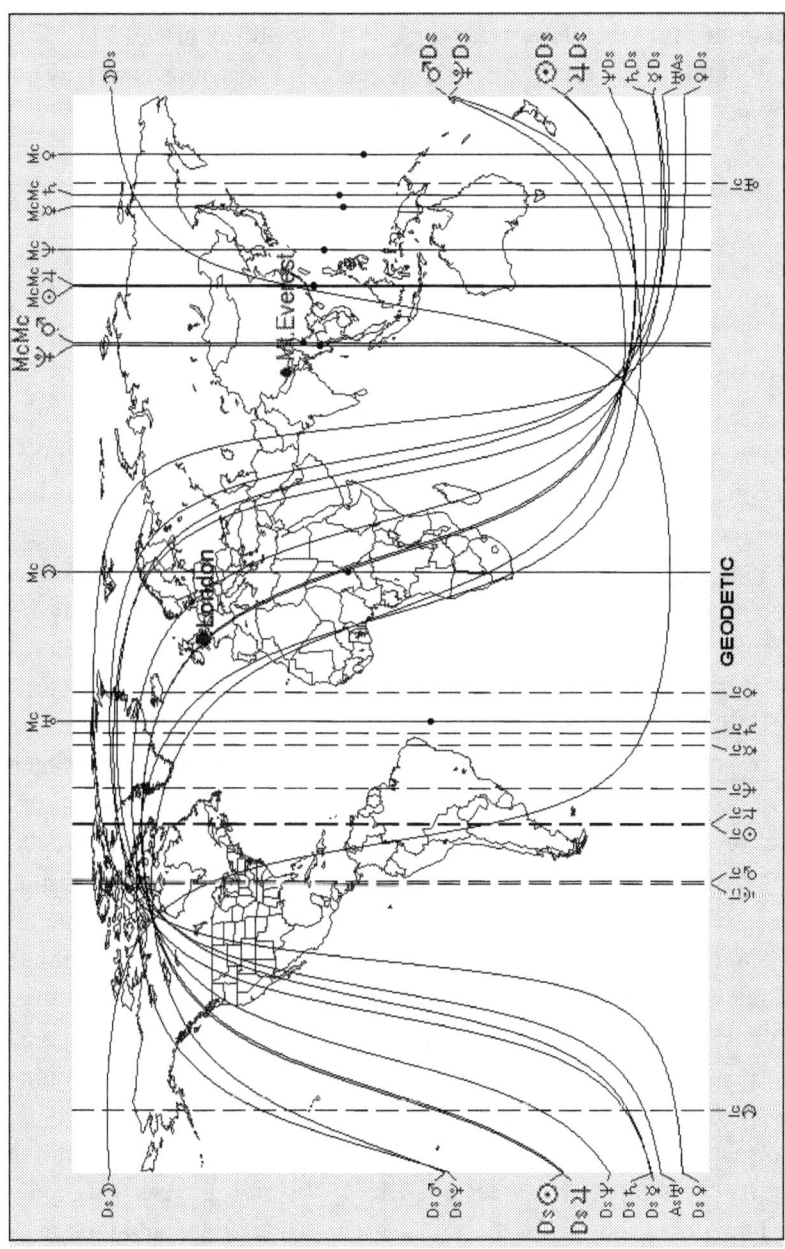

Figure 4 – Geodetic World Map with Sir Edmund's natal planets

Geodetics for Mundane Astrology in determining global hot spots

In mundane astrology, one needs a reference or structure as well as tools to work with. We do have a choice of systems, as follows:

1. Chart of a nation
2. The corresponding Astro*Carto*Graphy map of the nation's chart
3. Four cardinal ingress charts per year
4. Geodetic equivalents.

Tools, of course, would include transits, great conjunctions,[5] progressions, eclipses and lunations.

This chapter is focusing on the geodetic equivalent. The map is exceptionally handy for observing where a powerful eclipse or other planetary influence will have its greatest impact. It may indicate a powerful storm if it is within a hurricane, tornado or cyclone area. It may indicate a political disturbance if such an event is ready to shift. It may be a geophysical disruption, again, if the region is prone to such activity.

It is noteworthy to look at the eclipses that influenced the Gulf of Mexico, the Caribbean, and Florida during the year 2005. That year witnessed the most number 5 intensity hurricanes since 1960 and had the most major hurricanes since 1954. Katrina raced into the Gulf, stormed into New Orleans and up the Mississippi River from August 21–31, 2005, ranging in intensity from a number 2 to a number 5 hurricane. Damage was estimated as the most ever, at $100 billion plus. Then, on October 27th, along came Wilma that devastated the resort areas of the Caribbean. Wilma was reported to be the strongest hurricane in recorded history.

Eclipses can signal such events and when they fall on or in geodetic angles where storms are likely to occur, that is an easy prediction to make. There are two eclipse seasons in a year, producing no less than two solar eclipses a little less than six months apart. I have observed that any pair less than 10 degrees apart in opposition, increases the power along a global range of those few degrees. Then one would look across the map to see where those degrees would be in an angle. Let's see how this works in practice.

It is important to note that from December 2001, eclipses traveled across Gemini and Sagittarius alternatively until the end of 2003. There were no eclipses in the signs of Taurus/Scorpio this time around the zodiac as they move backwards through the signs. They went from Gemini/Sagittarius right into Aries leading into the devastating year of hurricanes that swept across the Atlantic into the Gulf of Mexico. The following is a list of these Aries eclipses:

    April 19, 2004   Partial Solar 29°50' Aries   GMT 13:34:05
    October 14, 2004   Partial Solar 21°06' Libra   GMT 2:59:22
    April 08, 2005   Annular Total 19°06' Aries   GMT 20:35:50
    October 3, 2004   Annular Total 10°19' Libra   GMT 10:32:46
(This is by far the longest in the series being the only one to date that lasted over a minute at 4 minutes, 31 Seconds. I believe duration affects the strength of an eclipse.)

    March 29, 2006   Total 8°35' Aries   GMT 10:11:21

The next eclipse in the year 2006 shifted to mutable but it is noteworthy partly because its obscuration period is a whopping 7 minutes 09 Seconds, and secondly, because it still has influence within the Aries group. According to NASA, this eclipse was one of the longest possible in the annals of eclipses.

    September 22, 2006   Annular 29°20' Virgo   GMT 11:40:15

The next eclipse was on March 19, 2007. Only a partial, its significance was in being at 28°07' Pisces, which was exceptionally close in opposition to the previous one.[6]

One can see by these eclipses that the buildup continues past the noteworthy year of 2005, through 2006, which is the year of this article, and into the year 2007.

Go back now to the geodetic map, Figure 1, and see that these eclipses strongly influence the whole Gulf of Mexico, the Caribbean, and, indeed, even inland along the Gulf coastline. On the map, look for the area covered by the geodetic Aries Ascendant. Of course the corresponding geodetic Descendent, which is not shown, would be Libra.

Note that the Ascendant of 0° Aries also follows up along an area often referred to as "Tornado Alley", where those storms increased during this period, in both frequency and intensity.

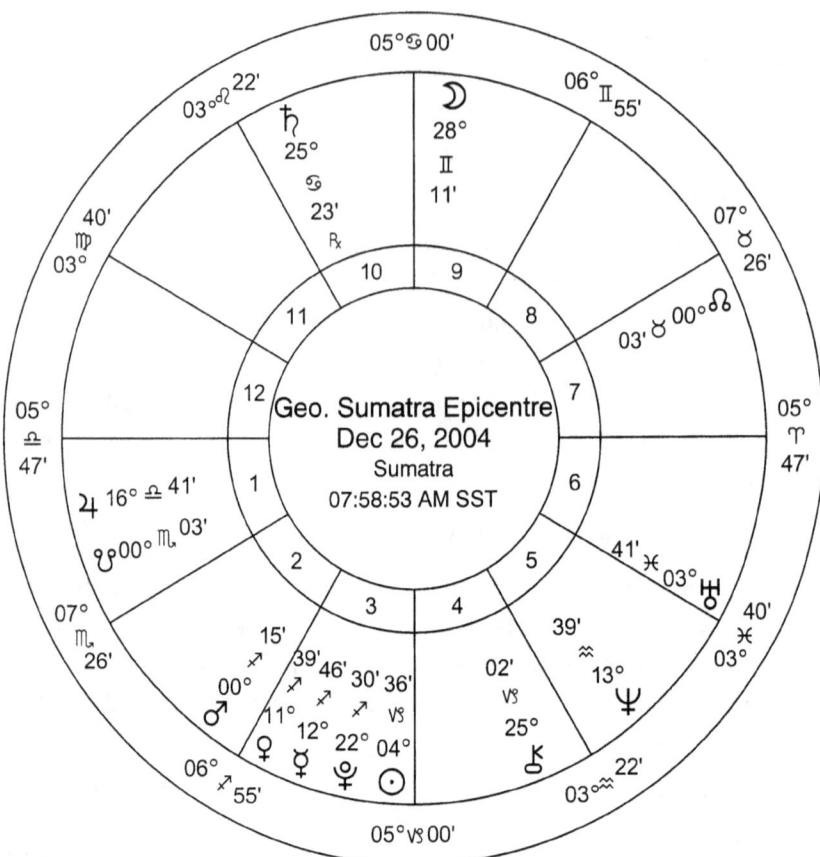

Figure 5 – Geodetic chart of the massive Sumatra quake and subsequent devastating tsunami.

The opposite geodetic Ascendant of 0° Libra, is located on the map at a geographic location of 90 degrees East Longitude in the region of Thailand, Sumatra and Malaysia. This would also be the point of an angular Ascendant. This is the region where cyclones are more prevalent globally than anywhere else. In fact, the great Sumatra Quake (9.0 on the Richter Scale) on December 26, 2004 that created such immense devastation and loss of life along relevant coastlines, was easily seen geodetically by the position of the aforementioned two previous eclipses at 29°50' Aries and 21°06' Libra. These eclipses lay across the geodetic descendant/ascendant angles, which formed a t-square with the position of Saturn at the time of the quake. See Figure 5, which is the geodetic chart for the epicenter of the quake. Then refer back to Figure 1, The geodetic map, and observe where the 0° Libra Ascendant is located, which starts at geographic longitude of 90 degrees East. The Descendant would be 0° Aries which is not shown on the map itself, but is assumed as the opposite point of the Ascendant.

The Life of Amelia Earhart, as seen both Geodetically and with Astro*Carto*Graphy

Let us start with a brief biography and the natal chart (see Figure 6) of this amazing woman pioneer aviator, lecturer and author who broke several records in the annals of aviation history. Various locations pertinent

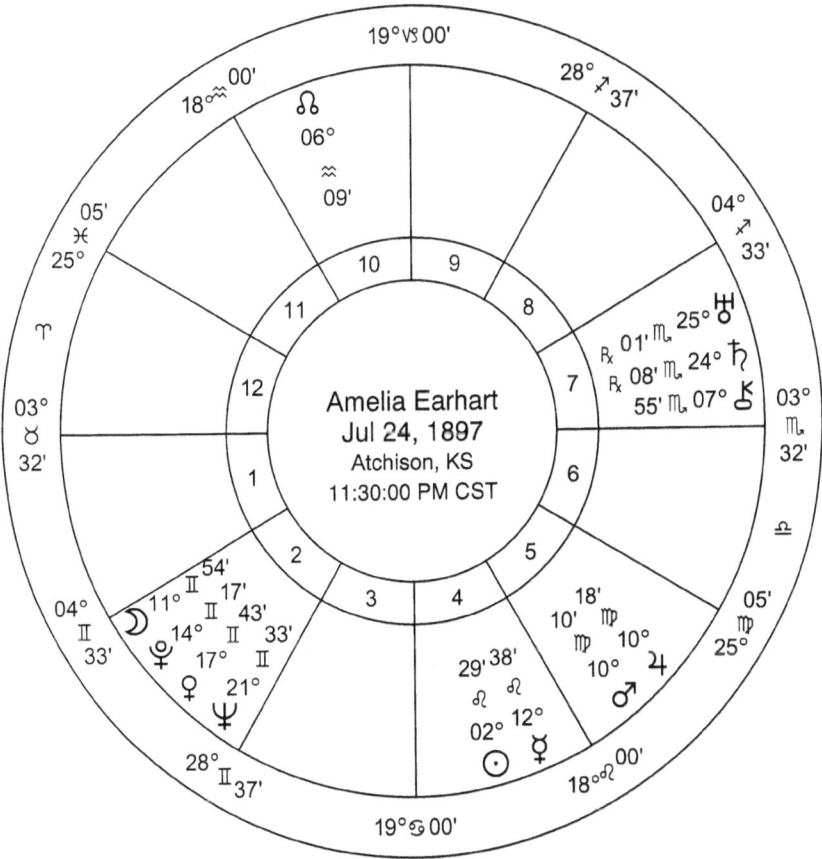

Figure 6 – Amelia Earhart, July 24, 1897, 11:30pm, CST, Atchison, KS, USA. Rodden rating A, from memory (AstroDataBank).

to her life are mentioned, so you can observe where her natal planets fall in both the Astro*Carto*Graphy and geodetic maps that will follow (Figures 7 and 8). This will allow us a comparison of the two relevant systems in this type of (locational) astrology.

Earhart's early years were far from ideal, with significant mother problems and an alcoholic father. However, due to helpful relatives and much perseverance, she was able to achieve a decent education, but her life purpose eluded her until she became captivated with flying. Prior to flying, one stint in her life took her to Toronto, Canada, where she was a nurse's aid, followed by odd jobs such as a settlement house worker in Boston.

It was in Los Angeles that she took her first flying lessons. Two years later she became the first woman to fly across the Atlantic, with two other pilots. Flying solo, she later set a transatlantic record. She was also the first woman to fly across the Pacific Ocean, setting out from the Hawaiian Islands.

Let's look first at her A*C*G map, Figure 7. There are a multiplicity of lines there, supporting new pathways (North Node Ascending) and travel – with the help of her navigator, Frederick Noonan (Mercury and Sun Descending). We can also note the nearby Saturn and Uranus Midheaven lines at the Islands, emphasizing the planning detail and hard work required for her journey, as well as the excitement and emancipation her journey represented. On the GE map, the Hawaiian Islands are at the midpoint of those positions to the east and her Gemini Stellium, represented by the Descending lines of Moon, Pluto, Venus and Neptune, all to the west (shown on the right hand side of the map to the north of Australia).

On July 2nd, 1937 she set out on a round-the-world flight with her co-pilot, Fred Noonan in an attempt to circumnavigate the globe flying along the equator. When they were flying from New Guinea to a scheduled stopover on tiny Howland Island[7] (note map position) they disappeared and their fate is, to this date, still unknown. The main conspiracy speculation of her disappearance has been that their plane either crashed or was shot down somewhere around Saipan[8] where there was a Japanese air base (note map position) but it is not known where they actually did go down. On the other hand, there is evidence that they had an erroneous

Looking at the World Geodetically 125

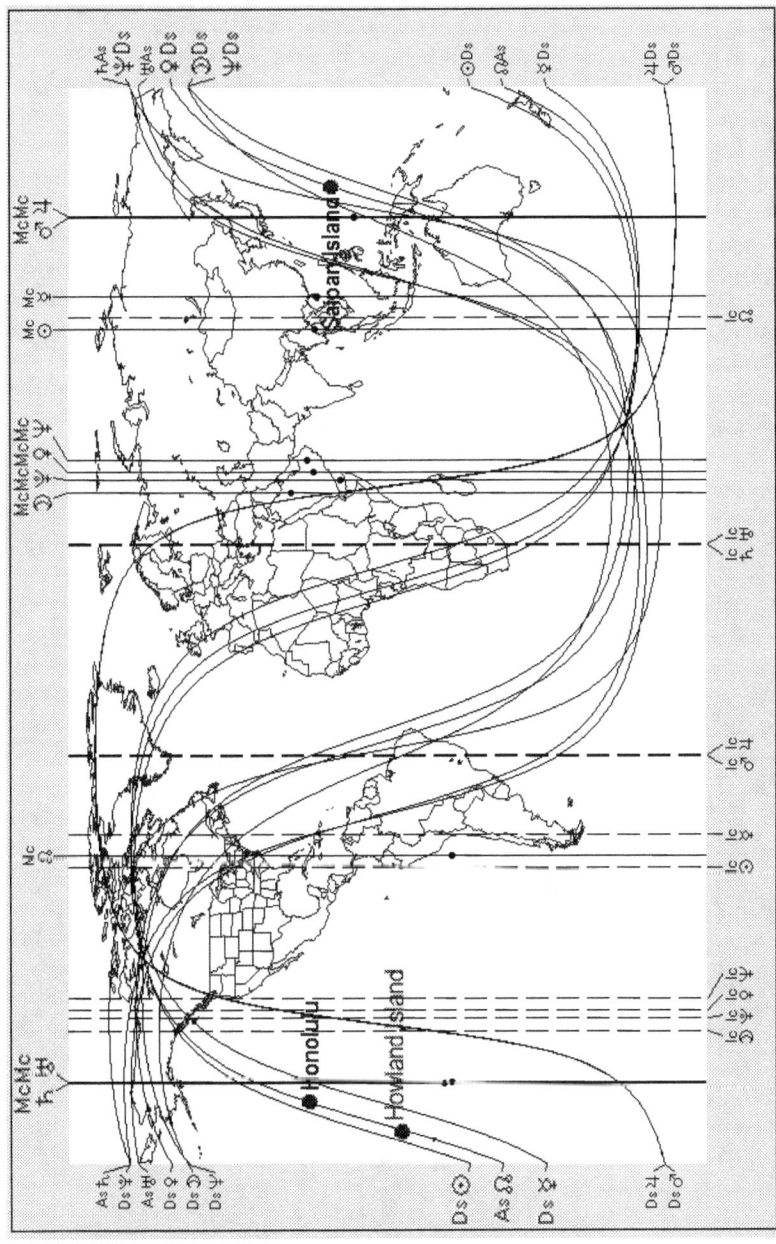

Figure 7 – Amelia Earhart, AstroCartoGraphy, Culmin/Anti/Rise/Set

126 *From Here to There*

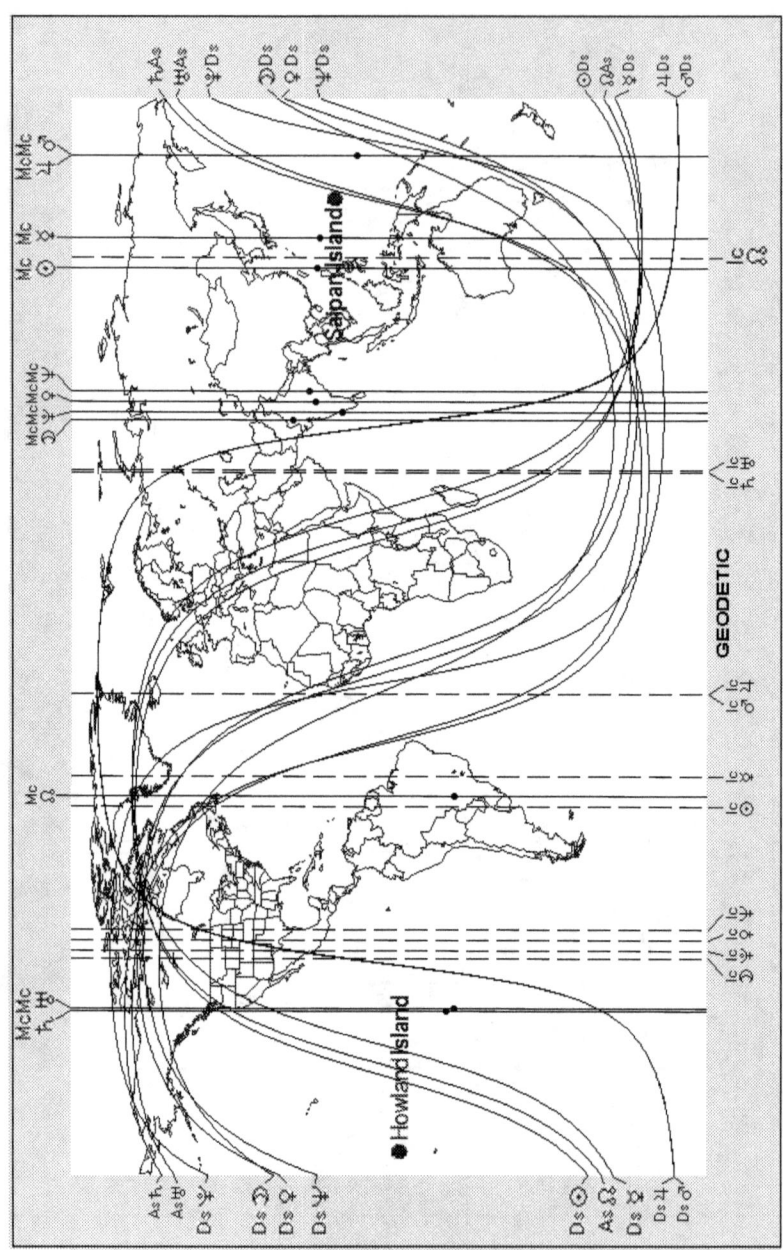

Figure 8 – Amelia Earhart, Geodetic MC/IC/Asc/Desc

map putting them about 200 miles off of Howland Island. Noonan had received slightly – though fatally – outdated naval maps. The error had been corrected but had not worked its way out to publication. Howland wasn't where they expected it to be. *The National Geographic Magazine*[9] alludes to this possibility, as does Earhart's biography, *The Sound of Wings*.[10]

On the GE Map (see Figure 8), the position of Howland Island is very close to her Moon/Pluto/Venus/Neptune Stellium of Gemini Descendant lines, which are square to Mars and Jupiter in her natal chart, adding a dangerous volatility to this planetary mix. Her Mercury/South Node/Sun Midheaven lines run down close to the Saipan area, perhaps indicating why the 'crashing and being captured by the Japanese' theory of her disappearance remains to this day. Her Saturn/Uranus conjunction Ascendant line is also close. This is a famous planetary combination of tension, perhaps even possible "breaking" or violence. Note on this map that her Mercury Descendant line runs right through Los Angeles where she learned to fly, and her Saturn/Uranus Midheaven lines are very close.

As a comparison, now look to these planetary positions on angles in the Astro*Carto*Graphy map, Figure 7. You will note similarities of a different description. Her Sun, and Mercury Descending and Node Ascending lines, as well as her Saturn/Uranus Midheaven lines are somewhat in the vicinity of Howland Island, although Saturn/Uranus Midheaven line may be a little too far away to be considered significant. In the area of Saipan we see a congestion of Mars/Jupiter Midheaven lines and Moon/Pluto/Venus/Neptune in Gemini Descendant lines. If you look to the position of Los Angeles, where she learned to fly and earned an international reputation, you will note the Jupiter Descendant line. Running through the vicinity of the Hawaiian Islands from whence she flew the Pacific, we see the Sun and Mercury Descending and the groundbreaking North Node Ascending line.

This article is primarily a description and use of geodetic equivalents as a framework to relocate a natal chart, or to observe mundane events. However, it has also been pointed out that other systems do exist. It is obvious that each of these systems must have some merit or they would not be used by so many notable astrologers. Each has a purpose and each is relevant in our work as astrologers. That is why a comparison has been shown between these two remarkable systems. One, A*C*G, shows where planets are angular and shift according to the chart being used. The other, geodetics, shows specific and unique, Earth-generated angles, into which planets can be inserted (plotted).

© Chris McRae 2007.

Editor's comments:
The fullest historical exploration of Earth zodiacs can be found in chapter 11 of the book, Mundane Astrology.[11] *Other important resources are appendix 9 of Nicholas Campion's* The Book of World Horoscopes[12] *and Chapter 5 in my book,* Astrolocality Astrology.[13]

NOTES

1. *The Geodetic World Map*, I.I. Chris McRae, published by AFA, AZ, USA, 1988.
2. Ibid, page 114. McRae also offers an accurate and beautifully printed Geodetic World Map, 3' x 5' wall size. For your own copy, email her at: cmcrae@interbaun.com
3. *"Go West Young Man"*, Indiana newspaper writer John Soule's 1851 advice, would be popularized by Horace Greeley and serve as the mantra for nineteenth Century American migration.
4. Hillary's data is rated DD in Astro Data Bank, as there are conflicting stated times. One source does give 12:30pm, however, and it is reported that his mother said the birth time was between Noon and 1pm that day, making the 12:30pm time a reasonable mid-range possibility. Some astrologers have proposed that geodetic angles be used for the location of birth when a birth time is unsure or completely unknown.
5. Great Conjunctions are conjunctions of planets from Jupiter outward. Conjunctions of Jupiter and Saturn are the original Great Conjunctions.
6. This article was written before March 2007, so no specific event could be tied to it at that time.
7. Howland Island, Oceania, is in the North Pacific Ocean, about half way between Hawaii and Australia.
   Location: Longitude 176W38, Latitude 0N48.
8. Saipan is part of the Mariana Island chain of Micronesia. Longitude 145E75, Latitude 15N25.
9. *National Geographic*, January 1998, "Amelia Earhart", by Virginia Morell.

10. *The Sound of Wings*, by Mary S. Lovell, Hutchinson, London, 1991.
11. *Mundane Astrology*, by Baigent, Campion and Harvey, Aquarian Press, UK, 1984.
12. The Wessex Astrologer, UK, 2004 – updated regularly.
13. *Astrolocality Astrology*, The Wessex Astrologer, UK, 1999.

Bibliography

The Geodetic World Map, I.I. Chris McRae, published by AFA, 1988.
Planetary Phenomena, Neil Michelson, ACS, 1990.
AstroDataBank computer program for chart data and biographies.
Biography.com website for biographies.

The Geodetic World Map, 3' x 5' wall size is only available from Chris McRae. She can be contacted at: cmcrae@interbaun.com

9

Would Relocation Change Your life?
A Look at Astrology's Answers[1]
Donna Cunningham, MSW

Donna Cunningham is a noted international astrologer whose extensive writing and lecturing have been important contributions to the Astrolocality field. She is the originator of the core locality aphorism, "Wherever you go, you take yourself along". Cunningham is active in the web's central A*C*G* resource, www.ContinumnACG.net. In this chapter she asks if relocation can change our lives.

A major geographic move is a huge displacement in your life and ranks high on the lists of stressful situations published from time to time. It is not something to be entered into lightly, for even the best of moves require an intense adjustment period of at least a year. You would want to read about your chosen location in *Places Rated Almanac*, a reference book that belongs in any astrologer's library. On the Internet, you also have a number of great tools for researching and getting to know any given area you might be considering.

However, astrology itself – particularly the branch known as locational astrology – provides helpful tools for making an informed decision about where and when to move. Locational astrology techniques can take much of the guesswork out of moving, especially the highly sophisticated tool of Astro*Carto*Graphy or other computerized maps that show the spots on earth where the various natal (or progressed) planets come onto the four chart angles (Midheaven, Ascendant, Descendant or IC). Working with this tool, I am often surprised at how many people are instinctively drawn to spots that are excellent for them – although others, with less trustworthy instincts, are strongly drawn to spots that represent their own worst nightmares.

The first consideration in relocation work is how accurate the birth time might be. Astro*Carto*Graphy and other locational astrology techniques are not forgiving of birth time errors.[2] A time of 3:20pm, for instance, looks promising, as it seems less likely to be a rounded-off estimate than 3:30pm would be. With a rounded off or vague birth time, some rectification may be required, and though a good rectification can be costly, so can a move that is several hundred miles off target!

Transits: The Moving Force Behind a Move
Transits are usually the stimulus for a major geographic change. Moving to a new home may be part of what happens under a transit to the natal Moon, the 4th house cusp (IC), through the 4th house, or aspecting a natal planet in the 4th. Such transits are the primary triggers for changes in residence. Relocation goes more smoothly under a trine, with the Moon/Uranus trine being the swiftest and the least hassle. A move under a Moon/Saturn trine, however, is more organized and more likely to be permanent. Under a Moon/Uranus or Uranus/IC aspect of any kind, you might as well keep nonessentials packed in their boxes, as you're likely to move more than once during the two or three aspects you will generally experience from transiting Uranus. Under Moon/Neptune transits, you're probably not thinking things through carefully enough and may regret the decision – *do not* buy a house until the transit passes. You're not so much moving *to* something as moving *away* from something because you've become disillusioned. Your fantasies about a wonderful new life tend to be unrealistic.

Generally speaking, when life conditions change dramatically at the time of a move, the change is not just due to the location but also the timing. You will probably find a similar message in transits to both the birth and the relocated charts. Often, someone who moves during an important transit is drawn to the exact area where that transiting planet is on one of the four angles. For instance, many 28-30 year olds who are undergoing their Saturn return seem unerringly drawn to an area where Saturn is on one of the angles. They are drawn to a place where the energies of Saturn are maximized. Whatever the planet, under transits like these, the new location makes the issues and lessons of that planet even more pressing to resolve – you might say it forces the issue – but that is not generally a good place to stay for any length of time.

A smooth move is a combination of two things: the right time and the right place. You may hit one of them and not the other; for instance, the location may be promising but the timing may stink! Timing is important even when moving to a positive location. Don't move when nothing is happening to your Moon, IC, or 4th house planets, or when Neptune or Saturn are aspecting them. If you do, you could just sit and spin your wheels for a costly year or two. Cyclo*Carto*Graphy, derived from the natal Astro*Carto*Graphy map, is the best clue to understanding why a location may be promising at one stage of your life and not at another.

"Wherever You Go, You Take Yourself Along"
When considering a move based on your map, it is important to refer to the birth chart for interpretation. Suppose you are thinking of moving to one of your Venus lines, generally considered the best places in the world to find love, believing it will improve your chances in relationships. First, you have to consider what your own natal Venus is like. If natal Venus has difficult aspects, then any undesirable long-standing patterns in relationships would be not only active but intensified there. For example, if you were born with Pluto on Descendant squaring Venus, and you move off the Pluto line to a place where Venus is on the angle, you are only increasing the strength of that already challenged Venus. In fact, now you probably have Pluto square the local angle. You'd be better off picking one of the Descendant lines, like Sun or Jupiter on the Descendant, if love were your goal.

Another example might be relocating to improve career potentials. You might expect that Jupiter or the Sun on the Midheaven would be an excellent choice. Suppose, however, that natally Neptune closely squares Jupiter. If you moved to your Jupiter/Midheaven line, you would at the same time be moving to a spot where Neptune squared the local Midheaven – an aspect that is easy to miss, and, under which, it is harder to diagnose a possible undertow of self-sabotage. Difficult conjunctions or oppositions in the natal chart can present a special blockage in relocation, for wherever one of the pair is on an angle the other one is as well. Thus highlighting that pair of planets by placing them on the MC or IC would not be a good career move.

Difficult aspects and placements in the birth chart represent ways that we create our own difficulties, so analyzing the behaviors represented by those astrological factors is essential to a successful relocation. What you need to consider is that your self-defeating attitudes and behaviors go right along with you when you move, so if the problems you are having in the old location are mostly of your own making, they will be with you in the new one as well.

You may get a temporary break from them, given new people and unfamiliar circumstances in which you are on your best behavior: a kind of honeymoon period. However, unless you have well and truly learned whatever lesson is involved and healed whatever wounds or patterns you kept tripping over in the old place, the old patterns will eventually creep back in the new location. Thus, if you entertain the thought of a move, you need also to examine your contributions to recurrent problems honestly. Take responsibility for shaping a new reality for yourself in the new location through new attitudes, behaviors, and relationship strategies. However, suppose that you have been working on yourself and have truly changed, and yet the people and situations in the old place have become so entrenched that they cannot allow you to be different and to grow. In situations like these, then a major change in location can give you the space to create a new reality. This is particularly true of long-standing roles that family or others around you have assigned you (Family Mess-Up, for instance, or Saviour of Us All), roles that you are no longer willing to fulfil. A whole new set of people will not have the same expectations, so you have room to grow.

Consider Your Motive in Moving
Sometimes we relocate for the wrong reasons, and when we do, we are likely to make costly errors in judgement. An ill-considered move can be a major roadblock in our lives. While the transiting planet involved shows the circumstances of the move, the real question is why are you doing it? It is generally due to an important shift in the lunar areas of life. Often, the reason is that the womb has gotten too confining. As a young adult, you leave your parents' house to go out on your own, or maybe with a

partner. Sometimes, because any aspect to the IC is simultaneously an aspect to the MC, either you or your partner may find a job in a new place. Maybe you have a family now and the house has gotten too small. Or, your family has grown up, and you don't need so much space. The Moon waxes and wanes, all within a life cycle. The pressure to leave the womb precedes the relocation. There is a lunar realignment before the move, followed by a long adjustment to the new home.

It has been especially interesting to me to observe what happens when people are struck by nostalgia and think along the line of a pilgrimage to their roots – maybe even moving back home with the folks for a time. This type of pilgrimage generally comes about with a major transit to the Moon, the IC/MC axis, or a 4th house planet by Saturn, Chiron, Uranus, Neptune, or Pluto. (When more than one of those points is impacted by transits, it is even more of a rite of passage). I forget who said that you can't go home again, perhaps Thomas Wolfe. That ringing phrase has become part of conventional wisdom, the sort of truism that people love to utter.

Like most bits of conventional wisdom, it is wrong as often as it is right. In observing people over these past 35 years – clients, friends, colleagues, and acquaintances – I've repeatedly been struck by how profoundly they are affected by returning home after a long absence. Often it is a deep healing of old wounds, especially when the Inner Child is still stuck in seeing the parents as all-powerful, spending time with elderly parents can provide a reality check. They become just people, maybe mellower or frailer and thus finally seen as life sized rather than the giants our unconscious makes them into. Often, based on exposure to the people your parents have become, you can begin to forgive them for what they did to you 30 or 40 years ago, and that forgiveness can be a great healing. Even if you cannot forgive, the experience of confronting them and seeing their humanness can be empowering. Yes, You *can* go home again, but you'll never be the same!

Often, major moves will entail purchasing a house, so I also look into the effect of transits on that particular decision. Buying a home, especially the first one, is a rite of passage into adulthood. Having a home of your own gives you a greater sense of security, roots, and belonging – for lunar types, especially. Moon/Saturn and Moon/Pluto aspects are the most likely to involve actual purchases of real estate, although Pluto as often accompanies major remodeling efforts. With Moon/Saturn or Saturn to the MH/IC, a home of your own may be the result of well-earned success. You may be conservative in your purchase. You may settle for something smaller or less luxurious than you'd like, because you are being realistic about not taking on too hard of a financial commitment.

With some Moon/Pluto contacts, the new house may be financed by something other than your own efforts. The source could be an inheritance, a gift or bribe from your parents with strings attached, a trust fund, or a divorce settlement – or, it may be a last-ditch effort to keep the marriage together. If you've suffered losses during this phase, take time to mourn the end of one chapter in your life. The grief may be intensified by a period of isolation in the new location.

If you buy property under a Neptune transit to the Moon or other points listed above, you probably haven't inspected the cellar or foundations. The realtor saw you coming, and you may have a lemon on your hands for a good, long time. What to do about it? Ah, well, it would be reprehensible of me to suggest you find a buyer who is also under a Moon/Neptune aspect, wouldn't it? Maybe you could donate it to the church, your guru, or some charitable organization. Or, hang in there for whatever deep spiritual lessons it may teach you – like the one about not signing anything you haven't read and understood.

What Relocation Charts Can and Cannot Do For You
You would want an Astro*Carto*Graphy or other computerized map if you are moving more than 500 miles east or west of your birthplace. Especially if you have no idea where you want to live, this tool can help you find optimal locations for business, love, home life, health, and travel. It can also help you avoid really serious relocation mistakes, like moving to a place where Saturn, Neptune, or Pluto fall on an angle. While you may want to order such a map from the various places that offer them, relocation is not a do-it-yourself project. Getting an Astro*Carto*Graphy printout can help you narrow down choices, but for all the complexities of the map you really need the advice of a trained Astro*Carto*Graphy professional, one who will take into account the natal chart features it

reflects. While such services may entail a fee of $100-$250, moving itself is extremely costly in life force energy, finances, and other resources.[3] Know that a geographic change cannot offset an important transit to the natal chart, though it might mitigate it somewhat or strengthen a supportive astrological aspect. Under a major outer planet transit to a natal placement, people often spontaneously gravitate to a place that puts that natal planet (or the transiting planet) on an angle, to intensify it for purposes best known to their higher self.

It would be important to have a relocated chart calculated as well, showing the new Midheaven, Ascendant, Descendant, and IC and any aspects natal planets form to them. (I do not experience the relocated house positions as overriding the natal interpretation). You need to scrutinize the resulting chart carefully to make sure you're not fooling yourself. You may move to a place where the locational angles are aspected by difficult planets. Suppose your motive is to get away from a difficult outer planet line at your birthplace. Did you really get away from that outer planet, or is it now aspecting a different angle? For instance, suppose you have Pluto natally conjunct Midheaven, only to find out that now you're living in a place where it squares the local Ascendant. In other words, I don't believe an individual can always cheat their fate by a move. In fact, this issue reminds me of that old song from the Seventies, *Games People Play,* which went, "They're gonna teach you how to meditate, read your horoscope and cheat your fate".

You would want to watch the transits to the angles of the relocated chart, also, as these transits have a strong, though not permanent effect. Suppose you move to a place where you have Aquarius on the Midheaven, and Neptune will be crossing back and forth over that Midheaven for two or three years. You are likely to have a devil of a time establishing yourself career wise. That transit to the local Midheaven would be particularly important if you were already sensitized to Neptune by natal impact on career houses. In considering going to a place where Neptune is emphasized, you may fool yourself into believing that what is coming is spiritual, creative, and therefore wonderful, but it may still mean several years of floating in space.

Relocation astrology becomes more complex the more people there are in a household. Often a desired location is excellent for one partner but the pits for the other. Or, it suits both parents fairly well but is a disaster for one or more of the kids. Especially when business is calling a family to that spot, situations like these become a very hard life decision. You can find out interesting things about the dynamics of a family, however, by comparing their relocation prospects. I have sometimes done relocation work for couples in which many regions of United States were promising career-wise for the wife, but none for the husband. Relocating abroad to satisfy the needs of both partners is not always feasible. In cases like these, explaining the situation in astrological terms has made it less frustrating for the couple to understand and deal with a role reversal in which the wife is likely to be more successful than the husband. Astrology is a superb tool for gaining detachment and letting go of needlessly blaming oneself or another for things that just **are**.

Getting Out of Dodge: Can Relocation Help the Outer Planet Person?

Outer Planet People (OPPs) are those with more than one of the outer planets emphasized in their birth charts, especially those with the outer planets on one or more chart angles.[4] If you have an outer planet on the angles natally, locations far east or west of your birthplace can change your life and career in very important ways. With Uranus, Neptune, or Pluto on the Midheaven, for instance your relationships with parents and other authority figures have doubtlessly presented an ongoing challenge in terms of having the freedom to pursue a fulfilling life work. (As mentioned earlier, this technique is not forgiving of birth time errors, and when dealing with such powerful planetary forces, you need to be exact. However, those with outer planets on the Ascendant natally have often had dramatic birth circumstances and other dramatic events that make it easy to check whether the birth time is in the ballpark).

    I hear from many OPPs who have struggled a lifetime with the complications an outer planet on an angle can entail. Having one on the Ascendant, for instance, can color their social connections with everyone they meet. Since mainstream individuals often have little clue about what to do with their own outer planets, they tend to be very reactive and rejecting when encountering a person who wears one of these planets as an outer garment. Consistently being treated this way can be alienating in the extreme. Moving half a continent away can mean getting out from under familial parental pressures and the projections of everyone around you so that you can start over afresh. But as we've discussed already, leaving home won't change all your problems so you can't avoid the work you need to do on your use of the outer planets, or the same patterns will catch up with you.

Suppose you don't have an outer planet on an angle natally, but the outer planets are strong in your chart in other ways. If the outer planets represent our genius – those ways we help ourselves and the collective to move beyond everyday reality – then could it not be argued that the OPP *needs* to move to where those planets are on the line? Should you not, in fact, put that planet on the locational Midheaven if you want your contribution to be recognized by the world? Still, you have to ask yourself if you are not biting off far more than you can chew, maybe even asking for a broken tooth or two. If Pluto, for instance, is strong in your birth chart, it will always be a strong part of you, but do you want to make it even more dominant by living in a place where you can **never** get away from its pressures? Since Plutonian types are prone to becoming the targets of other people's projections, would you want to live in a spot where others are continually projecting their disowned Pluto qualities onto you? Is that even safe?

Before making such a choice, assess how purely and how consistently constructively you are using the energies of the outer planet in question. Be honest with yourself, for when you intensify the energies by moving to a line on the map where that planet is angular, keeping it all in balance may become far more difficult. It becomes harder not to crash and burn dramatically. You will doubtlessly also find yourself surrounded by others of the same type – a mixed blessing, since it can be wonderful to find like-minded souls, but you'd also have to monitor your associates' expressions of those energies carefully, as they can pull you toward the negative expressions. As long as you are going to the considerable effort and expense of moving, you might instead wish to emphasize a more solidly grounded part of your chart.

The Outer Planet Person: City Mouse or Country Mouse?
Certainly there are individual differences, but it is my observation that the various outer planet types thrive in certain types of locales and are miserable in others, depending on the nature of the highlighted planet. Except for Neptunians, who are extremely sensitive to their environment, OPP often thrive in larger cities, where they are less apt to fall under the scrutiny of small-minded others and more likely to meet like-minded folks.

Uranians love the glitter and excitement of big city life, where they can stay abreast of all the newest trends, like seeing the newest film releases immediately. They love the intellectual stimulation and the concentration of bright, innovative, and often quirky thinkers. They finally have a chance to have a group around them who thinks like they do. Here, they find true peers who validate their counter-culture ways, so that they can be who they are without shame or social pressure to conform. (They may handle small town life better now with Internet access to the myriad of groups and email lists that flourish on the net). The less evolved Uranian loves excitement for its own sake.

Plutonians, too, may be happier in large cities, where they can have the privacy and anonymity they crave. They are often singled out or ostracized in small towns for their differences and even for their power, since nothing remains a secret in such places. All is judged and remembered. The less evolved Plutonian likes cities for the sleaze, especially the license to engage in sexuality compulsively and anonymously, without continually tripping over their discarded conquests on the town square.

Neptunians may not do so well in large cities, especially those who have become psychically and environmentally sensitive (as often happens under Neptune transits to the 6th, 1st, or 12th houses). Psychic sponges, they can become hyper-reactive to noise, neighbors, crowds, environmental toxins, and other disturbances in the force. As they become increasingly sensitive, they may not be able to handle cities any more and may need to go to a remote place where meditation and other spiritual practices are made easier. They thrive on quiet spaces to immerse themselves in creative pursuits, and they often thrive on being near water.

Moving Stress? Be Good to Yourself?
As you can see, relocating isn't just a matter of packing boxes and calling a mover. For instance, you may find that while packing, you take an intense trip down memory lane. Each object you touch has memories and feelings attached, which you may relive. The process of deciding what to keep and what to get rid of involves re-evaluating your priorities and values. The home is related to the Moon and to the sign Cancer, and a move is an immense readjustment in many lunar areas of life, for what is more basic than the home? A crab goes through a period of vulnerability when it sheds its shell.

We, too, may feel especially vulnerable for at least a year after a move – a complete cycle of lunations. There can even be strong somatic reactions, particularly to the stomach or menstrual cycle. In particular, lunar types – those with the sign Cancer, the Moon, or the 4th house prominent in their charts – can find relocation distressing. A move is nothing to take lightly: it is a major displacement requiring maybe a year or longer to recoup those forces and adapt to the new location. Give yourself plenty of space to feel the losses and insecurities and to lay down roots in the new home.

© Donna Cunningham 2005.

Donna Cunningham, MSW (Columbia University), has been an internationally-known professional astrologer for over 40 years, with numerous awards, books and classes to her credit. She is listed in several Who's Who volumes. For information on her astrological or web design services, visit her web site at: http://www.DonnaCunninghamMSW.com. Cunningham is now conducting an intermediate level astrology correspondence course by email, Chart Interpretation and Synthesis. For more information, go to http://www.moonmavenpublications.com/correspondancecourse.html

She has several ebooks which can also be found on her Moon Maven publications web site. They include: The Outer Planets and Inner Life, Volume 1: The Career Path of The Exceptional Soul, An Astrological Guide to Self-Awareness, (2005 Edition), *and the book this excerpt comes from,* Astrological Analysis: Selected Topics in Chart Interpretation.

Editor's note:

About her own professional travel Cunningham comments: "As a writer and international speaker, I've been fascinated with the effects of lines in other countries where I've spoken or had books translated into other languages. For instance, my book *Healing Pluto Problems* did extremely well in its German version (*Pluto Probleme*) and for many years earned me as much in royalties as the English version. However, when I spoke in cities along my Pluto MH line in Germany and Sweden, the audiences were very distant and unresponsive. One lecture that had audiences rolling in the aisles laughing in England and Ireland (My Sun and Jupiter on the MH there) got absolutely no response in Sweden. The sponsors said the audience loved it. I said, "Really, how would I know if they hated it." They said, "They'd get up and leave."

In Brazil, my Venus and Uranus are on the MH in all the major cities up and down the country. Every book I've ever written has been translated into Portuguese and does well there. I've been brought to tour three times to enthusiastic audiences, standing ovations, treated like a princess, and interviewed in the media. I was even recognized in the street once. Needless to say, though my traveling days are over, I'd go back there in a heartbeat!

NOTES

1. This article is an excerpt from Donna Cunningham's ebook, *Astrological Analysis: Selected Readings In Chart Interpretation.* To order a copy, visit http://www.moonmavenpublications.com
2. A difference of 13 or 14 minutes, for example, can erroneously place a MH or IC line from one border of a medium sized US state to its other side and across into a neighbor's state.
3. For a list of professional astrologers who are certified in this technique, visit the website of Continuum, the organization dedicated to preserving the work of the late Jim Lewis and to furthering knowledge of locational astrology: http://www.continuumacg.net. On that site, there is also a library of articles on this topic.
4. How does a planet become prominent? The Sun, Moon, Ascendant, or Midheaven could be conjunct, square, trine, or opposite that planet. Or, the Sun, Moon, Ascendant, or several planets could be in that planet's sign. A planet would be strong if it is in a major configuration like a T-square, grand trine, or grand cross. It gains strength if it is one of the most aspected planets.

10

Jyotish[1] Locality
Dennis Flaherty

In this chapter, I'm pleased to present an important work by Dennis Flaherty. He is one of a group of astrologers who are proficient in both Vedic and Western astrology. Much of this article was first published in the August-September 1997 issue of The Mountain Astrologer *magazine. In it, Flaherty explains how both Eastern and Western systems meet in locality, each using the same A*C*G map in their interpretations. Written just about two years after Jim Lewis' passing, he clearly details the basic principles of A*C*G and shows how the Vedic perspective can enrich our A*C*G studies.*

Ancient Vedic Astrology Meets Modern Astro*Carto*Graphy

Nearly every practicing astrologer has heard of the late Jim Lewis' research in relocational astrology trademarked as Astro*Carto*Graphy™. Today's astrologers owe a great debt of gratitude to Jim Lewis and his precursors, as he and his kind have forever enriched and changed the way we practice astrology.

Jim Lewis ingeniously built upon research in relocational astrology that already was a century ripe. The idea had fascinated astrologers well back to the 1800s. Before Lewis, the precursors of relocational astrology were A.J. Pearce in the 1870s, L. Edward Johndro, in the 1920s and 1930s, and the famed sidereal astrologer, Cyril Fagan, who extensively researched and wrote about it in the 1940s. The idea of movement in time and space is germane to the realm of astrology, and the concept of moving the astrological chart played itself out in the varying progressions and transits that astrologers utilize in their work. But the great minds of

Pearce, Johndro and Fagan extended this sense of movement to localities outside of the birth locality. It was Jim Lewis, however, who galvanized these ideas into a revolutionary modern tool he called Astro*Carto*Graphy.

Continuum magazine[2] succinctly summarizes Lewis' immense contribution to relocational astrology in a tribute entitled: "Jim Lewis and Astro*Carto*Graphy". Continuum explains: "Lewis' contribution was to take time and place beyond the narrow focus of a single horoscope and recast them onto a world map. Lewis' Astro*Carto*Graphy, then, is an angularity map that displays orbit tracks of the lights and planets for all horizons and meridians...for the birth moment. The premise behind it, again, is that people will experience the intrinsic natures of the planets at locations where their natal planets fall angular. Lewis himself received many thousands of letters, corroborating this notion, from customers who were so impressed with the technique that they felt compelled to write to him and explain the detail of their lives. He advertised that changing one's locale could substantially change the prevailing conditions of one's life circumstances. It's true. There is no advertising hype behind it." Those of us who have practiced what Jim Lewis developed can attest to the veracity of that statement.

Although Jim Lewis was a tropical astrologer, the techniques he developed in Astro*Carto*Graphy were never zodiac specific. One can be a tropical astrologer, or sidereal astrologer, or use any of the several ayanamsas (difference between the tropical and sidereal zodiac)[3] available, or invent one's own, and the relocation technology is still relevant. How can this be so? Let us examine the fundamental principles of how Astro*Carto*Graphy measures the planets as they come to the angles, that is the horizon and meridian of a given locality.

Astro*Carto*Graphy: How it Works
On any given day the planets have a specific spatial relationship with one another irrespective of where one is born on the planet. This planetary relationship changes slowly over time due to the slow orbital speeds of the planets. The planets also have a specific relationship to any given locality dependent on the rotation of the earth, and because the earth rotates so much more quickly than the planets move, this relationship

constantly changes over the course of twenty four hours as planets quickly rise in the East, culminate overhead, and set in the West, at the observers locality here on the earthly sphere.

Even though the Sun, or any planet for that matter, may not be rising or culminating or setting at the locality of your birth, at the time when you came into space, that is the moment you were born, it was specifically rising, culminating and setting somewhere on the earthly sphere. In fact, on the day at the time you were born, somewhere in the world all of the planets were rising, culminating, setting, and falling. Astro*Carto*Graphy measures this, and this measurement is profoundly simple. Just as parallels of latitude (north and south) and meridians of longitude (east and west) locate a place here on the earthly sphere, their celestial counterparts of parallels of declination and meridians of right ascension assist us in measuring planets on the heavenly sphere. By extending the Earth's equator into the heavenly sphere as a celestial equator, we can locate the planets in parallels of declination north and south along the celestial equator, and in parallels of right ascension east and west along the celestial equator. In this way the declination of a planet corresponds exactly with terrestrial latitude, and the right ascension of a planet corresponds exactly with terrestrial longitude. This system measures all of the planets through lines of extension to all terrestrial locations where the planets appear on the four angles: the ascendant, the MC, the descendant, and the IC. It's that simple, yet profound.

Most importantly: Astro*Carto*Graphy is locality specific, not zodiac specific. To further explain, Astro*Carto*Graphy uses a world map to measure the planets on the earthly sphere only in reference to the planets rising and falling on the four angles at given localities. This local activity of the planets is an observable phenomenon (except the IC, of course). It is determined by local observance, not by the zodiac or ayanamsa the practitioner uses. Like ancient astrology it returns us to an observance of the night sky, replete with the rising and setting of the heavens. It is therefore a valid technique for tropical, as well as sidereal astrologers. No one group of astrologers can claim a monopoly for Astro*Carto*Graphy, for the one thing we astrologers all share in common, and upon which our eyes must agree, is the local observance of the planets as they rise on the horizon in the East, culminate directly overhead, and set in West, as they fall out of our line of sight. Jim Lewis developed a tool which completely sidesteps the tropical/sidereal zodiac debate and returns us to an observable astrology we all can agree upon. As I am both a practicing sidereal and tropical astrologer myself, this is, in my opinion, is the definitive tool which joins East to West, where ancient astrological techniques meet modern techniques, utilizing the full potential of each zodiacal preference.

Let me show you how easily this modern tool of astrology can be incorporated into your practice of Jyotish (Vedic astrology) and how easily the ancient tool of Jyotish can augment and enrich your current practice of relocational astrology. You need not draw up special relocational maps. The Astro*Carto*Graphy maps developed by Jim Lewis, and marketed by several fine astrological software programs work perfectly regardless of zodiac. The Vedic relocational astrology I have researched and developed over the last several years is what I call *Jyotish Locality.*

In the Eastern school of astrology we have a tradition honoring our gurus and teachers. The ancient Vedas of India say we owe a debt of gratitude to our forefathers. I honor and pay homage to sage Parser for his gift of Jyotisha and I honor and pay homage to Jim Lewis as well. Knowing Lewis' fierce dedication to independent astrological thinking through our service together on the AFAN (Association For Astrological Networking) steering committee, I would like to think he would be pleased with the rise of a new star in the realm of astrological independent thinking as relocational astrology moves eastward.

Jyotish Locality: The Right Angle on Relocation
Ancient astrologers from both the Eastern and Western traditions observed that planets near the angles of the astrological chart (near the horizon and meridian) were imbued with great power to influence the life of a person. The fundamentals of Astro*Carto*Graphy are built upon this ancient principle. But the genius of relocational astrology lies in the principle that if you cannot bring the planets to the angles of your chart because of the time you were born, then by all means bring the angles to the planets by relocating in space to the various localities on terra firma where the planets were on the angles at the time you were born. In this

way you can bring Venus and Jupiter, or Mars and Saturn, to the horizon or meridian of your chart.

The conventional wisdom of contemporary relocational astrology suggests it is best to enhance the classic benefic planetary lines of Jupiter and Venus, and to prudently be prepared, or to avoid classic malefic lines, such as Mars, Saturn and Pluto. For example, the Jupiter line of angularity on the eastern horizon is said to increase personal influence and popularity, increasing a person's optimism. On the other hand, the Saturn line of angularity on the eastern horizon is said to increase personal power but decrease self-esteem and popularity. Venus angular on the eastern horizon is said to enhance the personal image, refine personal aesthetics and create an atmosphere of indulgence. Mars, however, angular on the eastern horizon, is said to increase a virile, machismo image, magnifying competitive and confrontational energies in the person's life, often subjecting the person to physically challenging and harsh life circumstances. As you can see, the conventional wisdom certainly favors the benefic planetary lines of angularity.

Vedic astrology also generally favors the benefic planetary energies of Jupiter and Venus over Saturn and Mars but there are important exceptions to this general rule and very important distinctions about which planetary energies to embrace and which to avoid. To understand this let's begin to weave a basic understanding of Jyotish, commonly called Vedic astrology, into our current understanding of relocational wisdom.

Jyotish Locality: Preferred Planetary Placement

The astrology of India is a sidereal-based system of astrology, which incorporates several distinct factors not currently used by today's contemporary Western astrologers.

Ancient Jyotishis (practitioners of Vedic astrology) observed and recorded that planets near or on the *kendras* (angles), bring great power to influence a life, just like today's contemporary Western astrologers utilize the angles for the most obvious and distinguishing characteristics of a person's life. The Ascendant (1st angle) indicates the appearance, the IC (4th angle) indicates the family of origin, the descendant (7th angle) indicates the significant other or spouse, and the MC (10th angle) indicates the profession. The same principles of relocational angularity of the planets apply equally to Vedic relocational astrology, for as previously noted, relocational astrology is locally specific, not zodiac specific. It makes no difference what ayanamsa (difference between the tropical and sidereal zodiac) the astrologer uses; the calculations of the planets angular lines will always be the same.

The Vedic sage Parasara, in his masterpiece, *Brihat Hora Shastra*, says further, that each of the planets has a preferred kendra (angle) where the planet gains its greatest directional strength. This system of planetary strength is called *dik bala* (directional strength). Parasara explains that each of the planets has a direction (North, South, East and West) in which it is most powerfully placed. Here is a table of these directional strengths.

Planet	Directional Strength		
Mercury	East	1st Angle	Horizon East
Jupiter	East	1st Angle	Horizon East
Moon	North	4th Angle	Lower Meridian
Venus	North	4th Angle	Lower Meridian
Saturn	West	7th Angle	Horizon West
Sun	South	10th Angle	Upper Meridian
Mars	South	10th Angle	Upper Meridian

Relocational astrology suggests that as planets come to angularity, they become more powerful. Vedic relocational astrology, or Jyotish Locality, agrees wholeheartedly, and further suggests that each planet has a specific angle at which it is most powerful. This implies preferred planetary lines of angularity for all of the planets.

For example, as you can see from the table, the Sun is best placed directly overhead, on the MC, the upper local meridian or 10th angle. That is the Sun's preferred and most powerful placement according to dik bala (directional strength). This will be the most powerful planetary line of angularity for the Sun, more powerful than the ascendant, the IC, or the descendant lines of angularity. This directional strength of the Sun is so obvious it is almost indisputable. The Sun appears strongest overhead and it casts little or no shadow. Both ancient and modern astrologers agree on this point. Jyotish Locality further suggests that each of the planets will correspondingly be most powerful on its preferred line of angularity. The Moon's most powerful preferred placement is the IC line of angularity, opposite the Sun. Saturn's most powerful line of angularity is in the West and Jupiter's line in the East, and so on and so forth for all of the planets.

Although, as we have seen, relocational astrology is predicated upon the principles of local planetary angularity, Jyotish Locality agrees, and further gives preferential treatment to one line of angularity over the others for each of the planetary lines. This preferred line further increases the power of the planet. But as a planet becomes powerful we need ask ourselves *powerful for what*? Modern relocational astrology suggests that the characteristics indicated by the specific planet will become more powerfully enhanced, such as optimism and friendliness for Jupiter's planetary lines, and realism and an increasing sense of isolation for Saturn's planetary lines. Jyotish Locality again agrees on these powerful enhanced planetary indicators according to the nature of the planets involved. But Vedic astrology further indicates that as planets become more powerful, the astrological houses these planets are associated with also become increasingly powerful. In fact, in Vedic astrology, the astrological houses a planet owns will singularly determine whether that planet will be powerful to help you, or to hinder you. Thus, again, some planets are preferred over others.

Yoga Karakas: Preferred Planetary Energies

As you have read, ancient and modern astrologers alike agree that the angles, or *kendras* of the chart are preferred planetary placements of power. The ability of a planet to make itself prominent in a person's life is attributed to its angularity. The four angles are powerful, that is why they are considered beneficial planetary placements. If a planet becomes powerful on an angle, then certainly the purpose behind this power is also a powerful consideration, for ultimately the purpose is a determining factor on whether the planet will become beneficially disposed or not.

Therefore the astrological houses of purpose are of special importance in Vedic astrology. These houses of purpose are called the *dharma* houses, and they ultimately determine whether the power of any given planetary angularity will be a positive or negative force in a person's life.

The dharma houses, commonly called the *trines* in Vedic astrology, are the 1st house, the 5th house, and the 9th house. The Sanskrit word *dharma* implies the inherent purpose, the duty of the soul to fulfil itself. The purpose behind anything reveals its intent. The intent of the soul is sacred, thus in Vedic astrology these astrological houses are especially auspicious. The 1st house does double duty as both an angle and a dharma house, called a trine. It is supremely auspicious because the planet that rules it is fully indicative of the self. The purpose of these trinal houses reveals the dharmic path of the soul through many lives. This makes these soulfully purposeful houses. Further, the planets that rule these houses are purposeful, benefic planets, that is, they are unusual for the astrological chart in question, whether these planets are the benefics (Mercury, Venus and Jupiter) or the malefics (Mars and Saturn).

In Vedic astrology, when it so happens that a single planet owns both an angle (houses 1,4,7,and 10) and a trine (houses 1,5, and 9), it becomes a supremely auspicious planet for the person in question, for when purpose and power are combined, it is truly auspicious for the dharma of the soul. Like ancient Greek astrology, ancient Vedic astrology uses the original seven planets (the Sun through Saturn) in its house rulership principles. Modern Vedic astrologers use the outer planets (Uranus, Neptune, and Pluto) but not in the house rulership principles. Again, like ancient Greek astrology, Vedic astrology utilizes a whole sign house system. So the planets will rule over each sidereal house/sign in zodiacal succeeding order. This order is determined approximately every two hours by the sidereal sign that is rising in the eastern horizon. So all the planets, with the exception of the Sun and Moon, will rule over two houses, as they rule over two signs each (Venus rules Taurus and Libra, Mercury rules Gemini and Virgo, Jupiter rules Sagittarius and Pisces, Saturn rules Capricorn and Aquarius, Mars rules Aries and Scorpio). When the two houses that a planet rule are each an angle and a trine, then that planet gains a special status of positively influencing the life of the person. This is because the planet that rules both an angle and trine has that aforesaid synergy of power and purpose behind it (because of its house rulerships) to lift it above the other planets and confer upon it a preferential status. In some cases two planets are necessary to create this linkage of power and purpose. The preferential status given to such planets is called a *yoga karaka* in Vedic astrology. Yoga karaka in Sanskrit means the best indicator of planetary combination. It is the best planet, or planets, benefic or malefic, for a given chart and this is entirely determined by what sidereal sign you have rising at birth. Below is a list of the highly beneficial yoga karakas for each of the twelve sidereal planetary ascendants:

Ascendant Yoga Kararkas

Aries Ascendant:	Sun and Jupiter
Taurus Ascendant:	Saturn alone
Gemini Ascendant:	Mercury and Venus
Cancer Ascendant:	Mars alone
Leo Ascendant:	Mars alone
Virgo Ascendant:	Mercury and Venus
Libra Ascendant:	Saturn alone
Scorpio Ascendant:	Sun and Moon
Sagittarius Ascendant:	Jupiter and Sun
Capricorn Ascendant:	Venus alone
Aquarius Ascendant:	Venus alone
Pisces Ascendant:	Jupiter and Moon

Jyotish Locality suggests that these are the best planetary lines of angularity for each of the twelve ascendants due to the auspicious house rulerships of the given planets.

So if you are a sidereal Capricorn or Aquarius rising, the benefic Venus is your yoga karaka, and thus your best planetary line of angularity. If you are a sidereal Cancer or Leo ascendant, the malefic Mars is your yoga karaka, and thus your best planetary line of angularity. It is the same for the sidereal Taurus and Libra ascendants, where the malefic Saturn is the yoga karaka and thus the best planetary line of angularity. When malefic planets such as Mars and Saturn are yoga karakas, they become temporarily benefic for those sidereal ascendants only. This is how Mars and Saturn, usually malefic energies, become highly beneficial lines in Vedic relocational astrology, because of their specific status as yoga karakas for Cancer, Leo, Taurus and Libra ascendants. To begin to practice Jyotish Locality, you will need to remember the yoga karakas for each of the twelve differing ascendants as these are the most auspicious planetary lines.

Devas and Asuras: Friendly Planetary Groups
The concept of *yogas* (planetary combinations) and especially yoga karakas is fundamental to the workings of Vedic astrology. You have already seen how certain planetary lines of angularity become exceedingly auspicious because of the preferred astrological houses over which the planets in question have dominion. Vedic astrology further divides planetary energies into two planetary camps: Devas[4] and Asuras[5]. Just as the yoga karakas work well with one other, planets from the same planetary grouping have a natural affinity and also work well together.

The planets that rule the fire and water signs in Vedic astrology are friendly members of the Deva planetary group. These planets are the Sun, Moon, Mars and Jupiter. They generally work well together. The planets which rule the air and earth signs are friendly members of the Asura planetary group. These planets are Mercury, Venus and Saturn. They also work very well together. Vedic astrology mimics life. We generally can do no wrong in the eyes of our friends and do no right in the eyes of our enemies. Below, please find the table of planetary friendships for easy reference:

Planetary Friendships

Planets	Friendships
Mercury	Asura Planetary Group
Venus	Asura Planetary Group
Saturn	Asura Planetary Group
Sun	Deva Planetary Group
Moon	Deva Planetary Group
Mars	Deva Planetary Group
Jupiter	Deva Planetary Group

Jyotish Locality suggests that next in importance to your yoga karaka planetary line of angularity you can't do much better than relocating to the line of a planetary friend. The first line of preference, next to the yoga karaka, should be the planetary line of the ascendant lord. No man or woman can be a better friend to oneself than by relocating to the planetary line of the planet that represents self. Next in order of importance will be the planetary lines of the planets from the same planetary grouping. Planetary friends will be supportive and beneficial for the chart as a whole.

So you see, Jyotish Locality follows the same principles of modern relocational astrology when it comes to assessing local planetary lines of angularity. It then distinguishes the planetary lines by giving preferential treatment to the planetary line of angularity, which has dik bala, or the directional strength, for a given planet. It further qualifies planetary lines preferentially in the order of yoga karaka, ascending sign ruler, and lastly by planetary friendship lines of angularity. Each technique from ancient Vedic astrology enriches our understanding of modern relocational astrology, giving, in my opinion, a more distinctive and in-depth analysis of each of the traditional seven planetary lines. Jyotish Locality is just that profound and yet simple.

Planetary Dasas: Preferential Planetary Periods
Vedic astrology has a time-tested, unique feature, which has no equivalent in modern Western astrology: planetary *dasas*. The dasa system is one of planetary periods lasting anywhere from 6 to 20 years each, somewhat the eastern version of planetary progressions.

The classic dasa system utilized by today's Vedic astrologers is the *Vimshottari dasa* system. Each person will start life in one of nine planetary periods, including the seven original planets and the two nodes of the Moon. According to the principles of Vedic astrology, you will receive the indications, and thus the karmic results, of each of the planets in your chart over the course of time, as you change from the planetary period of one planet to that of another. There is no need to discuss how to calculate the planetary dasas, as any of the several fine Vedic astrology software packages will easily calculate these planetary periods for you.

The premise behind the planetary periods is that some planetary periods deliver better results than others do. This has much to do with how powerful the planet is in the chart, i.e. whether the planets are in their own sign or exaltation, and how powerfully the planetary period lord is placed, i.e. whether the planet is in one of the aforesaid angles or trines. The periods of well placed planetary friends are generally said to give the most favorable and supportive results. Jyotish Locality will take the dasa system one step further.

Jyotish Locality suggests that if you are running the planetary period of a planet that is friendly to your chart, then, this planetary line usually becomes the best possible line of angularity to embrace if you are relocating during the planet's dasa. The concept is simple. If a person is running a planetary cycle of a planet friendly to their chart, say the planet Mercury for example, for a Taurus sidereal ascendant, then they are experiencing the karmic results of the planet Mercury during his cycle, which generally would be favorable for a Taurus sidereal ascendant. This is because Venus, the ascendant ruler, is a friend to Mercury in the system of planetary friendship groupings. If the person wanted to move in Mercury's cycle, Jyotish Locality would suggest the Mercury lines of angularity, especially the eastern horizon line, as there Mercury receives dik bala, his most powerful directional strength. The reasoning is again straightforward. Mercury's cycle will generally bring about auspicious results for a Taurus sidereal ascendant, and these results will greatly be enhanced and magnified by relocating to a Mercury line of angularity. This, in my opinion, will bring about the greatest possible planetary confluence, linking the current planetary period lord-with the planetary period lord's best line of angularity. This technique of Jyotish Locality is to be employed only when the current planetary period lord is from the same planetary friendship group as the ascendant lord. But what happens when the current planetary period lord is not that of a planet from the same planetary friendship group as the ascendant lord? What does Jyotish Locality have to say then?

Jyotish Locality *Upayes*: Remedial Relocation Measures

When a person is running the period of a planet that is not friendly to the ascendant lord, the results of a such a planetary cycle are generally not as favorable for the person, unless other mitigating factors are involved.

Vedic astrology utilizes a number of remedial measures to ameliorate difficult planetary energies. These are called *upayes* in Sanskrit. These upayes range from the use of prayer and mantras to the use of spiritual ceremonies (yagyas) and gemstones to propitiate difficult planetary energies. In ancient India, people did not relocate as readily and as easily as we enjoy today in modern Western culture. Because of our recently acquired mobility, Jyotish Locality can now be employed as an additional remedial measure. This technique of Jyotish Locality is again very simple and straightforward. If a person is wishing to relocate, and is running a difficult planetary period, simply suggest moving to a line of planetary angularity friendly to that person's chart! In my opinion, this, along with other suitable measures, will help propitiate the negativity of the difficult planetary cycle by realigning the person's energy with the positive resonance of a friendly planetary line of angularity.

For example, imagine a person with a sidereal Leo ascendant is running the cycle of Venus. Venus is not part of the planetary friendship grouping that is friendly to the ascendant lord, the Sun. So if the person wanted to enhance their life by relocation, Jyotish Locality would suggest that they first move to their Mars line of angularity, for Mars is the yoga karaka for the Leo ascendant. Jyotish Locality further suggests the Mars line of angularity on the upper meridian, the MC, as this is where Mars gains dik bala, or directional strength. We would further suggest the planetary lines of the ascendant ruler, the Sun, and Jupiter, all of which are from the same planetary friendship grouping. These lines will bring out the best planetary resonance for the Leo sidereal ascendant.

Case Histories

Now that we have established the fundamental principles of Jyotish Locality, let us see just how well this system functions using actual case examples researched over the last two years from my private client files[6].

Practicum One:
It Must Have Been the Right Place But the Wrong Time
The first case history is that of a man who wished to relocate for personal and business reasons. John was born April 16, 1947, at 11:50am, MST, in Bozeman, Montana. Let us systematically establish the aforesaid

principles of Jyotish Locality so we can begin to interpret his A*C*G map for the best locality for relocation. See Figure 1, John's A*C*G map. John's Vedic chart has a sidereal Cancer ascendant. Mars is the planet who is yoga karaka for the Cancer ascendant. Mars gains dik bala, or directional strength, on the MC, the upper meridian planetary line of angularity. Therefore, according to Jyotish Locality, the Mars line, particularly the MC line of angularity, is the best possible relocational planetary line of angularity for John's chart. The Moon is the ascendant ruler and so the planetary friendship grouping of the Sun, Mars and Jupiter are the lines of planetary friends. These are the next best planetary lines of angularity.

Now, according to the principles of Jyotish Locality, we will want to examine what planetary period John is running, and whether that planet is friendly to his chart. When John called me he was just finishing the balance of the planetary period of Saturn, a planet which is not friendly

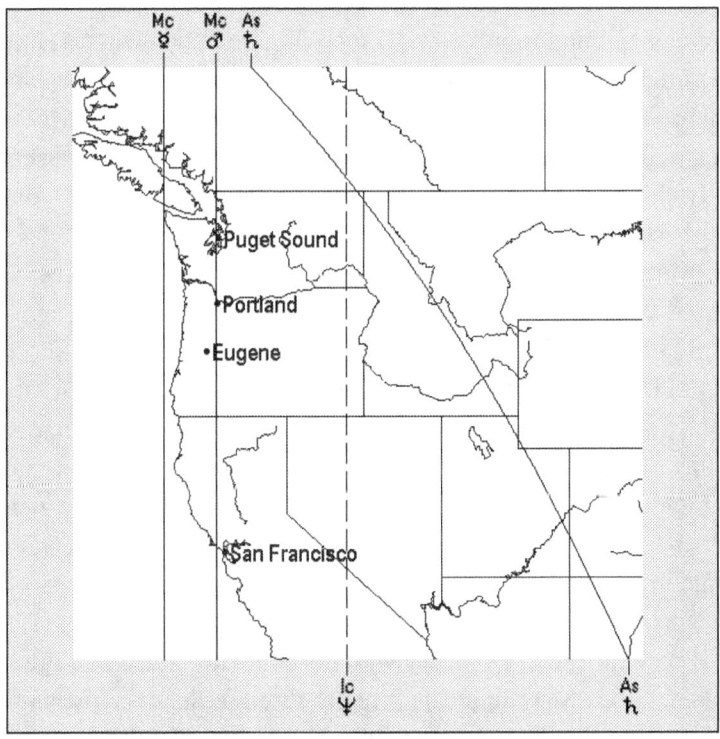

Figure 1 – John's A*C*G map, USA, West Coast detail

to his chart. Saturn is within degrees of the ascendant. At the time of the consultation he was unhappily involved in a relationship with a woman from the eastern part of Washington State. This is where, in fact, his Saturn planetary line of angularity was rising on the eastern horizon. It is thought that we receive the positive or negative energy represented by the planets from the people who come from the localities which their planetary line of angularity run through. This concept seems to work in Jyotish Locality as well. Saturn, in John's Vedic chart, rules the 7th house of relationship and the 8th house of joint finances for a Cancer ascendant. As John's Saturn planetary period of time was finishing, he was simultaneously also finishing the karmas of this very difficult relationship, which involved aspects of deep personal rejection and financial difficulties reflecting the Saturn house rulerships. Amazingly he was fulfilling all of this not far from his rising Saturn line of angularity in Eastern Washington just as he was finishing the difficult cycle of Saturn. The synchronicity of Jyotish Locality can be incredible!

In examining John's A*C*G map (Figure 1) you will certainly see the Saturn line rising through eastern part of the state of Washington. You will also notice a Mars line, in fact the preferred Mars MC, upper meridian line of angularity running along the whole western coast, going directly through the Puget Sound area of Washington. This would be John's best planetary line according to Jyotish Locality. In John's Vedic chart, Mars was with Mercury in the sidereal sign of Pisces, in the preferred 9th trinal house. He was a successful technical writer in the Puget Sound area of Washington. There he had been financially successful on his Mars and Mercury lines of angularity. But, in the Puget Sound area the Saturn rising, eastern horizon, planetary line of angularity was just too close for comfort, even though it went through Eastern Washington. The memories of a long-term difficult relationship were just too much to bear for his Cancer ascendant. The sorrows of the relationship culminating in Saturn's planetary period ultimately made this locality unacceptable. It was time for a move.

I recommended a transfer with his company to the San Francisco Bay area, as his Mars line cuts directly through this locality, as well a Mercury planetary line of angularity for his technical writing skills. John has since relocated to his Mars yoga karaka preferred planetary line of angularity in the San Francisco Bay area, directly on the MC, the local upper meridian, where his confidence and business assertiveness skills are currently flourishing. That is exactly what Jyotish Locality would expect, bringing out all the positivism and confidence of a Martian, that is what Mars as a yoga karaka for a Cancer ascendant promises.

Practicum Two: Fairy Tales Can Come True
The second example is that a woman who wished to relocate for personal and vocational reasons. Joan was born September 13, 1965 at 4:30pm, CST, in Dumas, Texas. Joan had just finished a very interesting time in her life, felt she was waiting for her life to take off again, and wanted to relocate to fulfil emerging career ambitions. Once again let's follow the fundamental principles of Jyotish Locality in interpreting the best locality for relocation.

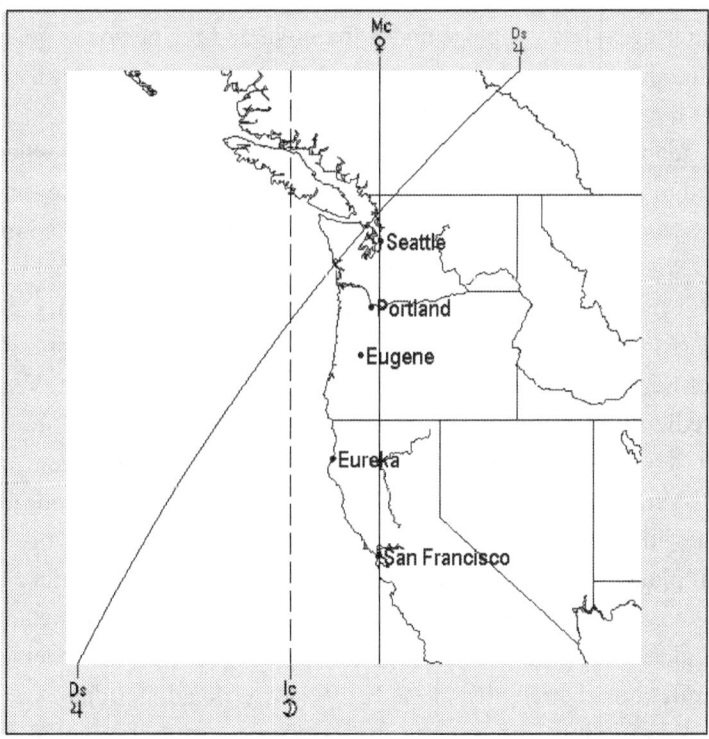

Figure 2 – Joan's A*C*G map, USA, West Coast detail

Joan has a sidereal Capricorn ascendant. Venus is the yoga karaka for Capricorn ascendants. Therefore, Joan's Venus line of angularity holds the best promise for relocation. Especially good is the Venus line on the IC (the lower meridian) as this is Venus' preferred planetary line of angularity. It is where she would receive dik bala (directional strength). Next in order of preference would be the planetary line of angularity from the same planetary friendship grouping as the ascendant lord Saturn. This includes the grouping Venus, Saturn and Mercury, in that order.

When Joan spoke to me she has just finished the planetary period of Venus, the dasa of her yoga karaka planet, and potentially her best planetary period of time. She was now well into the planetary period of the Sun. Joan's Venus is well placed in its own sidereal sign, Libra, in the 10th house. Her Venus forms a powerful planetary configuration called *Malavya Yoga*. Certain yogas, that is, certain planetary configurations in Vedic astrology, confer positive attitude and have great power to lift up one's life. Malavya Yoga is one such yoga. Venus's Malavya Yoga is said to confer great beauty, poise and refinement and the person is generally well liked by all. Such a planetary yoga delivers its powerful results during the yoga planet's planetary period of time.

Joan had already experienced the results of this yoga, when she entered the Venus planetary period in 1971. Venus' cycle was to run for a full twenty years, until 1991. During that period of time she had moved form Texas to the greater Seattle area. Why Seattle? By referring to Joan's A*C*G map (Figure 2) you will see that her Venus planetary line of angularity on the MC (the upper meridian) goes directly through the greater Seattle area. She came here to be a teacher to children. Venus in her Vedic chart rules the 5th house of children and the 10th house of career. There are no coincidences here, only the law of karma in full effect! Venus as yoga karaka for a Capricorn ascendant was conferring 'karmic bliss' through relocation during her planetary cycle, as the Venus line of planetary angularity on the MC went through the greater Seattle area. As good as this planetary line is, it is not the greatest planetary line of angularity for Venus. That is the IC line for Venus, as she receives dik bala (directional strength) on the IC, the lower local meridian.

What is most astounding in examining Joan's life is that during the Venus major planetary cycle she also left the country to teach abroad.

She received great personal recognition when she moved to Oman to teach the children of a royal Sunni Muslim family. Oman is directly on that aforesaid best Venus line of planetary angularity: the Venus IC, its lower meridian line of angularity.

All this glory behind her, Joan wanted very much to recapture the fullness of her Venus period of time, but she was no longer in the cycle of Venus, and had well over a year remaining in the present cycle of the Sun. According to Jyotish Locality, the Sun is not a planetary friend to the Capricorn ascendant planetary friendship group. Further, her Sun was in his own house, the 8th house of the Vedic chart. It was a time for seclusion, something of a retirement from the high energy of the Venus cycle. In 1997 her Moon planetary cycle was to begin. Although not a planetary friend, the Moon in Vedic astrology really has no true enemies. The cycle of the Moon promises to be a much better period, as the Moon in her Vedic chart is placed in the 4th house, where she gains dik bala and rules one of the angles, the 7th house of relationship.

I recommended that Joan continue to reside in the Puget Sound area, or perhaps relocate to Northern California, as she entered the planetary period of the Moon in 1997. This locality is where the Venus MC, upper meridian planetary line of angularity is strong. Venus, after all, as yoga karaka is a great friend to her ascendant lord, Saturn. A Venus line will act as an upaya, a planetary propitiation, and offer much support for a Capricorn ascendant during the concluding difficult cycle of the Sun. In concluding her consultation, I recommended staying in the Puget Sound area because her Moon IC was just off the west coast, much closer to the Puget Sound area than Northern California.

Conclusion
The Vedas of India explain that, "a king without an astrologer is like a man who is blind in his own home." Jyotish in Sanskrit means the 'knowledge of light'. In ancient India, astrology is given special distinction as being the 'eye of the Veda'. Astrology gives us sight through the light of the Divine. The usual processes that go on in the dark proceed very differently when those processes take place in the light. What takes place in the dark can no longer remain the same when the light of astrology shines. We are then no longer blind.

If you are a tropical Western astrologer, think of the techniques of Jyotish Locality as shining an additional ancient light on your current astrological practice. If you are a sidereal Vedic astrologer, think of the techniques of Jyotish Locality as shining an additional modern light on your astrological practice.

In my opinion, Jyotish Locality is one place where ancient Eastern astrology meets modern Western astrology. Don't just take my word for it; try its dynamic techniques for yourself. Relocational astrology maps can't distinguish the difference between the two systems of astrology.

Must we?

© Dennis Flaherty 1997.

Dennis Flaherty is an internationally known astrological consultant, lecturer, teacher and mentor with over 25 years experience. He is one of the few westerners experienced and practiced in both Western and Vedic Astrology, having been the recipient of the prestigious Jyotish Kovid and Jyotish Vachaspati, awarded by the late BV Raman of the Indian Council of Astrological Sciences and the Jyotish Navaratna by the American Council of Astrological Sciences.

Flaherty is the first elected President Emeritus of the Council of Vedic Astrologers, and one of the original founding board members of the American Council of Vedic Astrology. He is a past president of the Washington State Astrological Association and has served four terms on the board of AFAN, The Association for Astrological Networking. He writes regularly for The Mountain Astrologer. He is the author of "Mythic Measurements of the Moon's Nodes" and "The Eastern Moon Through Western Eyes", and is featured in anthologies from Llewellyn and Samuel Weiser.

Flaherty teaches Jyotisha through his audio correspondence course, which has been distributed widely and in several foreign countries. He is the founder and director of the Northwest Institute of Vedic Sciences in the Seattle, Washington area, where he teaches, consults, and tutors a curriculum in Vedic astrology. Over 25 of his personal students have graduated at Level I and Level II from the American College of Vedic

astrology. He can be reached through his web site:
www.vedicsciences.com

NOTES

1. "Jyotish" is the Hindu system of astrology; the Sanskrit word means "light, brightness", but in the plural also "the heavenly bodies, planets and stars". Idiomatically, it is "the knowledge of light".
2. *Continuum* magazine, 1997 edition, "Jim Lewis and Astro*Carto*Graphy", by Ken Browser.
3. From www.eastrovedica.com: The Concept of Ayanamsa: The Date of Coincidence of the Tropical and the Sidereal Zodiacs was found to be 285 AD and the Ayanamsa (precessional distance) was called Lahiri's Ayanamsa. Different scholars gave different dates but the Indian Government, in order to standardise the Ayanamsa value, took the initial point of the Zodiac as the point in the Ecliptic opposite the star Chitra (Alpha Virginis), which was the vernal equinoctial point on the Vernal Equinox day of 285 AD. The rate of precession of the Vernal Equinox was taken as 50.3 seconds per sidereal year.
4. Deva: Sanskrit for god, deity, angel and/or celestial being.
5. Asuras: Sanskrit for power-seeking deities, sometimes referred to as demons. They were opposed to the Devas.
6. Although these are actual case histories, the names have been changed.
7. As has been stated, note that the A*C*G map would be exactly the same if the birth chart had been of the tropical zodiac, rather than sidereal.

11

A Locality Tale

Kathryn Cassidy

Astrologer Kathryn Cassidy has travelled widely, especially during the years she worked as a flight attendant. Here we have the narrative of how locality astrology actually played out in her real-life experiences.

When I turned seventeen years of age, astrology was already my passion. It was not, however, something that the careers officer at my college recognized as being a 'proper job'. Not wishing to get into the tick-tock of office-bound life, I decided to indulge my Venus in Sagittarius and earn some money working in the travel industry. In my early twenties I began working as a flight attendant for British Airways. I spent an entire decade operating either short haul (European) or long haul (worldwide) routes. This satisfied my Mars in Cancer and Uranus in the 10th perfectly – a service industry (Mars Cancer) that gave me freedom to roam (Uranus). It also didn't escape my notice that there was a wonderful correlation between my desire to work towards helping people reach their higher potential, and this work, which found me soaring high in the clouds!

In the mid 80s I was introduced to Jim Lewis's Astro*Carto*Graphy technique. As I had the added advantage of being an astrology student who was constantly on the move across the planet, I was able to directly apply, and test, the fundamental tenets of A*C*G. What I found was that Lewis had developed the most incredible and accurate technique for describing the events and feelings I had experienced, or was yet to experience, at locations across the globe.

Armed with my map and the little accompanying A*C*G booklet, I began to investigate where I had planetary angularity and parans and how my experiences matched up to 'my lines'. As a control for my experiment, I also recalled events that had already happened in the first few years of my flying. I wanted to satisfy myself that I wasn't subconsciously manifesting events as a result of my newfound A*C*G knowledge.

The results were astounding. I can personally attest to the use of these maps and lines to elaborate on the type of energies and resonances encountered at given locations.

Hooray for Venus!
Venus is primarily the planet of relationships. In my birth chart it is in trine (flowing 120 degree) aspect to my Uranus and in wide conjunction to Jupiter. I have Venus and Jupiter angular nearby Dubai. On every trip to Dubai, I loved the opulence and beauty of the hotels and the value of goods I could get for my money. Being considerably younger and perhaps a little more materialistic, I would shop, shop, shop 'til I dropped for luxury items in the souks and duty free outlets. This is a very Venusian pastime. On one trip I went for a sumptuous meal and met a man (I was single then) who was a Taurean. Taurus is the sign ruled by Venus. We got chatting and it transpired that he was on a business trip and actually lived very close to me in England. We dated for about two years and I ended up having a live-in relationship with him in London. Venus/Uranus perfectly describes my delight, but surprise, at meeting a man in Dubai and quickly establishing an unexpected romantic relationship.

If I look back over my life I have also always been a magnet to people of Middle Eastern origin. The received A*C*G wisdom is that you don't have to actually travel to the lines; the energies can come to you. In other words, I have a particularly sympathetic resonance in the area of Venusian matters with people who were born, or reside, under my Venus lines. As another example, I have my Venus Local Space (LS) line (more of Local Space later) running near to my Venus IC through the Caribbean. One year, before I knew of A*C*G, I took a week's holiday to Antigua with my mother. When we arrived we appreciatively surveyed our resort and glanced at the yachts moored in the bay. I turned to my mother and said to her jokingly, "Now all we need is the millionaire with the yacht". The very next day (remember I have Venus trine Uranus) a man approached us on the beach and, to cut a long story short, he turned out to be a very wealthy Californian who had a holiday home on the island (Venus IC). We spent the entire week with him; he flew us over to St Maarten where he hired a yacht with crew and we sailed to St Barts, all expenses paid and no strings attached, other than a bit of harmless flirtation. He remained a friend until we drifted apart a few years later.

I should also note here that in later years, when I was married and no longer flying for a living, I won a national newspaper competition to fly to the Caribbean island of St Lucia for a week. Here we have Venus at work again.

Mercury and Neptune Undermine and Infiltrate
Another example is a trip I made to Southern Mexico, which lay near both my A*C*G Mercury/Neptune IC lines and my Mercury and Neptune Local Space lines (called a "destiny crossing" of those planetary energies). Mercury is the planet of movement, especially by car. Neptune is associated with liquids, especially alcohol. It also has correspondences to the emotion of fear. In this location, I was involved in a car accident when my inebriated taxi driver ploughed into a midline road barrier. I wasn't hurt but, from that day to this, I have had a phobic fear of being driven by anyone I don't know well.

In 1989, on a subsequent trip to this location, (under those Mercury/Neptune lines) I contracted an illness that put me, upon my return, in the Hospital for Tropical Diseases in Isleworth, London. The doctors were baffled and originally thought I had contracted typhoid. Subsequent tests showed that I had *mycoplasma,* a genus of bacteria that lack cell walls and is transmitted via microscopic, airborne water droplets. Neptune is associated with illness that is hard to diagnose and also anything that lacks boundaries. The microbes gave me pneumonia; Mercury has astrological resonance with anything tiny (and this includes the microscopically small) and with the lungs.

Incredibly, later in my life, whilst on a trip to Kuwait, which also lies directly under my Mercury /Neptune LS lines, I contracted dysentery. This is an illness in which micro organisms are transmitted by contaminated water.

Mars and Saturn pose a threat
Mars is a planet whose energies are usually very unsubtle. It has

correspondence with the adrenals, violent events and physical injury. My Mars line stretches up through the mid-Atlantic Ocean. Whilst working for British Airways, flying back from Brazil, and crossing close to where Mars MC links with my Saturn LS line (a MA/SA destiny crossing) I had my worst in-flight experience when, as a result of air turbulence we suddenly lost altitude. We were going to put down in the Azores but the captain made the decision to fly on when none of the injuries were life-threatening. The incident certainly got my adrenaline pumping overtime! Mars/Saturn can be read in astrological parlance as 'the tendency to get hurt or injured'.

Local Space Helps Out
Since making astrology my career in the early 1990s the field of Astromapping has grown phenomenally. New methods and techniques have been added and in 1996 I was fortunate to be introduced to Martin Davis. He hails from St Louis, USA, which is exactly on my Sun IC and within miles of my Uranus Ascendant line; perfect symbolism for the male astrologer who is now bringing my experiences to public attention via this book. Martin has also led a very peripatetic life and his knowledgeable writing and lecturing on Local Space (LS) techniques empowered me to explore my own maps with a greater understanding.

Pluto
It was only after I learned more about Local Space that I was able to see the pattern in another event. Local Space projects your potentials out across the globe. My Pluto LS line arcs through Paris over to Los Angeles. In 1989 I had met someone special to me who lived in Paris but came from California. He put in an appearance as transiting Pluto was conjoining my Sun. I spent almost two years commuting back and forth to Paris to see him. I later lived in L.A. for a year. This suggests that my Pluto Local Space line assumed greater significance when Pluto conjoined my Sun. As I am a Scorpio, I would expect to have a naturally strong resonance with my Pluto lines anyway but the Sun highlighted it and I was subconsciously drawn to locations along this line.

Cyclo*Carto*Graphy (C*C*G): Because Timing is Everything
Another technique we can utilise with modern day A*C*G computer programs is that of secondary progressions. This is one ingredient of what is called Cyclo*Carto*Graphy or C*C*G.

Here's a story which illustrates C*C*G: Though I have a natural affinity (Uranus 10th) with astrology and airlines, within weeks of joining British Airways, I was surprised to learn I had come top of the training course, with the reward, or prize, for this being an around-the-world ticket. I chose to go to across to Hong Kong and then down to Australia. If we were to look at the C*C*G for the period of my trip – bearing in mind I hadn't even heard of A*C*G at this time let alone C*C*G – we would see that both my progressed Sun and progressed Uranus had cycled to their MC's, straddling Hong Kong and going down to Western Australia. My Jupiter LS line cut right through Hong Kong and down through Sydney. I visited both Sydney and Perth on that trip and these lines all perfectly describe the unexpected nature of my visit.

Parans Are Important Too
From looking carefully at all my travels I also feel that parans are of vital importance in pinpointing an exact line of latitude where planets find expression. The Sun-Moon paran is *the* paran for describing 'you' as it links the masculine and feminine, the past and present, the emotional and the physical. Local Space lines add a truly personal flavour; linked as they are to your birth location, whilst the actual lines of angularity, i.e. ASC, DESC, MC and IC, have quite a wide orb but serve to highlight areas of countries, or continents, which will be of significance in the life of the individual.

I have had particular success, whenever I have been ill, in using Tibetan Medicine. I choose to see practitioners in England who are visiting from The Tibetan Medical & Astrology Institute (Men-Tsee-Khang) in Dharamsala. This is near to where my Saturn, Mars, Neptune and Mercury A*C*G lines converge with my Venus LS line. This location lies exactly on my Sun/Moon paran latitude.

In Conclusion

I believe the angularity of planets at the time of our birth sets up a field of vibration, or a natural resonance, with various locations on Earth. Just as aspects in the birth chart can manifest on a whole host of levels, so too do our lines describe areas where manifestations of the archetypal meaning of the planet and its harmonic aspects can arise. I highly recommend that all practicing astrologers make careful study of this knowledge in order to understand where, and with whom, their client might increase their chances of avoiding difficulties and embracing love, success and fulfillment.

© Kathryn Cassidy 2007.

Kathryn Cassidy is a UK based astrologer who writes extensively on astrology, A*C*G and the ancient Hermetic wisdoms. All of her writings and videos can be accessed via www.kathryncassidy.com

12

The Stars and Stripes
The USA Presidential Inaugurations and the Complex Sky

Bernadette Brady

Bernadette Brady is well known for her innovative work in Visual Astrology, the astrology of working with the whole sky. I'm pleased to be able to include this important and previously unpublished article by her. In it, she alerts us to the idea that the earth is not intrinsically a neutral canvas waiting for locality lines 'to impregnate it'. Rather, places and regions have inherent qualities, some of which come from their relationship with the sky.

Places and calendar dates have a relationship. We raise monuments at these places and hold ceremonies at these monuments on the calendar dates of the events enshrined in that time and place – the anniversary. Two such times and places for the USA are the events of 9/11 in New York City and Pearl Harbour in the Pacific. For Australians, one of these is the cold and windswept cliffs of Gallipoli. Culturally we acknowledge time's relationships to certain places.

But as astrologers our knowledge of this relationship is generally retrospective. Our astrology is better suited to looking at what has happened, rather than providing a tool which we can use to explore the potential of a place to produce an event. Granted we do have the technique of Astro*Carto*Graphy but this method views the Earth as a neutral canvas, blank and empty, waiting for a planet line to impregnate it. Yet the Earth is not a neutral canvas. Places and regions have an inherent quality, and some of this quality, I believe, comes from a location's relationship with the sky, the whole sky.

If we focus solely on the planets and their movement along the ecliptic, then we tend to forget what is meant by the word *fixed* when referring to the stars. The earth rotates on its axis and every day the whole sky, stars, planets, ecliptic, sun and moon, appear to rise and set. Yet unlike the planets, the stars are, for all observations and purposes, fixed in their place in the dome of the sky and therefore, since the dome of the sky appears to rotate, they will, for any given place, always rise in the same place on the horizon, set on the same place on the horizon, and culminate at the same degree of elevation above the horizon. They do not wander around the sky, changing their times and positions of rising, setting and culmination like the planets. They are fixed. To change this we must either wait seventy-two years for precession to move these positions by roughly a degree or, and this is the important point, *change our location*.

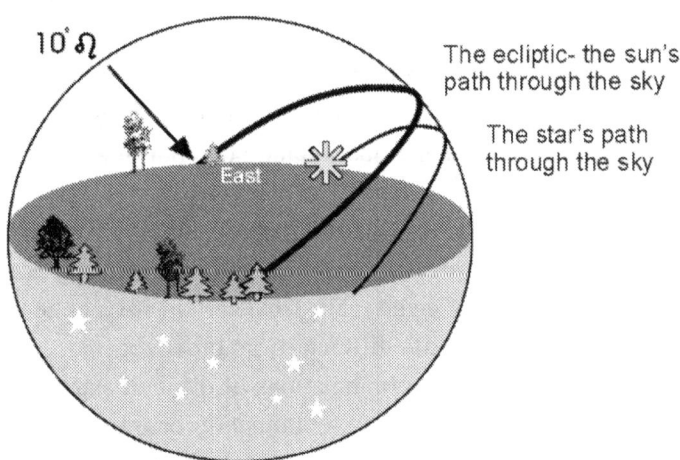

A star rising when 10 ♌ is rising on the ecliptic

Figure 1 – Ignoring precession, for any given location, a star will always rise with the same degree of the ecliptic and at the same place on the horizon. As transiting planets or the luminaries move into the 10th degree of Leo, then when that planet rises it and the star will be in a paran relationship.

The Quality of a Latitude

Given the fixity of the stars for a particular location, a star will always rise (or set, culminate or be on the IC) when a certain degree of the ecliptic is rising (or setting, culminating or on the IC). The star may be further around to the north or south of the ecliptic but when it (the star) touches the horizon, we can look to see what degree of the ecliptic is also touching the horizon.

For example, the star Sirius, the brightest star in the sky (the Dog Star, known to the Egyptians as The Scorcher), will always co-rise with 10° Leo for the latitude of New York, NY but for Tokyo, Japan it co-rises with 5° Leo. So for New York every year the Sun co-rises with Sirius on the 2nd August (when the sun is at 10° Leo), but for Tokyo this date is around the 27th July (when the Sun is at 5° Leo). Further south, down in Sydney, Australia, Sirius co-rises when 14° Gemini is rising and this corresponds to the 4th June (when the Sun is at 14° Gemini). So it can be seen that these three cities all have a relationship with Sirius and the Sun but this relationship is expressed on different calendar dates which in turn are a reflection of the latitude of the city.

So fixed stars are fixed and this fixity gives us an important tool with which to examine the quality and potential of a particular latitude for the unfolding of certain types of events.

Therefore, as astrologers we can recognise that specific bands of latitude on the globe are coupled with specific fixed star combinations. We can look at the globe and realise that certain areas or zones will have potentials, which are quite different from other zones or latitude bands. Some latitudes will have combinations of difficult stars that will move onto the angles (rising, setting, culmination or on the IC) at the same time. Other latitude bands may have a combination of stars which are more productive or successful. Additionally, a single band of latitude will contain times when a certain ecliptical degree will align with difficult stars, and times when another ecliptical degree will align with easier stars.

Every line of latitude on the Earth is rich with these combinations; rich with its own stories, history, qualities and potentials – and these have been seriously neglected by astrologers.

Thus, we can examine a line of latitude for its key degree positions on the ecliptic and if transiting outer planets move into these sensitive degree positions, a nexus is formed between stars, planets and the Earth. This nexus will be unique for that particular latitude. These patterns can be seen if one examines historical events which are sorted by latitude. Additionally, if we involve the Sun in paran to a star, then the events will also occur around the same calendar date. Consider the following events:

- The San Francisco earthquake of 1906 happened on 18th April at latitude 37N36.
- The Oklahoma City bombing of 1995 happened on 19th April at latitude 35N29.
- The assassination of Abraham Lincoln in Washington, DC, in 1865 happened on 15th April at latitude 38N54.

These events occurred in mid-April, for a latitude band around 36° North, which is the period in which Sirius rises when the Sun is culminating.[1] Every year the Sun and Sirius are tied together in mid-April at this latitude. There are many years where no events occur but the key issue here is that this potent combination speaks of a potential between place and calendar.

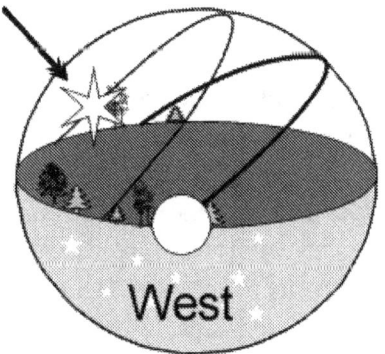 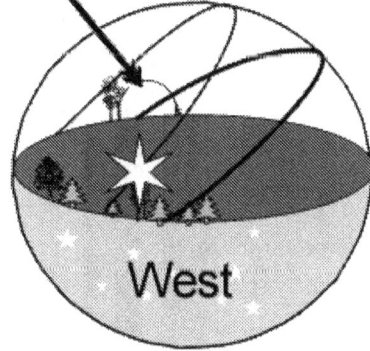

Figure 2 – For this latitude band in mid-April when the Sun culminates (24-25° Aries), 6-7° Leo are rising. This is also the degree at which Sirius will rise every day for this latitude in mid-April, therefore, the Sun and Sirius are in paran for the cities in this latitude band.

When the outer planets form a difficult pattern and also occupy one or more of these key degree positions for this latitude, then the stage is set for memorable events to occur. See Figure 2.

The San Francisco earthquake occurred in this 'charged time' when a tight Uranus-Neptune opposition was in paran with Alhena, the heel of the twin Pollux. In mundane work this star is known as *a ground shaker*. The Oklahoma City bombing occurred in this 'charged time' when a Uranus-Neptune conjunction was in paran with Altair the Eagle, meaning in mundane terms: *ungrounded, ill-planned or fanatical actions*. The assassination of Abraham Lincoln occurred in this 'charged time', when transiting Pluto had moved into a key zodiacal position so that it was in paran with Algol at this latitude: *assassination, to kill one's enemies*. (All star meanings taken from *Starlight*).[2]

Places and times have relationships. When those relationships involve the Sun, as in these three examples, then places also have a relationship to a calendar date. For latitudes of around 36° North, the time of mid-April is a potentially difficult time and if other factors become involved via the movement of the outer planets, then ill-omened events can unfold.[3]

These types of dates are littered throughout history. For example the Great Fire of London erupted on September 2, 1666, and the London Blitz of World War 2 began on September 7, 1940. At both of these times London was nearly destroyed. Is this a coincidence? No. From an astrological point of view, London in early September, every year, is governed by a star called Alphard, the heart of the Serpent.[4] Some years there are also difficult planetary patterns which coincide with these degrees. For the Great Fire of London it was a Saturn-Neptune conjunction; for the London Blitz, Saturn and Neptune were not in aspect to each other but, by a strange quirk of the mathematics of that latitude, they both formed parans to the same stars as for the Great Fire.

Place and time do have a quality and one of the ways we can explore the potential this creates is to examine the possible unions of stars and planets for a location.

Star Phases – How Stars Govern a Place and Time
This fixity produces more than just stars that rise with the Sun. It also

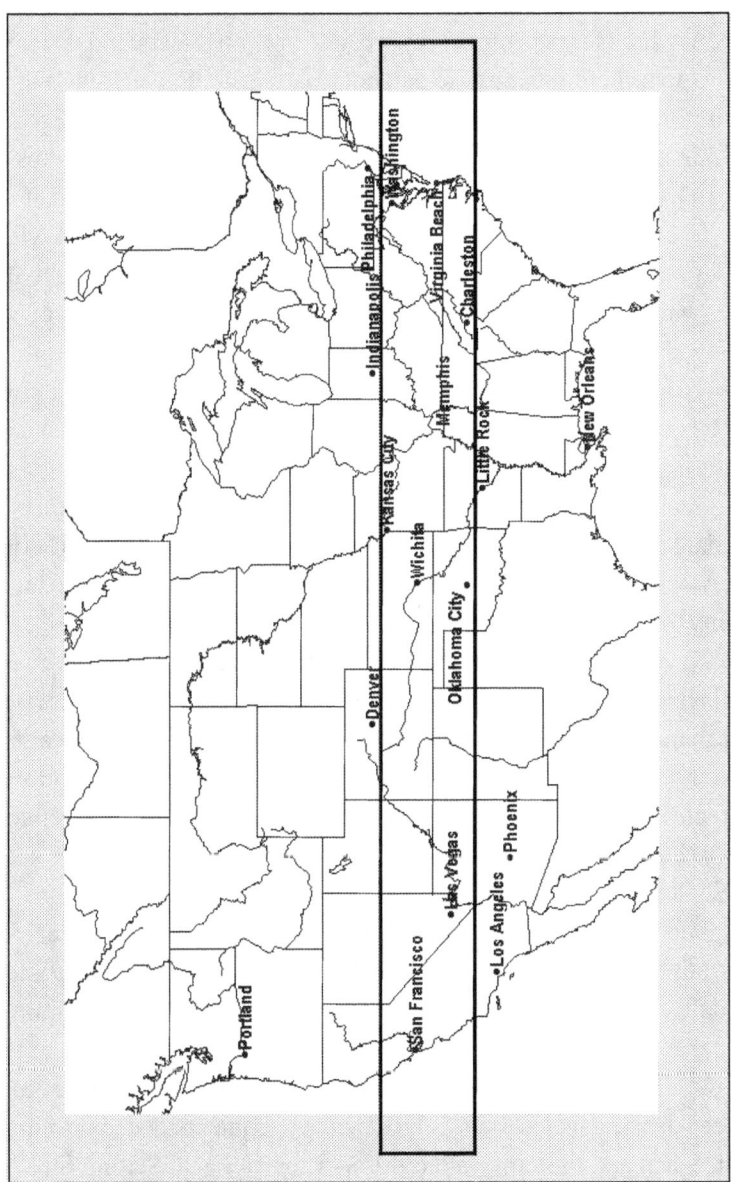

Figure 3 – Some stars can, at fixed times of the year, be seen in the east at sunset and still be visible in the night sky the following dawn. Such a star does not touch the horizon and is therefore said to have lost touch with the mortal Earth and joined the realm of the immortal deities, which are the circumpolar stars.

produces a type of ballet, an annual dance of stars over a particular location, which few astrologers appreciate or even understand. Over your city or town there is a precise calendar pattern to a given star's annual rhythm. Stars have their own individual path through the sky. For some stars this pathway can be shorter than the path that the Sun takes (see Figure 1) and these stars will disappear from view at a set calendar date. Even if you watch the night sky from dusk to the next dawn you will not see that star. However, after a while (days or months) the star will be seen to rise again just before the Sun. Now if you watch the star over the next few days and weeks it will appear to rise earlier and earlier until one evening it will set just before sunset and not be visible again until the same calendar date next year. Then you will see it rising again just before the sunrise.

Such a star, when seen in the predawn light, was considered by the Egyptians to be born again. The star had travelled into the realm of the Underworld, died, and was now reborn. This star was called by Claudius Ptolemy[5] the Heliacal Rising Star.[6]

Nevertheless, if you really are star watching, you would also notice another group of stars that have a pathway through the sky longer at times than the path of the Sun. These stars will set in the west at some time during the night. Each night, these stars will set closer and closer to dawn, until one night the stars will not set at all. Instead, they remain in the sky the whole night and the Sun will rise *before* the stars are seen to set. (See Figure 3.)

Such a star will 'lose touch' with the Earth on the same calendar date from one year to the next for that location. This star was deemed to be a deity visiting the realm of the Immortals, those beings who never died because they never set – the Pole Star, Polaris is the most obvious example of an immortal star. When a star returned from this realm and was seen to set again just before the dawn, it was understood to be rejoining life on Earth and Ptolemy called this star the Heliacal Setting Star.[7]

The Governing Star
When a star returned from its journey from the Underworld or returned from its annual visit to the Immortals, it was believed to govern (I have used the term 'govern' in preference to 'rule' to avoid confusion with the

Date of change of Governorship	Heliacal Rising Star	Heliacal Setting Star	The quality of the governorship
January 2	Acumen		Scandal and Rumours
January 4		Mirfak	A time of action
January 16		Capella	Independently minded
January 23		Pollux	A painful truth coming to light
January 25		Castor	New ideas, new knowledge
February 9	Rukbat		A time of steadiness, a time of no change
February 17	Deneb Algedi		A time of the Establishment and the law
February 19		Regulus	A noble, righteous act that inspires the nation
March 31		Zosma	The small person, or underdog, takes centre stage
April 5		Denebola	Clashes with the Establishment
April 9	Fomalhaut		Idealism, illusion, and even deception abound
April 29		Vindemiatrix	A time of gathering people or ideas together

Figure 4 – A partial parapegma for Washington, DC, latitude 38N54 (and other cities at this latitude). Each period has two governing stars which hold their influence until the next star in their column takes over.

relationship a planet has to a zodiac sign) that time and place until the next star took over and returned to once again touch the Earth. Two millennia ago the calendar was measured by these star risings and settings. Such a star calendar was called a *parapegma*. The parapegma was originally a peg board or stone in which markers or pegs were moved to measure the days of the year as different stars rose or set before the dawn.[8]

I believe that once a star governs a period of time the nature of that star will dictate the quality of the period of time until the next star takes over. Thus, any given location will have an annual rhythm with set times of the year being governed by set stars that hand over their governorship on the same dates each year. This is the potential of a place, the rhythm of a city. For the city of Washington, DC, the parapegma for the first four months of any year of the 20th and 21st century looks like this:[9]

Every latitude band has such an annual calendar and every one will be different. Compare the above parapegma for Washington, DC with that of London, UK in Figure 5.

Date of change of Governorship	Heliacal Rising Star	Heliacal Setting Star	The quality of the governorship
January 1	Facies		The shadow of war, the darkness of cruelty or aggression
January 6	Aculeus		A period of strong debate or criticism
January 22	Acumen		Scandal and rumours
February 4		Pollux	A painful truth coming to light
February 17		Castor	New ideas, new knowledge
February 21		Regulus	A noble, righteous act that inspires the nation
February 22	Deneb Algedi		A time of the Establishment and the law
April 28		Denebola	Clashes with the Establishment
April 29		Zosma	The small person, or underdog, takes centre stage

Figure 5 – A partial parapegma for London, UK, latitude 51N31 (and other cities at this latitude). Each period has two governing stars which hold their influence until the next star in their column takes over.

The pattern for Washington, DC has the potential for scandal and rumours for all of January, then a shift to the focus of law and order which holds sway from mid-February till early April, where a period of illusion is encountered. Whereas for the city of London, UK the new year opens with a potential for darkness or the worries of war, which rapidly (by 6th January) shifts to a debate. This debate is followed by rumours and the flushing out of the truth, and the whole period from late February to late April is governed by the themes of law and order. It is not until late April that there is the opportunity for challenging the establishment line. This calendar is affected by precession but only one day in seventy-two years.

It is important to understand that these events will not happen every year, but if there is, for example, in late April of a given year, a planetary combination which lends itself to a clash with law and order, it will have a greater chance of gaining expression at the latitude of London than at the latitude of Washington. The stars prime a location and the stars for London at that time are conducive to clashes with the law.

So, we can think about a relationship between calendar and place in terms of the stars. Some periods of the year will be blessed with joyful or creative stars which provide a background of potency. For a given city or place, some days will be naturally happy, while other days will hold sadness. Some days will contain the potential for tragedy while others the potential for more positive outcomes. Sometimes this will occur over a period of only a few days; other times it can be a few weeks as a star holds sway over a particular city until the next star returns from the Underworld or from its journey with the Immortals. But each year will be different as the quality of this governorship will vary from one year to the next via the other star and planet parans happening at that time.

Time and Place - The First Tuesday in November

As a society we tend to organise events to fall on set calendar dates and in set places. In Melbourne, Australia, the first Tuesday in November is devoted to a horse race called the Melbourne Cup. By a good chance, rather than design, at that latitude for that time of the year the Sun rises with Procyon, a bright star linked with glamour and glitter.[10] In mundane work, I have delineated this in Starlight as simply: *A time of sporting success or short-lived, ephemeral glories.*

This is the perfect background for the nature of this event and is, I believe, one of the astrological reasons for its growth from a small provincial race, starting in 1861, to one of the major racing events of the sporting world. But what would happen if the Melbourne racing authorities moved the event to another month? In effect, they would be placing the event and all of its importance into another type of time, charged with different stars, which may or may not be supportive of the horse race.

In the USA, however, in every fourth year, the first Tuesday in November is a race of a different nature. It is Election Day. On that date, for the latitude of Washington, DC, the governing stars are Spica and Alpheratz. Spica, the Wheat sheaf of Virgo, symbolises making the most of an opportunity or a choice, and Alpheratz in Pegasus, the flying horse, is concerned with making changes, asking us to take action, to not be restricted.[11] This is a good combination for a political election. This is the potency of that time of the year for that latitude.

All elections are different from each other and depend, according to astrology, on the position of the planets and how those planets relate to other stars on any particular election day. Nevertheless, the background energy is in rapport with the intentions and actions of the population.

Any changes to this date, as in the example of the Melbourne Cup, could have serious long-term consequences, for, according to my hypothesis, it would open the door to different energies and flood this important event with energies that may not be so supportive.

Yet a key date in US political events has been changed; firstly in its location and secondly in its calendar date. When George Washington became the first US president, he was inaugurated[12] on April 30th, 1789, in Wall Street, New York City. After that inauguration the event was moved to Philadelphia, PA, and the date was changed to March 4th. It was then moved to Washington for the 1801 inauguration of Thomas Jefferson. Having settled on that place in 1933, the date was changed from March 4th to January 20th for the second inauguration of Franklin D. Roosevelt.

1789	April 30 – George Washington	New York, NY
1793	March 4 – George Washington	Philadelphia, PA
1801	March 4 – Thomas Jefferson	Washington, DC
1937	January 20 – Franklin D. Roosevelt	Washington, DC

Figure 6 – A summary of the changes to the inauguration dates and places for the US presidents. The president listed in the table is the first president to be inaugurated on that calendar date.

So the important event of the inauguration of the presidents of the USA has been placed into different places and different dates. Like a seed, it has been planted into different types of soil, each one having different qualities. What were and are these qualities? And have these changes been of service or disservice to the presidency?

George Washington's Inauguration
George Washington was inaugurated on 30th April, 1789 in New York, NY. His inauguration stars are as follows: [Note: All the following meanings are from the delineations that I researched for the software Starlight. Starlight is also designed to take the date of an event and search back in time to find the dawn where a star was returning to the Earth – either becoming the newly-crowned Heliacal Rising star or Heliacal Setting star].

> **30 April, 1789 – New York, NY**
> **Themes that Occur for this Latitude Every Year in this Era**
>
> Heliacal Rising Star
>   Fomalhaut – Rising before Sunrise
>   *Idealism, illusion and even deception abound*
>
> Heliacal Setting Star
>   Vindemiatrix – Setting before Sunrise
>   *A time of gathering people or ideas together*
>
> Sun – The stars in paran with the Sun on this day
>   Setting when Mirach is Setting
>   *The promotion of peace, or order, in a territory*
>   Rising when Altair is Culminating
>   *Bold or daring actions by a group or a person, military matters*
>   Rising when Vindemiatrix is Setting
>   *People gather together, an event that unites*

These are the star themes that repeat themselves every year for New York, NY, at this time of the year and they are fairly self-explanatory. Here we see that the ritual of the first presidency was planted in a rich, supportive soil. The act of creating a republic and a president was a noble idea, full of dreams held together by ideals which united people; a bold venture, a pathway to peace, the victory of self-government after the military matters of the American War of Independence. This was a good day and a good place for George Washington to stand on a balcony on Wall Street and take the oath of office. It gives the fledgling nation the best chance to grow into its dreams. And grow it did.

However, for the second inauguration both the date and the place were changed. George Washington's second inauguration was on March 4th, in Philadelphia.

> **March, 1793 – Philadelphia, PA**
> **Themes that Occur for this Latitude Every Year in this Era**
>
> Heliacal Rising Star
> > Deneb Algedi – Rising before Sunrise
> > > *A time of the Establishment and the law*
>
> Heliacal Setting Star
> > Regulus – Setting before Sunrise
> > > *A noble, righteous act that inspires the nation*
>
> Sun – The stars in paran with the Sun on this day
> > Setting when Sualocin is Setting
> > > *The talented long-shot takes centre stage*
> >
> > Culminating when Rukbat is Setting
> > > *A leader stands steady, or a leader is seen to be stubborn*
> >
> > Rising when Regulus is Setting
> > > *To engage in a noble, or military, endeavor*

As can be seen from the quality of this date for Philadelphia, the shift of the inauguration put the presidency, with all its new dreams of nationhood, on a more solid footing. Gone is the idealism of the 30 April, New York inauguration and now, in its place, we have the energy of Deneb Algedi, the tail of the goat of Capricorn. This is the mark of law and order, the establishment acting in a ritual which is about nobility, an act that inspires a nation (Regulus is the heart of the Lion and one of the royal stars of Persia). Present also is a statement concerning the new concept of a republic which elects its leaders based on their ability, rather then anointing the heir to the throne (Sualocin in paran with the Sun). The inauguration in Philadelphia was a good move.

But there were still changes to come. Thomas Jefferson became the third president of the United States. His inauguration on 4 March, 1801 was held in the new seat of power, Washington DC. His presidency ended twelve years of Federalist rule. There was only a small shift of latitude, with Philadelphia being sited at 39N59 and Washington DC at

> **4 March, 1801 – Washington, DC**
> **Themes that Reoccur for this Latitude Every Year in this Era**
>
> Heliacal Rising Star
>   Deneb Algedi – Rising before Sunrise
>   *A time of the Establishment and the law*
>
> Heliacal Setting Star
>   Regulus – Setting before Sunrise
>   *A noble, righteous act that inspires the nation*
>
> Sun – The stars in paran with the Sun on this day
>   Setting when Alphecca is On Nadir
>   *(Strength and leadership found through hardship)*
>   Rising when Regulus is Setting
>   *To engage in a noble, or military, endeavor*
>   Rising when Mirach is Rising
>   *The promotion of peace, or order, in a territory*

38N49, so the stars are quite similar and as for Philadelphia they also talk of law and order, but there is an important difference.

The only change is the star Sualocin which has been replaced by Alphecca, the alpha star of the Northern Crown. The Greeks called this constellation the Wreath, and the star is linked to the action of being offered a crown. Now the presidential candidate who will be offered the crown needs to be a hardworking respected leader; skill alone is not enough.

Of course each president had his own unique natal chart as well as his inauguration chart. However, during this period of US history all of the presidents placed their inauguration charts into this quality of time which promoted successful growth for their country. We can see how some parts of an inauguration chart will be encouraged by the stars, while others are not.

182 *From Here to There*

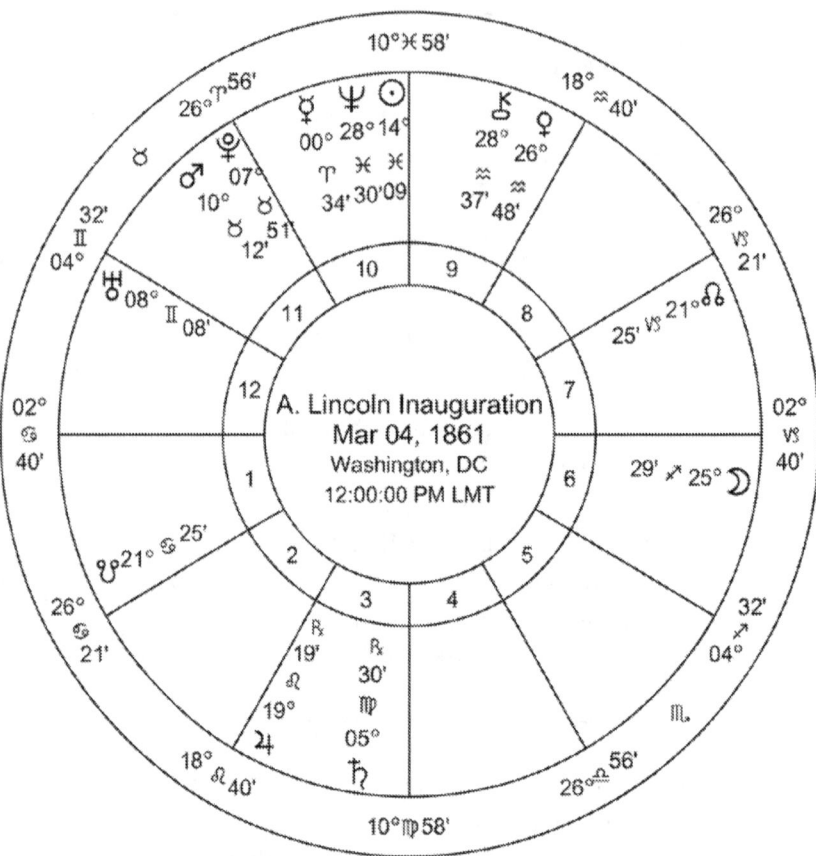

Figure 7 – The first Inauguration of Abraham Lincoln. March 4, 1861 at 12 noon LMT (estimated time) in Washington, DC 38N53, 77W02.

Lincoln's Inauguration: a March 4 type

The chart for Abraham Lincoln's first inauguration, I have set to noon[13] on March 4, 1861 in Washington, DC. One of the features of this chart is the Mars-Pluto conjunction.

Given that we already understand the *quality* of this time and place, we can expect that this stellar quality will enhance certain planetary combinations in the chart that are of a similar nature while reducing the potency of other planetary combination which are not of its nature.

The quality of this time and place already contains the theme of leadership in the face of hardship, as well as the theme of military activity, enabling us to highlight the Mars-Pluto in Lincoln's inauguration chart and say that there will be military endeavours of great hardship. Indeed, it was Lincoln who took the Union into the Civil War; the most bloody of conflicts. And the Civil War began April 12, 1861, within five weeks of his inauguration. One can then look at the actual Mars and star links (parans) for the period of the day of his inauguration and see not only the bloodshed but also the potential for the Union victory:

Mars was in paran to two stars on the day of his inauguration: firstly, to Facies, the meaning of which in Starlight is: *Matters of endurance or great hardship*, and secondly to Sualocin, which I have delineated in Starlight as: *Assuming mastery of the territory, to take the upper hand*.

Planet Combinations Supported by Star Parans

This is a key point: one needs to look for support for a particular theme at *both* levels of the astrology, on the ecliptic – that is in the chart –as well as in the sky, using the full dome of the celestial sphere. This point bears repeating: one should look for an issue firstly in the chart and *then* look for its nature or expression being reflected in the stellar background. In Lincoln's inauguration chart we have a difficult planetary combination of Mars/Pluto, this is supported in the star parans for the inauguration and thus can grow and gain expression.

The Change of Inauguration Date

In order to allow enough time for officials to gather election results after election day, as well as for candidates to make the long journey in the winter months to the north of the country, the United States had enshrined in its constitution that the inauguration would be held on 4 March, unless that was a Sunday, in which case it would be held on 5 March. However, with improvements in communication, as well as travel, the lengthy time until the transition of power now seemed unnecessary and in 1933, with the passage of the Twentieth Amendment, the constitution was changed to move the date to 20 January, or 21 January if that was a Sunday.

Hence, with the second inauguration of Franklin D Roosevelt (his second of four), the seeds of nationhood and presidency were to be planted into a different type of soil. A different time, and therefore a different quality, was being used as the foundation for the presidency.

> **20 January 1937 - Washington DC**
> **Themes that Reoccur for this Latitude Every Year in this Era**
>
> Heliacal Rising Star
> > Acumen – Rising before Sunrise
> > > *Scandal and rumors*
>
> Heliacal Setting Star
> > Capella – Setting before Sunrise
> > > *A period which favors the independently-minded*
>
> Sun – The stars in paran with the Sun on this day
> > Setting when Schedar is Culminating
> > > *The people, or an exalted woman, act with dignity*
> >
> > Rising when Algol is On Nadir
> > > *A person who destroys through passion*
> >
> > On Nadir when Alpheratz is Setting
> > > *To take independent action*
> >
> > Culminating when Altair is Culminating
> > > *Bold or daring actions by a group or a person, military matters*
> >
> > Rising when Menkar is On Nadir
> > > *A time of extremes of action or weather*

This is a vastly different theme to the 4 March date. Gone is the nobility, the honor, the action that inspires a nation. Not all presidents will be hounded by scandal and rumors and not all presidents will be driven to the extremes of the nuclear attack on Japan (symbolized by the joining of the two stars Algol and Menkar with the Sun) but this is the potential, into which the US presidents – and thus US history – were embedded from 1933 onwards.

A few inaugurations of the 20 January type
To date, Richard Nixon has been the only president to resign in office. The second inauguration of Richard Nixon on 20 January, 1973, is shown in the following chart:

The Stars and Stripes   185

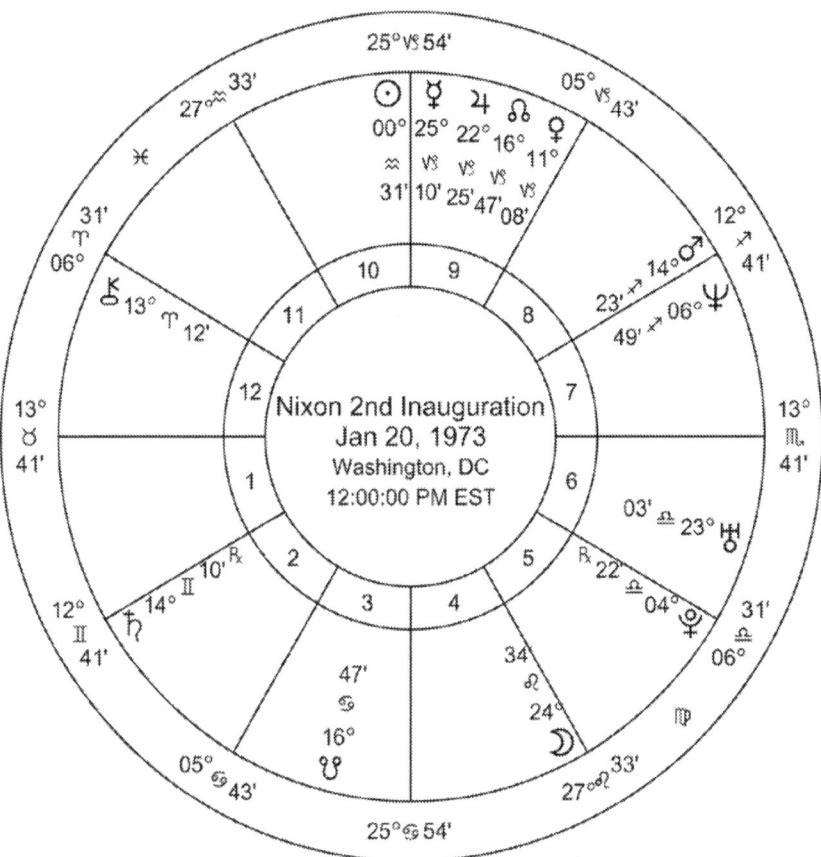

Figure 8 – Richard Nixon's 2nd inauguration. 20 January, 1973, 12 noon EST (estimated time), Washington, DC. 38N53 77W02.

This chart contains a strong Mercury conjunct the MC, as well as a partile Mars-Saturn opposition with a wide separating conjunction between Neptune and Mars.

Mercury and Scandal

The background star theme for this time and place *already* contains the potential for scandal or rumours (Acumen, one of the stings of the Scorpion, being the Heliacal Rising Star governing that time period).

So into this star theme is laid an inauguration chart which has a strong Mercury tightly conjunct the Midheaven, and its ruler, Saturn, is linked with Mars and just happens to be in Mercury's sign of Gemini. Additionally, Mercury forms a square to Uranus and a conjunction to Jupiter. There are many ways such a strong Mercury could be delineated.

We could say that detailed knowledge of Richard Nixon's dealings will keep expanding and growing (Mercury conjunct Jupiter) with totally unexpected outcomes (the square to Uranus) which have difficult or even fatal results (bringing in the nature of the Saturn-Mars opposition). However, when we consider the background star potential, then we begin to understand that, combined with the Acumen, this could open the doorway to scandals and rumors.

The unfolding story of the strong Mercury in the inauguration horoscope has a tendency therefore to flow into the Mercurial themes of rumor and scandal present in the background star themes. There is a match, a sympatico between horoscope and stars.

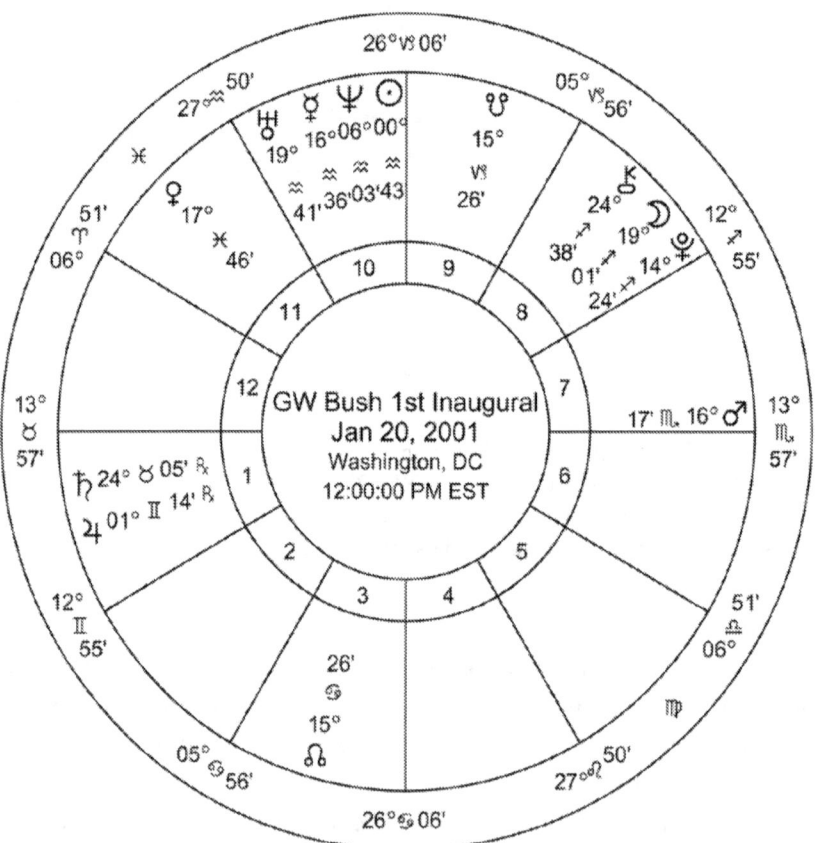

Figure 9 – George W. Bush's first inauguration, 20 January 2001, noon EST (estimated time), Washington, DC. 38N53 77W02.

There are other supporting star and planet parans in Nixon's second inauguration chart that indicate difficulties, but the main point is to show how the stress on Mercury in the chart expressed itself via rumours, which grew stronger. These rumours, of course, lead to Nixon's resignation.

In looking at another example, George W. Bush. Bush has had two inaugurations. The first was on 20 January, 2001, in Washington, DC.

George W. Bush was elected with a minority of the popular vote; the potential for scandal, rumors and the muttering of corruption was a rich legacy from the elections. His inauguration chart contains among other planetary combinations a Mercury-Uranus conjunction squaring both Mars and Saturn. We see in this horoscope the potential for a sudden and unexpected event or piece of news which could herald hardship or even war. This could be economic, military or social hardship. We still have the annual star theme linked to this date and place, which, for Bush's first inauguration was:

Heliacal Rising Star
    Acumen – Rising before Sunrise
        Scandal and rumors

Heliacal Setting Star
    Capella – Setting before Sunrise
        A period which favors the
        independently minded

Sun – The stars in paran with the Sun on this day
    Rising when Algol is on the Nadir
        A person who destroys through passion
    Culminating when Al Rescha is Rising
        A person who unites or polarizes
    On the Nadir when Alpheratz is Setting
        To take independent action

When considering the quality of this time, we would bias our interpretation more towards the difficult Algol with the Sun and its passion and destruction predominating, rather than the rumours or scandal which was the focus with Nixon's chart. Keep in mind that we are looking for themes being repeated in both the sky and if found, are the ones on which we should focus. In Bush's first inauguration chart we have the themes of sudden upset and new hardships, so these are what we seek in the stars. If they are there as well, it is a strong indication of the nature of the unfolding of events.

We can expand this information by looking at the star parans to the planets involved in the particular combination. For Bush's first inauguration the following star planet parans were also in effect:

Uranus with Alphard – (The heart of the Serpent) – *Outrage in the community because of threats to families*

Mars with Zuben Elgenubi – (One of the claws of the Scorpion) – *People helping people*

Mercury with Alkes – (The Cup) – *Important news that will be remembered by many* and with Antares – (The Heart of the Scorpion) – *Anxiety and worry*

For **Saturn** there are several stars but one that stands out is:
With **Pollux** (one of the twins of Gemini) – *People's lives altered by a disaster or the actions of an aggressive group*

Given this additional information, the sudden news item is more likely going to be a disaster affecting innocent people and/or families than a presidential scandal, as was the case for Nixon. Within eight months of this inauguration the events of 9/11 unfolded in New York City.

This marriage between sky and chart reveals a focus to the planetary patterns in the chart and enables us to gain clearer insights into the potential indicated by the inauguration charts.

The 2005 Inauguration
The second inauguration chart for George W. Bush was for 20 January 2005.

In this chart Saturn is in detriment conjunct the IC. Once again, as with the inauguration chart for Abraham Lincoln, there is a Mars-Pluto conjunction. Additionally, there is a Jupiter square Mercury-Venus, while the other major aspect is the Moon squaring Uranus.

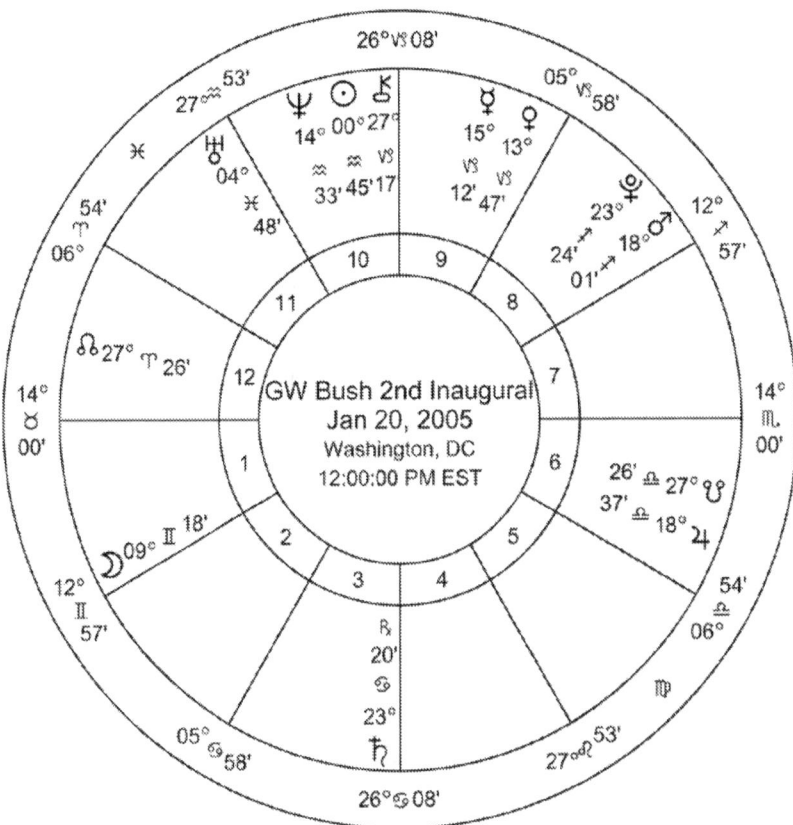

Figure 10 – George W. Bush's second inauguration. January 20, 2005, 12 noon EST (estimated time), Washington, DC. 38N53 77W02.

Before considering this chart let us examine the stellar themes that are also present. We already have the difficult themes inherent for this time and place produced by the Heliacal Rising and Setting stars and the parans to the Sun but we can also consider the themes which are unique for this event. The following is the full printout from Starlight of star parans, apart from the solar annual themes already discussed.

The rest of the stellar themes for January 20, 2005 Washington, DC, Stellar period commencing January 16

The background themes which can be active for many months:

Uranus – Public opinion, public expectations
    On Nadir when Ras Algethi is Rising
        A sudden upset in the political balance of power

The acute themes that are active just for this time period

Moon – The emotions of the people
    Culminating when Spica is culminating
        The hope that new technologies, or a new plan, will save the day
    Culminating when Murzim is Rising
        Emotional speeches, emotion-charged announcements

Mercury – Business and the media
    Rising when Hamal is On Nadir
        Jolting news, the truth unveiled
    On Nadir when Sirius is Culminating
        A publication, or the words of a person, have far-reaching repercussions

Venus – The social conventions
    Culminating when Alhena is On Nadir
        Social reform issues
    Culminating when Denebola is Setting
        Society's ideas or standards ruffled
    Rising when Al Rescha is On Nadir
        Recognizing what lies underneath a social issue
    Culminating when Vega is Culminating
        A celebration of the arts, a charismatic person takes centre stage

> Culminating when Facies is Culminating
>> *A ruthless approach to social problems, or savage artistic comment*
>
> Rising when Thuban is Culminating
>> *Protecting society's values and culture, even at the expense of other groups*
>
> Mars – The events of the day
>> Setting when Acumen is Setting
>>> *To act against social opinion*
>>
>> Setting when Aculeus is Setting
>>> *The hardships endured by people*
>>
>> Setting when Ankaa is Rising
>>> *Seeing the previously unknown potential of a group or person*
>
> Jupiter – The type of action which is favored by this period of time
>> Culminating when Diadem is Culminating
>>> *By helping others, old problems can be solved*
>>
>> On Nadir when Mirach is Culminating
>>> *Greed and excesses*
>>
>> On Nadir when El Nath is Setting
>>> *Aggressive actions or people rule the day*
>
> Saturn – The law and civic order
>> Rising when Ankaa is Culminating
>>> *Strong leadership comes out of chaos*

Are these horoscopic themes supported or altered by the stellar themes?

Not all of these stellar themes will come to pass, just as not all the possible expressions of the inauguration chart will come to pass. This is one of the dilemmas of astrology: what to emphasise and what to ignore? This is easy in retrospect but harder in the art of prediction. However, by looking at the horoscope and then looking at the stars for supporting or similar themes, we can focus our delineation of the inauguration chart.

Mars-Pluto Theme

The star parans indicate that the Mars-Pluto of the inauguration chart is not as violent as it was for Lincoln's first inauguration, as it seems to be focused more on the themes of social opinion coming from hardships suffered by a particular group. So, instead of a bloody conflict, such as the Civil War of Lincoln's era, we are more likely to see the angry social uprising of a particular group within the community. This possible civil unrest will be fuelled by a heavy-handed or even aggressive action taken by those in power.

Additionally, the star themes are indicating that from this turbulence a leader emerges.

Jupiter Mercury and Venus themes

This planetary pattern is focused into the expression of an orator, a leader who can talk on social issues. This person could be from the political arena or they may be a spokesperson from a grassroots cause. The shadow side of the Jupiter-Venus combination is that of greed or over-indulgence, gross waste or neglect, and this is also reflected in the stellar themes with Jupiter in paran with Mirach, the potentially artistic but also self-obsessed or over-indulgent star in Andromeda. So corporate greed or personal greed, or waste and excess may well be one of the unfolding issues of Bush's second term.

The Moon-Uranus theme

Moon-Uranus in any chart can suggest turbulence and upsets, but here we see that this is also supported by the stellar themes. Both the full dome of the sky and the horoscope are producing the same message: political upheaval.

Future Inaugurations

If the US continues to inaugurate its presidents on 20 January, in Washington, then it is not until the inauguration of Tuesday, January 20, 2037, that a new stellar background theme emerges via the action of precession. This inauguration theme will still contain the same Heliacal Rising and Setting stars of Acumen and Capella and the Sun will still form a paran to the difficult Algol. But gone is the theme of the independent, free-agent style president. The parans are:

Sun – The stars in paran with the Sun on this day
    Rising when Algol is on Nadir
        A person who destroys through passion
    On Nadir when Alphecca is Rising
        Strength and leadership found through hardship
    Culminating when Zuben Elgenubi is Setting
        A time of salvation, a leader is sacrificed

Interestingly a particular star returns that was first present for the inauguration in Washington of Thomas Jefferson on 4 March 1801. This star is Alphecca and it represents the Wreath, 'to be handed a crown'. Linked with this is a socially-aware and humanitarian star, Zuben Elgenubi. Accordingly, this will herald a new era of US presidency, one with less emphasis on the glory or power of the individual and more on the needs of the people. This theme will stay with the presidency, with variations, until the end of the 21st century.

In Conclusion
For most readers the concepts that I have expressed may be quite foreign, different to the astrology to which they have become accustomed. Yet by combining both the sky and the chart, by using the full dome of the heaven with the horoscope, we find that there is a great deal more information at the astrologer's finger-tips. Without doubt, this type of astrology is more complex, and harder for the astrologer to glance at and give quick judgement. Indeed, it is because of its complexity that the Greeks abandoned the stars and concentrated on the planets and the ecliptic. For them, this was based in necessity. But we live in the 21st century and astrologers now sit with their hands on a computer keyboard, not an armillary sphere, and therefore, unlike the Greeks, we can quickly and accurately reproduce the full dome of the sky for any time and place. If astrology is to reflect life then, like life, it will be complex. Surely now it is only the naïve or very new to astrology who believe that a simple aspect or midpoint can explain or even be used to predict a forthcoming event with all its complexity.

The sky is a vital and key principal of our craft and we should not run from it or try to reduce it down to a neat, simple line; we need to allow it to have its full complexity and grandeur. The parans and phases of the fixed stars provide us with a tool to gain a greater understanding of the unique relationship between the sky, the Earth and time. This unique relationship gives us the nature of the quality of times that flow across the different cities and locations on the globe. By accepting the complex sky we not only enhance our ability to delineate charts, we also gain a technique which tells us about the quality of a location itself.

© Bernadette Brady 2005.

Bernadette Brady, M.A., is a professional consulting and teaching astrologer who lives in Bristol, UK. She holds a masters degree in Culture Astronomy and Astrology from Bath Spa University, UK. In September 2006 the Astrological Association of Great Britain presented her the prestigious Charles Harvey Award for 'exceptional service to astrology'.

In her capacity as an astrologer she lectures, teaches, designs software and writes. Her books include, Brady's Book of Fixed Stars, Predictive Astrology: The Eagle and the Lark *and her latest,* Astrology, a Place in Chaos. *Bernadette Brady can be reached via her website:* http://www.bernadettebrady.com/

NOTES

1. The Civil War commenced on April 12, 1861 in Charleston, South Carolina. This is another mid-April date for the US but it is at a latitude of 320N47 which falls outside of the range given in the example. However, Sirius was also forming a paran with the Sun on that day for this latitude.
2. Starlight software, authors Bernadette Brady and Barnswood Ltd, published by www.zyntara.com
3. All non-polar latitudes will have annual dates where the Sun is in paran to Sirius. This example is simply showing one of the background stellar influences for this latitude which history has shown to be sensitive to being amplified by other planetary and star events happening at the same time.
4. Allen (1963) p. 249.
5. Ptolomy, Claudius (1993), *The Phases of the Fixed Stars.* Translator R. Hand. Berkley Springs, WV:Golden Hind Press.

6. For a more detailed explanation of Star Phases see Brady, 1998; Evans, 1998.
7. For a more detailed explanation of Star Phases see Brady, 1998; Evans, 1998.
8. Evans (1998) p.200.
9. The meanings of these star periods have been taken from Starlight.
10. Brady (1998) p.89.
11. Brady (1998) pp.51, 271.
12. Inauguration is defined in this article as the organised ceremony of the president elect taking the oath of office. This is different to a swearing-in which occurs upon the death of the incumbent president and is held as soon as possible at the location of the vice-president, or next in succession to the presidency.
13. The US Constitution states that the term of the President expires at noon on the day of the inauguration. Therefore, I have set all the inaugurations charts to this time. Additionally any debate about the exact time of the beginning of a new president's term is not relevant for fixed star work as parans only require a date and place.

REFERENCES

Allen, Richard Hinckley. (1963) *Star Names, Their Lore and Meaning.* New York, USA: Dover Publications.

Brady, Bernadette. (1998) *Brady's Book of Fixed Stars. Maine.* USA: Samuel Weiser.

Evans, James. (1998) *The History and Practice of Ancient Astronomy.* Oxford, UK: Oxford University Press.

Ptomley, Claudius. (1993) *The Phases of the Fixed Stars.* Translator R. Hand. Berkley Springs, WV: Golden Hind Press.

Starlight software (2001-2006) Zyntara Publications, UK – www.Zyntara.com

13

The Solar Return Astro*Carto*Graphy Map
David Meadows

David Meadows has researched and written extensively on the use of Solar Returns with Astro*Carto*Graphy. In this chapter he describes how he works with the Astro*Carto*Graphy solar return map, giving us a real life example of its use as a predictive tool in his own circle of family and friends.

Astrologers use various techniques when they examine how the natal chart is temporarily influenced. These include transits, secondary progressions, tertiary progressions, minor progressions, solar arc progressions, solar returns and lunar returns. Most astrologers do not have time to use all these techniques, as there is too much work involved.

Cyclo*Carto*Graphy is the main technique to find temporary influences on an Astro*Carto*Graphy map. I decided to embark on research to find out whether an Astro*Carto*Graphy map for a solar return chart can provide additional information about locations.

Solar Return chart

This is a chart that is calculated every year when a person has a birthday, so it can be also called a birthday chart. It shows what a person will experience in life during the next twelve months.

The solar return chart is calculated for the date and time when the Sun returns to its exact position in the natal chart. This occurs once a year, either on the birthday, the day before or day after. For example, if the natal Sun is at 24° Libra 12', then a chart is calculated for the exact date and time that the transiting Sun reaches this position.

Location for Solar Return chart

The first problem when calculating a solar return chart is which location to use. Some astrologers will calculate a solar return chart using the birthplace, and not consider the person's present living location. Other astrologers insist that the place of residence should be used for the solar return chart. Then there is the theory that a person can change a solar return chart by being in a different location for their birthday. If, for example, a person goes on holiday for two weeks in Spain and celebrates their birthday there, then the coordinates of the holiday location should be used for the solar return. But what if a person is travelling on a long plane journey at the time of a solar return? This makes it extremely difficult to calculate a solar return chart for where a person happens to be at this time.

The problem of deciding which location to use for a solar return is avoided when Astro*Carto*Graphy is used. When a solar return is drawn on a map of the world the planetary influences can be found for any location. Using this technique, it doesn't matter which location is used for the solar return, so I would recommend that you keep to the birthplace. Other locations can be examined after the solar return is drawn on a map of the world.

With or without precession

The next problem that an astrologer faces when calculating a solar return chart is whether or not to allow for precession.

In astrology two types of zodiac can be used, the *tropical* and the *sidereal*. Each year when the Sun returns to zero degrees Aries this is not the same place in relation to the fixed stars. The vernal equinox (zero degrees Aries) moves backward 50.25 seconds of a degree each year through the fixed stars. This movement is called precession, which is attributed to a wobble in the Earth's axis. The tropical zodiac (moving zodiac) is the one used by most astrologers, but very little thought is given to the effects of precession. The sidereal zodiac (fixed zodiac) is used mainly in Hindu astrology and is unaffected by precession. There are two ways of overcoming the effects of precession:

1. Use the tropical zodiac and allow for precession[1]
2. Use the precession-free sidereal zodiac

Using the tropical zodiac we need to consider the following: As a person gets older the *natal planets* should be corrected for precession. As zero degrees Aries is moving backwards it means that the natal planets are moving forward in the tropical zodiac. A few astrologers take precession into consideration when examining transits. The amount of precession is added to all the natal planets before looking at the transits.

Robert Hand[2] gives a table for the precession correction values in *Planets in Transit*.[3] At age 72 the amount of precession will be one degree, which can make a difference in the timing of transits. The effect of precession becomes more noticeable when a solar return chart is calculated. At age 18 the difference between a solar return calculated with and without precession will be six hours! The difference is 12 hours at age 36, and an entire day at age 72.

The two types of solar return charts will have totally different angles, so this will obviously change where planets are on the angles when an Astro*Carto*Graphy map is drawn.

The key question is which type of solar return chart is used in Astro*Carto*Graphy?

Having used both types of Astro*Carto*Graphy solar return maps it was very clear to see which chart was the correct one. I was amazed to find out that an Astro*Carto*Graphy map with precession was the one that provided accurate information. After I arrived at this conclusion I asked Jim Lewis if he had done any research with Astro*Carto*Graphy solar return maps. He told me that his research showed that solar returns with precession were the most effective when applied to Astro*Carto*Graphy.

Interpretation of the Astro*Carto*Graphy solar return map
The same techniques used to find the planetary influences at locations on an Astro*Carto*Graphy map are used for the solar return map. That is, planetary lines and latitude crossings (parans) at a location.

It is important to remember that the Astro*Carto*Graphy solar return map shows the temporary influences for one year. The information obtained should be added to that found with Cyclo*Carto*Graphy to get a broader view of the temporary influences.

With the Astro*Carto*Graphy solar return map further information is obtained about the temporary influences at specific locations. It is also possible to examine the birthplace on an Astro*Carto*Graphy solar return map to find out which temporary influences will have a worldwide effect.

Is it possible to time events on an Astro*Carto*Graphy solar return map? Quite a few astrologers use various techniques in a solar return chart to time events. I have tried these techniques myself, applied to the Astro*Carto*Graphy solar return map, but found that they did not provide accurate information about when events would take place.

Example: an event predicted from an Astro*Carto*Graphy solar return map.

On 18th March 1989 I got married in Dresden, which at this time was in East Germany. It was extremely difficult to get married behind the Iron Curtain as permission had to be obtained first from the authorities. From the time of the engagement it took 18 months to obtain permission from the East German government before it was possible to get married.

The solar return map for my 33rd birthday was valid from 21st March 1988 to 21st March 1989. When I examined an Astro*Carto*Graphy map of this chart with precession I saw very clearly that I would get married in Dresden before my 34th birthday!

On the Astro*Carto*Graphy solar return map with precession I had MO-MH, VE-MH and PL-IC near to Dresden (see Figure 1). I was convinced that this indicated getting married in Dresden against the odds. The same planetary lines have an influence in East Berlin where the application to get married was processed. I couldn't help but think that some kind of miracle would happen in East Berlin for this prediction to come true.

When I told my fiancée this she said it would be impossible to get married before my 34th birthday as it could take years to obtain permission from the authorities. This was confirmed when the East German authorities turned down our application to get married after we had waited six months for a decision. When I visited Dresden at Christmas in 1988 the East German government had just turned down a further application for our

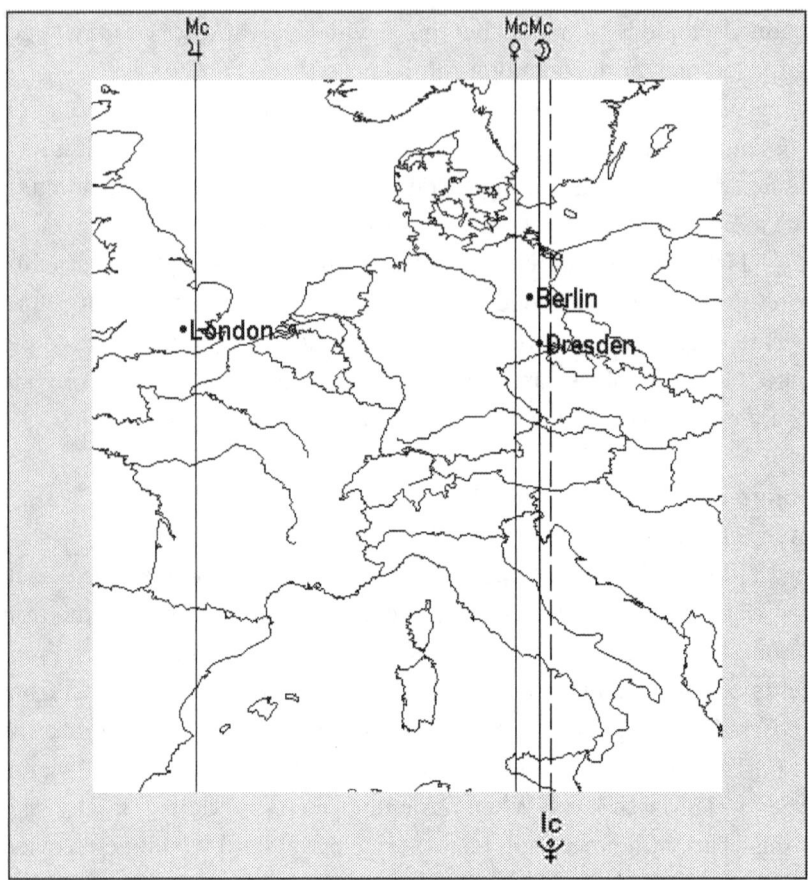

Figure 1 – Astro*Carto*Graphy solar return map, with precession

getting married. This meant that we had to make yet another application and wait a further six months for an answer. With only three months till my 34th birthday I couldn't see how my prediction would come true.

The British Embassy in East Berlin was doing all it could to help me obtain permission to get married. The Foreign Office in London was also putting pressure on the East German government to change their minds and my local MP became involved as well. Finally, much to our amazement, on 18th January 1989 we were given permission to get married. But before a wedding date could be arranged all my documents had to be re-translated, as they were more than six months old!

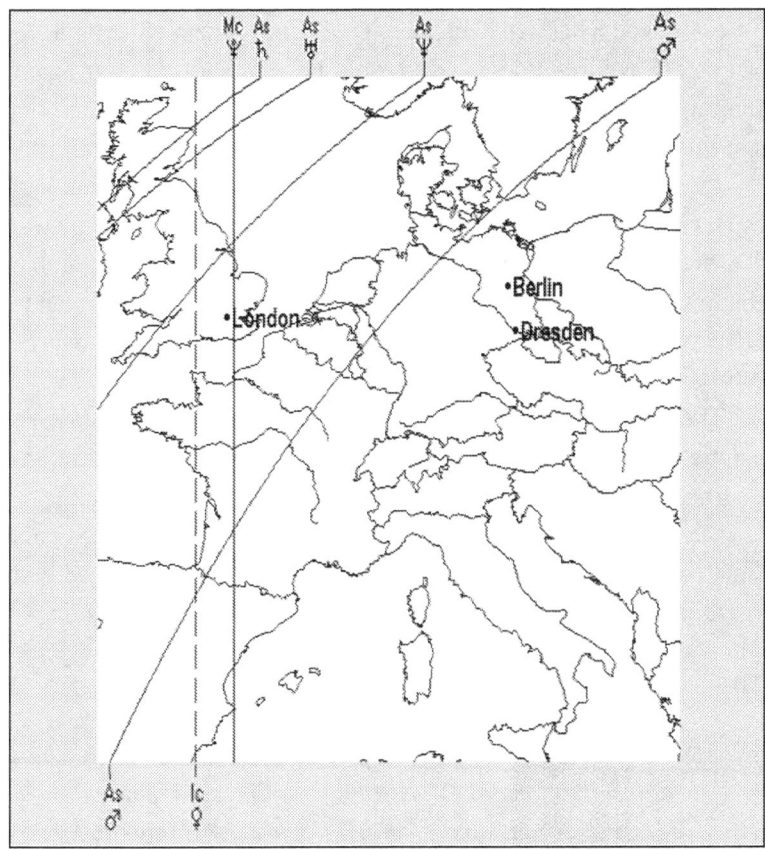

Figure 2 – Astro*Carto*Graphy solar return map, without precession

During the time that all my documents were being re-translated I told my family it would be best to arrange visas to visit East Germany. My family couldn't understand this as no wedding date had been arranged, but reluctantly agreed to do so. It usually took four to five weeks to obtain a visa to visit East Germany, which was then valid for six months. There was still a chance that I could get married before my 34th birthday.

After the translation work was completed, my fiancée was informed on 28th February 1989 that she could now go to the registry office to arrange a date for the wedding. At this registry office my fiancée was told that only one date was available. This was 18th March 1989 at 9.00am or 10.00am!

She asked what would happen if we didn't accept 18th March 1989. If this date was turned down, we would have to start all over again by making a new application to get married. So we had no choice but to accept this date.

As my family and I had applied in January 1989 for our East German visas it was possible to get married at short notice. Had we waited until a wedding date was arranged there wouldn't have been enough time to obtain visas to visit East Germany. So the information I obtained from my Astro*Carto*Graphy solar return map certainly helped to overcome the obstacles in getting married.

The marriage took place four days before my 34th birthday. Yet in December 1988 it was very hard to believe that my prediction would come true, so it really was a miracle that made this event possible.

Map 2 shows my Astro*Carto*Graphy solar return map calculated without precession. There is no way that I would have predicted getting married in Dresden looking at the planetary influences on this map.

© David Meadows 2007.

David Meadows is a British born astrologer who now lives in Finland. He has specialised in locational astrology for 20 years. One of Europe's most active locality practitioners, with a world-wide clientele, Meadows is known for his techical grasp of Astro*Carto*Graphy. He is the author of Where in the World with Astro*Carto*Graphy.[4] *His blog on locality issues can be found at: http://astromapping.blogspot.com/*

NOTES

1. Adding procession correction to Solar Return calculations is easily and automatically done as an option in astrological computer programs.
2. Information about the noted astrologer Robert Hand can be found on his website: http://www.robhand.com/
3. *Planets in Transit*, Second Edition, May 2002, Schiffer Publishing, Ltd, USA.
4. American Federation of Astrologers, Tempe, AZ, 1998.

14

The Business of Place and The Place of Business
Making Astrolocality Techniques Useful
Faye Cossar

Faye Cossar has successfully brought astrolocality into her practice as both a business consultant and therapist. In this article she shares some of her extensive experience from the business realm with us.

> "To be on a quest is nothing more or less than to become an asker of questions."
> *Sam Keen, American author, professor and philosopher.*

All the techniques involved in astrolocality are fun to look at and can offer insight. These include Astro*Carto*Graphy, relocation, Local Space and Geodetics. We should, however, choose the right tool for the job, so we first need to identify the question or problem we are attempting to address. I want to focus here more on business questions, but first a word on the personal side.

The Personal

Examples of the types of personal questions that I have been asked are:

- I have been offered two jobs, one in France and one in Portugal, which one should I take?

- I felt really at home and alive in South Africa – why is that?

- Where is the best location for me to buy a house in Amsterdam? Where should I look?

- I am redesigning my house – where would a good place for my desk be?

- My husband is going back to the States, I have never been there – how will that be for me and our dog?

Where there is a specific place mentioned, I would normally go straight to using a relocation chart as this provides more depth and more to work with than other techniques involving place. It provides an entire chart. When we relocate, we take our whole chart with us with all the aspects, so we are not just getting planetary lines as in the other techniques and we need to take this into account. By moving we are simply reorienting our basic nature. Different facets of ourselves can be expressed in different life areas.

Where there is a general question, such as "Where should I go on holiday?" I would look at both the world local space map and the global Astro*Carto*Graphy map to get a general view of where planetary lines run and then home in for a closer look at a few places. I would tend to focus more on the Astro*Carto*Graphy map as this gives more information. It is actually a type of summary of all the relocation charts for the world, showing where planets aspect or fall on the angles and, thus, where we will find powerful locations. Together with the client I would discuss the question further to see what the issues and wishes might be, and then give advice on the specific places based on these discussions.

For issues relating to a smaller scale, such as the question about where to buy a house in Amsterdam, and where to place a desk, the Local Space chart is the only way to go.[1] This chart is what I like to think of as your personal compass or direction-meter. If this chart is printed out on acetate it can then be placed on a map of the location, in this case Amsterdam, with the centre in Dam Square (the central point in Amsterdam), to ascertain where all the planetary lines run. As an example, I have had success with using the Moon line for this specific 'where to buy a house' question. We appear to be more likely to feel nurtured and comfortable (Moon) with houses (the kind we live in!) that are on this line.

Similarly, the acetate can be placed on your house plan. By placing the centre of the chart at the centre of your house (you sometimes have to guess where this would be), you can see where the lines run in your house. Advice can then be given, in discussion with the wishes of the client, as to how the energies might be used[2] – a Western Feng Shui if you like. So that's the personal in a nutshell.

Mundane issues

Then we can have mundane questions like:

- What will happen in China over the next few years?
- Who will win the US elections?

There are several ways astrolocality techniques can be used. All the techniques already mentioned can be used for the horoscopes of countries. For example the Pluto on the Midheaven line for the US chart (I have found July 4th 1776 17:10 Philadelphia, with Sagittarius rising, to be effective) runs through the Middle East, exactly through Baghdad – enough said perhaps.

Geodetic charts and maps are also often used for mundane issues but this is outside what I wish to cover in this article.[3]

The Business

The topic I do want to focus on here is business. Questions such as:

- I have a problem with supply in China – what's going on there?
- I love Italian design, should we incorporate that into our products?
- I am thinking of expanding our international group, which countries should I look at?
- Will I have a problem with importing from India?
- Our head office is in Amsterdam and we want to merge with another company whose head office is in Paris. What issues will we face?

And many other questions that have to do with anything involving other countries or places.

One of my friends, who is a finance director and is very supportive personally, is an absolute astro-sceptic. However he once said, "If you can help me with where to expand our business, I might be convinced that astrology is useful!" So there is the challenge for astrologers in business. How can we make astrology useful? In my view, that is the only way to make it acceptable to a wider audience. If we can give advice on these very real questions, our image will improve.

So how to attack this? What is happening in a specific country may be relevant for companies, so mundane issues may be of interest. The charts and maps of directors may also be interesting, however I wish to focus on company charts. The first thing to do is to obtain a chart for the company that works. This sometimes requires a bit of research. You may need to delve into the history of the company to see which chart works better at times when major transits or progressions would have been active. I usually use the incorporation chart as this seems to work well, but that is not always available. Once you have a company chart you can produce all the maps and choose your weapon!

The question

So, the main choices for companies are the Astro*Carto*Graphy map, the relocation chart and the Local Space map. And again it depends on the question as to how to select the right tool for the job. In my experience most clients have a country in mind, so I would start by looking at which lines run through those countries on both the Local Space and the Astro*Carto*Graphy maps. I will try to give an explanation of the difference between these two and will start with Astro*Carto*Graphy as I can get my head around what that represents and therefore how to use it! Let's take the horoscope of a company, say KLM.[4] Their birth date is 7th October 1919 in The Hague, midnight, because from then on the company exists. Figure 1, shows the chart using Koch houses, which I use because of the Huber Age Points but that's another story.[5]

For what I want to discuss here, the house system is irrelevant. What is relevant is the aspect pattern. I have my own preferences but you should use whatever aspects you like *except* the aspects to the MC and the Ascendant. I never put these in as they are a different type of aspect: they indeed show our relationship to our place of birth – the actual location – and should be used as such.

Visually, we have an aspect pattern here that has three 'pointy bits' to the right. I like to see this whole aspect picture as KLM's (or whoever's) 'crystal'. It is their own specific centre, which always remains the same.

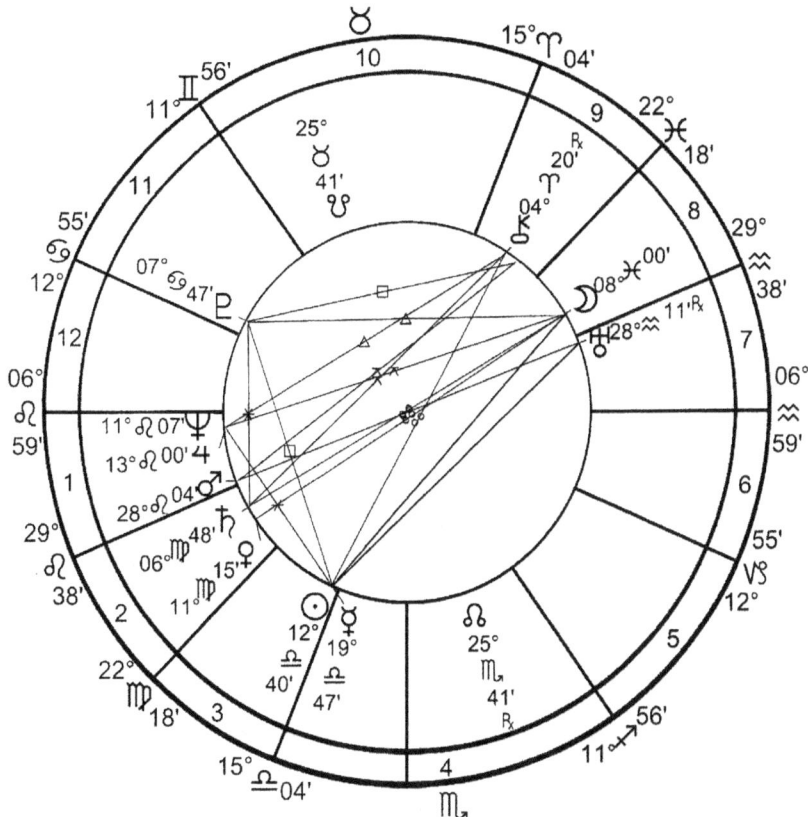

Figure 1 – KLM Founding, 7 October 1919, Midnight, The Hague

This pattern is inherent in the time but not the place, so this pattern will be present anywhere in the world at that moment. When we relocate we effectively roll this aspect pattern around so the three pointy bits will be pointing up or down or to the left as we move around the globe. The relocation chart (a horoscope made for a specific location at exactly the same time as the birth chart) will show the orientation of the crystal – i.e. our orientation in that place. The Astro*Carto*Graphy map simply shows the summary of all of these (so it shows everywhere where specific planets would be on an angle or making aspects to the angles). Although, with the software, you can look at all the aspects to the angles, most people concentrate on planets *on* the angles, which is what is done here.

Figure 2 – KLM founding moment, USA detail

For KLM, the Sun is on the descendant through the US near Minneapolis, Minnesota. We can see this from the Astro*Carto*Graphy map, Figure 2.

What this actually means is that at the exact moment KLM started (midnight in Holland) the Sun was exactly setting in Minnesota. So, we can then interpret that as we would a normal chart. Places where KLM has its Sun on the Descendant line might be seen as locations of partnership possibilities. There is something about the places on this line, where the Sun is setting, that makes KLM notice them. And KLM certainly did. A bit of history taken from the web:

July 1989: KLM takes an important step towards being a global airline by acquiring a 20% share in Northwest Airlines.

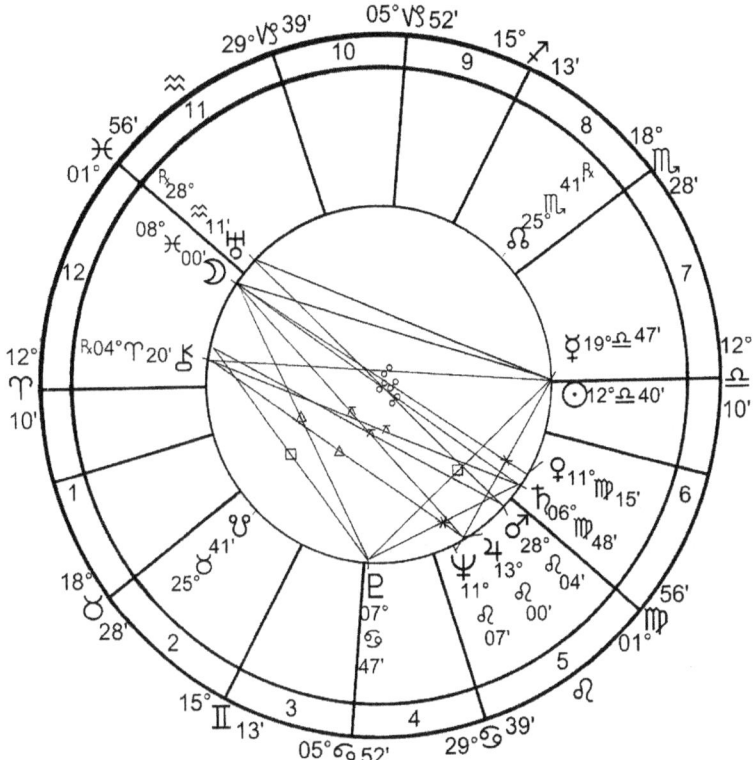

Figure 3 – KLM founding moment, relocated to Eagan, Minnesota

September 1993: All KLM and Northwest Airlines flights between Europe and the USA are operated as part of a joint venture.

March 1994: KLM and Northwest Airlines introduce World Business Class, a new product on intercontinental flights.

February 1998: KLM-Northwest Airlines alliance honoured with 'Airline of the Year Award' by influential US trade magazine Air Transport World.

The head office of Northwest Airlines (NWA) is in Eagan, Minnesota. Figure 3 is set for Eagan and as we can see, the Sun is exactly on the Descendant. Note that the aspect points are now to the left but the aspect picture remains the same.

This is after the event of course, but we could have said this beforehand and we could still say that other places on this line would also provide potential for partnership. Anything coming from places on that line, be it companies or people, may be potential partners for KLM. KLM doesn't have to go there for this to work. But what we do need to take into account is that it is not just a Sun in Libra looking for a partner with Sun on the Descendant. KLM also has a powerful square to the Sun from Pluto and Pluto is on the IC near Minneapolis, making this indeed a very powerful place. It could also mean, though, that Northwest Airline (NWA) has all the power. With the relocated Moon now in the twelfth house, KLM's feelings or the staff of KLM (as the Moon in a company chart represents staff in my view) may not be seen. A discussion about this with KLM would be necessary to see how this works in practice.

Interestingly, KLM's main partner now, following a merger, after many attempts, is Air France. The Sun on the IC line for KLM runs exactly through Paris, so, although Paris is not far away from The Hague the natal Sun in the 3rd moves enough to put the Sun on the IC, again with the square to Pluto. For KLM this is a powerful foundation (IC) for further development, which so far has proven to be true, although KLM are definitely the smaller partner, as again the Sun-Pluto aspect is brought into focus. How much KLM can use this Pluto energy could only be ascertained by discussion with them, but the potential and the possible problems can be seen. So that's one example of Astro*Carto*Graphy and relocation and how it can be used to foster discussion with clients.

Local Space lines
So what's the difference between local space lines and the Astro*Carto*Graphy lines? This can best be explained visually. Let's take KLM again.

What we see in Figure 4 is the KLM compass, also known as the local horizon chart or Local Space directions. The solid lines show the actual direction of each planet.[6] The lines of course go in two directions; the dotted lines represent the extension of the line in the opposite direction. If we take the Sun in this example, which is close to the IC (due North) then we see a solid line near the North. If we keep extending the lines and continue around the globe, we get the lines shown in *Figure 5*, in which KLM Local Space lines as shown on the globe. As we continue around the globe this line will approach the starting point from near the

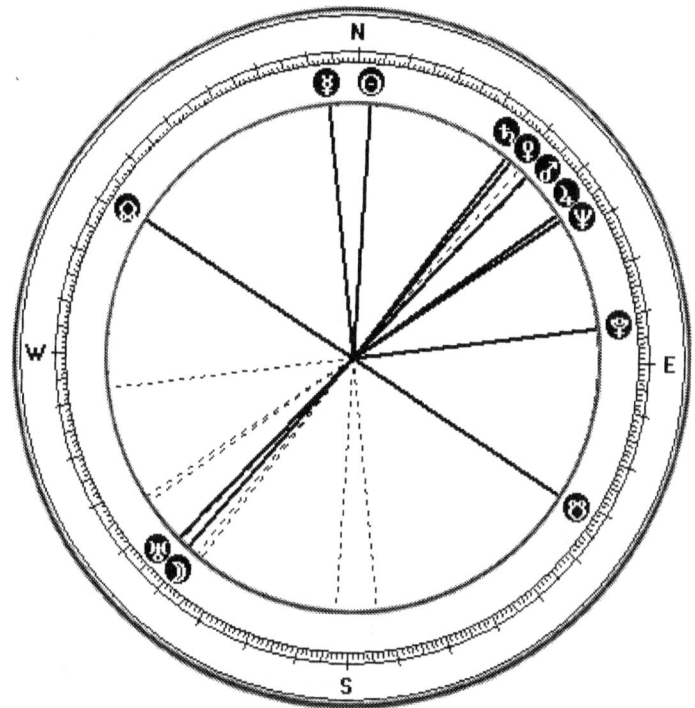

Figure 4 – KLM Founding
Local Space Compass (Local Horizon Chart)

South – the MC. So, the Sun line in this case runs close to N-S. See the Sun line in Figure 5.

So, if we had a KLM plane we could fly all around the world on the Saturn line, probably not one I might personally choose, and we would end up back at The Hague. We might have more fun flying on the Venus line, or experience more unexpected things on the Uranus line. Travelling on the Sun line would mean going almost due north or south and we would have Sun experiences on or near this line. Although I can see that these lines represent places where these energies are present, I find it difficult to get much more out of this technique on a global scale, although places that have meaning for clients are interesting to discuss. For me, the Local Space compass has more use in the office or in the local environment, as mentioned in the personal examples. I would need to do more company research to say anything more sensible about this.

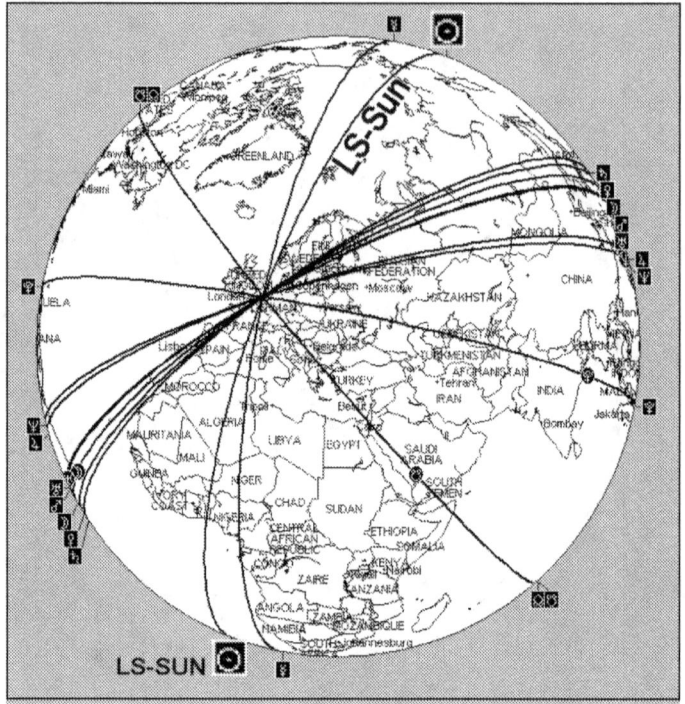

Figure 5 – KLM Local Space lines

Bums on different seats – Studio Schrofer

To finish I would like to give an example of a current client to show how I work with these techniques. Studio Schrofer was started as a one-man company on 1st January 1984 in The Hague in Holland. Later, on 1st January 2001, it was registered at the Chamber of Commerce. See Figure 6, Studio Schrofer. The January 2001 date is the one I use for them (midnight), having checked which one seems to work better now, although both charts have relevance.

The directors are husband, Frans Schrofer, and wife, Sonia Sin. Frans is a gifted furniture designer who heads up the design team. Sonia's background is in PR and marketing, although she does more than this for Studio Schrofer. Generally, their clients are manufacturers, who also market the products. In the past seven years, their company has rapidly expanded with the number of clients growing in Asia and Europe. Design is a tricky area, as there is a lot of intellectual property theft and copying

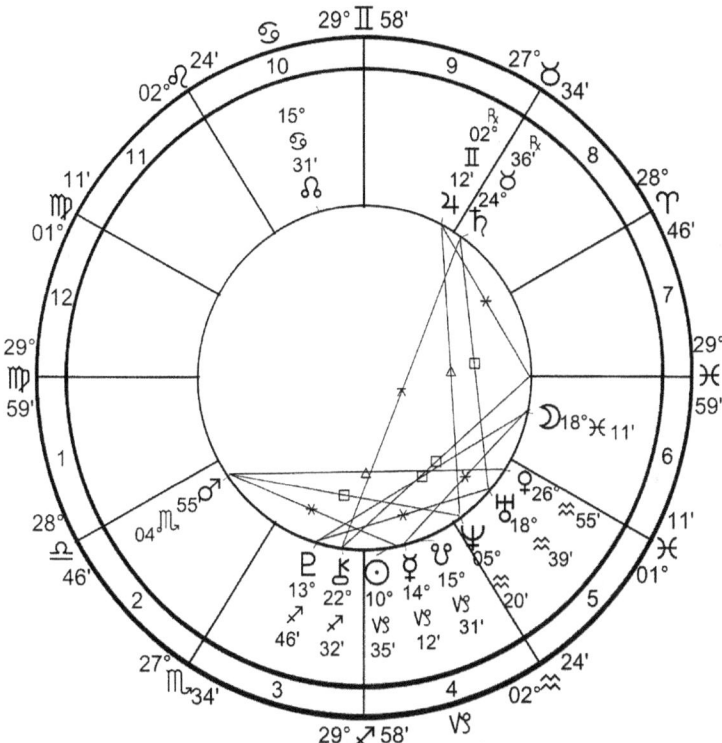

Figure 6 – Studio Schrofer Registration, 1 January 2001, Midnight, The Hague

that goes on in this industry. As their products receive more international recognition, so the number of intellectual property right infringements grows, especially in China.

First questions

I first had a quick discussion with Sonia Sin, the co-director, to ascertain where their international clients are located. For the discussion here, I will cover only international clients. As Sonia is sales and marketing based, she gave me information concerning these areas and mentioned the China problem, which was her question, although not in detail. Their goal (and therefore mine) was to try to see if any other countries might be interesting for them in any way and I wanted to see if I could throw any light on the China problem to see if I could offer some advice. As always, I wanted information from them so I could learn how these lines work *for them*. Only the client knows this and we can never guess how

214   *From Here to There*

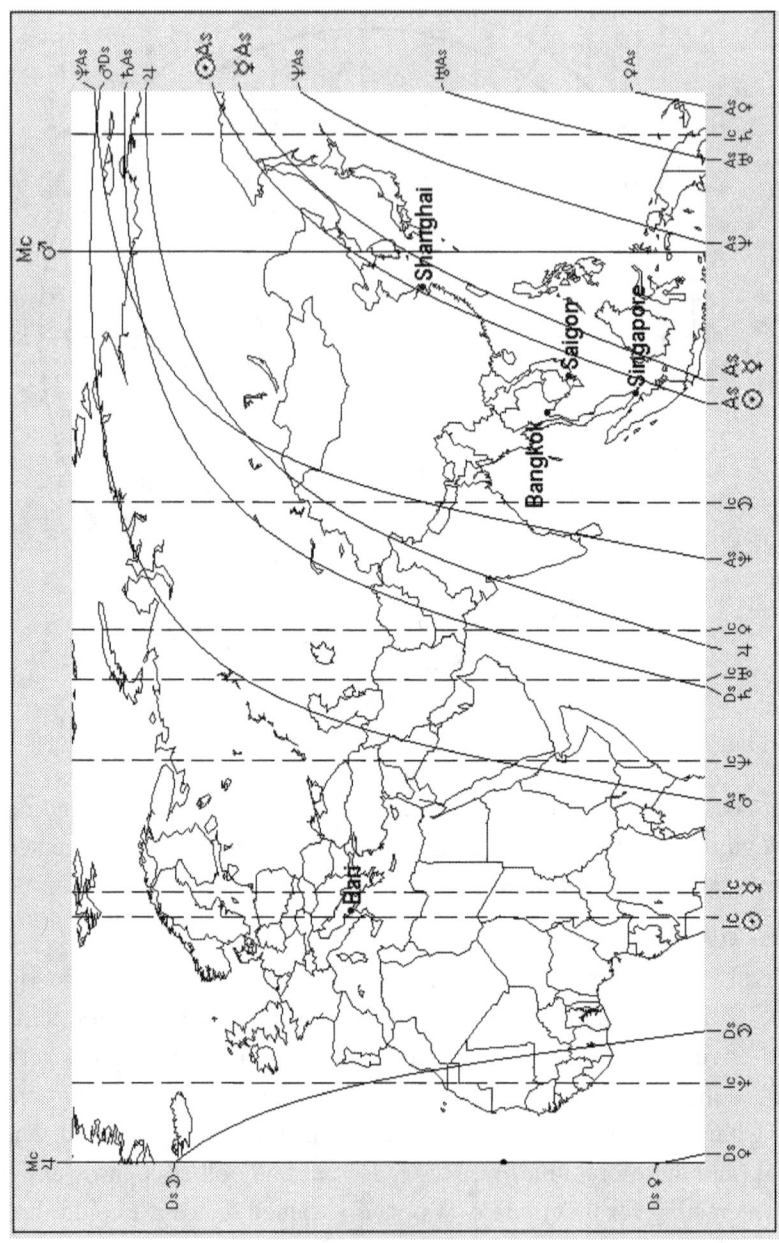

Figure 7 – Studio Schrofer, A*C*G world map

creative clients can sometimes be with these energies. We also need to ascertain this to see if the lines are working in a positive or negative way. After all, if they are working positively there is little we can add.

My preparation

I looked at the global Astro*Carto*Graphy and Local Space lines, and again found the Astro*Carto*Graphy lines to be of more interest. The Local Space lines did not touch anywhere they mentioned. See Figure 7 for the Astro*Carto*Graphy map.

Of particular interest is the Sun on the Ascendant line which goes through China very near Shanghai, which is where the problem lies, and also near Singapore and Ho Chi Minh City in Vietnam, where they have clients as well.

I also noted that the Sun on the IC line goes quite close to Bari in Italy where they have a major client. Bangkok in Thailand, where they also have a client is nowhere near any line, so I was interested to find out how this works. Now I had my questions and I had my suspicions about how their Sun on the Ascendant might work. Are they being too self-focused? Is there too much attention for Studio Schrofer where the client feels overshadowed? (Incidentally, both directors are Leos!)

The discussion

We talked about the lines in general, which they found fascinating, and they asked about specific places they were considering as possible markets. I gave general information about these; however, we also wanted to focus on current problems and current clients. In Sonia's words:

> "In Shanghai, a Dutch client sold to a Shanghainese ex-employee, so we are actually holding the original Dutch holding company responsible for infringements. The Shanghainese want our designs, so does the Singaporean based firm (who has manufacturing in Indonesia and China) owned by Germans. In Ho Chi Minh City, there is a Danish owned manufacturing firm, who want our designs as well."

In all of these, communication and commitment are tenuous.

> "They will take our designs and agree to paying advances for the design concept, but when it comes to keeping us within the loop of design concept expansion and informing us exactly of their developments, we get radio silence."

The following gives information on specific places.

Shanghai, China – Sun near the Ascendant: Schrofer's design collections propelled this client to international recognition ten years ago with a collection that is now considered mainstream. Unbeknown to Schrofer, the company was sold, breaching the contractual agreement. Discussions involving lawyers are underway concerning theft of one of their designs. The client is postponing action and Schrofer believe that the client does not realise the legal implications and complexities of international design infringement. There is simply no response from any correspondence.

    I suggested that maybe the correspondence is too self-focussed, although this is of course necessary in this case. The other possibility is that they are being too careful. Sun on the Ascendant would imply that they want to be seen and acknowledged. Perhaps if they can get publicity for a great design somehow, the money may not be the top priority. They are considering these options and it has given them something to reflect on.

Ho Chi Minh City, Vietnam – Sun near the Ascendant: Schrofer has made several different proposals to help expand the client's collections, incorporating more technology and more eye-catching models. Communication with the client entails a lot of designing, but the client lacks a clear design strategy. Because the client has tremendous production capacity and deals with predominately the mass middle market, they are hesitant to create a true market differentiation and an identity. A recent reorganisation has created more open-mindedness. The communication with their management team has been increasingly synergetic and transparent. However, strategic design direction gets dissolved by unfocussed 'mid-market' trends, resulting in a lack of clarity and commitment for Schrofer.

Singapore – Sun near the Ascendant: What came out of the discussion is that the client here is for some unknown reason stalling with the contract. The client refuses to agree with financial transparency. Again, I suggested that the contract may be all about Studio Schrofer, with not enough focus on the client. I am of course happy to give feedback on this contract and they are considering this. Again, it has given them food for thought.

However, to give more information on this problem it is vital to go back to the whole chart. It is interesting to note that in all these locations the Mercury can be seen in that there are *communication* problems – a lack of response or no clarity. What needs to be discussed with this client is how clear and structured (Capricorn) the contract is. Or is Capricorn working negatively in that the contracts are too limiting? How are discussions being handled with clients? Is there enough clarity before the contract stage? Maybe lessons could be learned here.

If we know that the Sun is near the Ascendant in these three places then we also know that this is actually a Sun-Mercury conjunction in Capricorn, near the Ascendant. It is obvious that these archetypes are being brought into focus at these locations. Communication (Mercury) and commitment (Capricorn) and 'radio-silence', a wonderful description of this conjunction in Capricorn, are among the problems.

I always say the solution is in the problem, so the solution is the positive use of this aspect, particularly in these places. Actually, what I notice is that there is usually a basic problem in the company that happens to come to light in these locations. So what would be a positive use of this aspect? The issue is likely to be one of authority. Studio Schrofer need to be authoritative, clear and state the goal. Capricorn calls for very structured communication. If I were the client I would want to know exactly what I was agreeing to in having to provide information about my developments. As is, that requirement would be too vague and broad for me. What might lie behind radio-silence is a fear of Studio Schrofer being able to block developments or their being too authoritative or strict. How far does a design concept go and what are clients buying? Clients would need to have a clear idea of what is allowed. Silence puts the client back in the lead.

Capricorn has an air of the teacher about it; this can also be positive or negative. It brings up ideas of punishment but Studio Schrofer could think about acting in a sort of mentor role, which would work much better. Perhaps a clear contract based on Studio Schrofer having an advisory role might stand a better chance of being signed. This still needs to be discussed with the client but it gives ideas for possible solutions.

Bari, Italy – Sun on the IC: This is indeed a big client and is a good basis for them. It is going well. What I enjoyed most about this client is that the director of the company is also a Leo! Advice here is to keep this client happy and maintain contact. They will want attention and I confirmed it is an important base for them. Sometimes confirmation is very important to clients.

Bangkok – no lines: There was a mild reaction to Bangkok: it seemed to be neither good nor bad; nothing special, which seems to reflect the lack of any lines.

Although the lines do not run through all the places exactly, they appear to be near enough to have an influence and if you look at the relocation charts you will see that the Sun is no more than three degrees from the specified angle, usually much closer. The only other aspects the Sun makes, apart from the conjunction with Mercury already mentioned, are, for those of you who use them, a semisquare with Venus and a sesquiquadrate with Saturn.

Sun-Venus can be too nice. How is this working? There is a dilemma here with the Sun in the spotlight at these places aspecting Venus. Does Studio Schrofer need the limelight (Sun) or is the relationship and the customer (Venus) more important? How can they achieve a balance (Venus) here? The aspect with Saturn is similar to the discussions on Capricorn above.

I have tried to show how the charts and maps can be used as input for discussions. The client always knows more about any issues than we do but it is possible to give new ideas, suggestions and advice. Astrolocality adds a valued tool to your company toolkit.

© Faye Cossar 2007.

The combination of Faye Cossar's background in business, together with her therapy training and her long experience with astrology, makes her unique. Currently, as well as consulting, she teaches in Amsterdam and lectures frequently in Holland and London. Cossar offers astrology training from her school, The Amsterdam School of Astrology [www.asastrology.nl], and business services from her organisation, juxtaposition b.v. [www.juxtaposition.nl]. Her business clients have included KLM in Amsterdam, (consultant for culture study), NIBC Bank in The Hague (consultant for staff development) and the Ministry of Justice in The Hague (management consultant). Cossar can be reached through either of her websites.

NOTES

1. See the local horizon chart in Solar Fire/Solar Maps (Esoteric Technologies) or the Local Space chart wheels and Local Space map wheels in Win*Star (Matrix Software).
2. Steve Cozzi's book, *Planets in Locality*, has good examples of how this can be used.
3. For more in depth information on this topic, I recommend the book *Astrolocality Astrology* by Martin Davis. Chapter 5 covers this topic in more detail.
4. KLM, Royal Dutch Airlines, founded 1919 in the Netherlands. This makes KLM the oldest international airline in the world.
5. For more information on this see www.api-uk.org/artageprog.htm
6. Directions are worked out in Azimuth, so you need a special program to do this. The directions are not easily seen from the birth chart, even though the MC is due South and the IC due North (Northern Hemisphere).

15

Locality and the Question of the USA Birth Chart
Dale O'Brien and Martin Davis

This chapter includes the work of astrologer Dale O'Brien and myself. It has its roots in a talk I gave at the Tucson Astrologers' Guild in November 2005 on Astrolocality techniques. One point of discussion was that a 'good' birth time (chart) for the USA, should exhibit a strong correlation between its locality maps and the country's origins and history. O'Brien was present and added his overview of USA chart possibilities. His important insight is that there have always been two valid birth charts for the USA. One, on 04 July 1776, he calls, "the chart of the American people". The other, for 15 November 1777, he calls, "the chart that reflects the American elite". Input from myself and O'Brien follows. The points of focus are on two charts, one chart for 4 July 1776 and an Articles of Confederation chart for 15 November 1777.

Local Space in Mundane Astrology
Martin Davis

A fertile area for Local Space (LS) analysis is in the field of mundane astrological research. LS maps, for example, indicate the 'directionality' associated with the politically related events for a country or world region. This in turn can help us with rectification studies when a mundane birth time is unknown or in dispute.

There is currently a divergence of opinion as to the 'best' chart for the birth of the USA or even whether one chart alone can ever provide us a satisfactory amount of information. After many years of detailed research, British astrologer Ronald W. Howland proposed an American birth time of 11am, Local Mean Time, on 4 July 1776, Philadelphia, PA. His well-researched work is presented in his book, *A Chronology of*

Locality and the Question of the USA Birth Chart

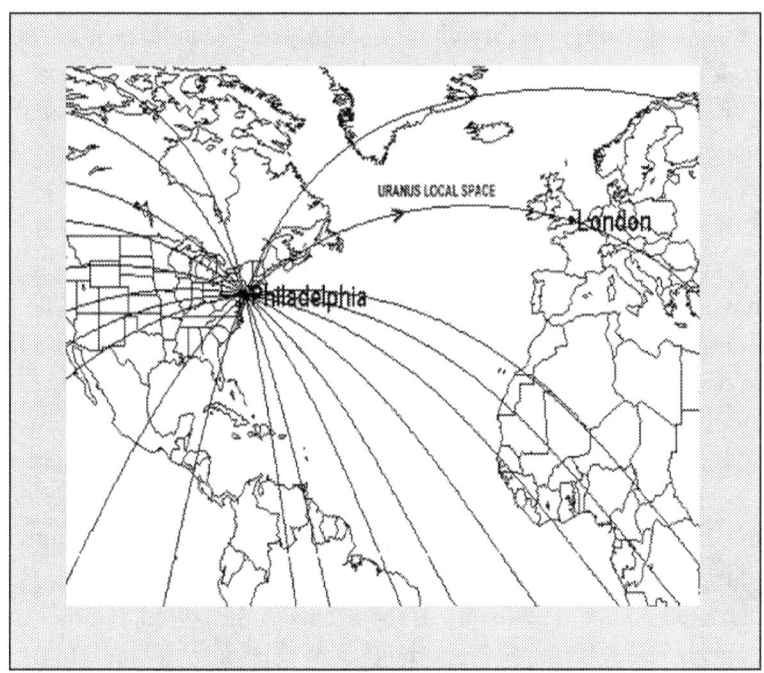

Figure 1 – USA Howland, Local Space lines

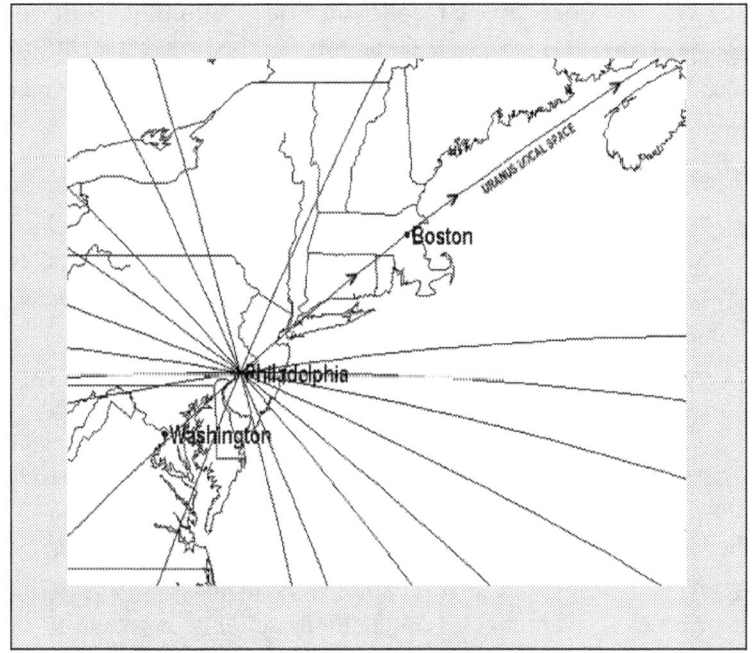

Figure 2 – USA Howland, Local Space Uranus line

American Charts.[1] Is this chart a good one? A look at it from the Astrolocality perspective shows some startling correspondences that indicate that yes, it's certainly worthy of further serious study. An analysis of the chart itself can be found in Chapter 4 of my book, *Astrolocality Astrology.*[2]

Let's begin by looking at the telling Local Space map for the Howland chart. Figure 1 shows the Uranus line, its origin in Philadelphia, running across the Atlantic and right over to London, England. Uranus lines are associated with the issues of freedom. We often find rebellious behavior along its pathways and directions, springing from a need for liberation from past patterns. This of course is a *perfect* representation of the radical and rebellious relationship that the founding fathers had with the English monarchy at the time of the Revolution. Figure 2 is a detail of this map. Note that the Uranus line from Philadelphia curves upward, running exactly through Boston harbour before connecting with England. To those who know the history of the events of the colonial uprising this is truly amazing. The most important act of American defiance to British rule happened in Boston harbour in what has become known as 'the Boston Tea Party'. The Local Space map for an 11am 'birth time' confirms the historical connection of the events in Philadelphia, Boston and England. Uranus issues and Uranus lines seem to play a role in Anglo-American relations even today:[3]

- Boston (via the Irish-American community) remains the centre of anti-British feeling in the USA to this day.
- Most Americans acknowledge and appreciate what is called the 'special relationship' (another Uranian keyword) between their country and Great Britain.
- One can note the testimony of British visitors to the USA, who state they feel 'free' when traveling there.

There is more. Figure 3 shows that the same Uranus line running southwest from Philadelphia is 25 miles from Atlanta, Georgia, Martin Luther King's birthplace ("Free at last, free at last!"). The Uranus line also runs within 35 miles of Montgomery, Alabama. It was here that the Union experienced another act of rebellious defiance, less than 100 years later, when the Confederate states declared Montgomery to be their

Locality and the Question of the USA Birth Chart   223

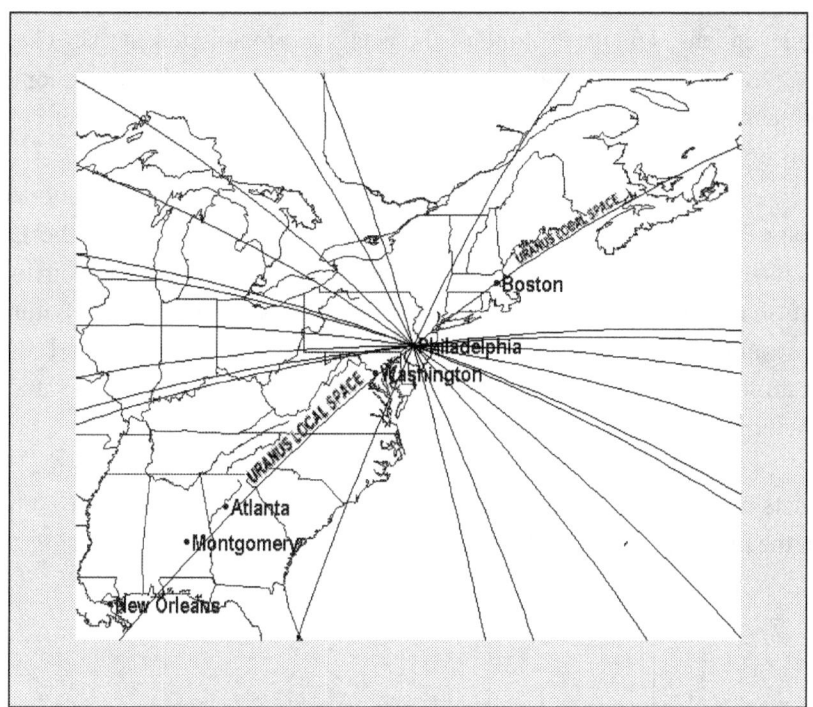

Figure 3 – USA Howland, Local Space Uranus line

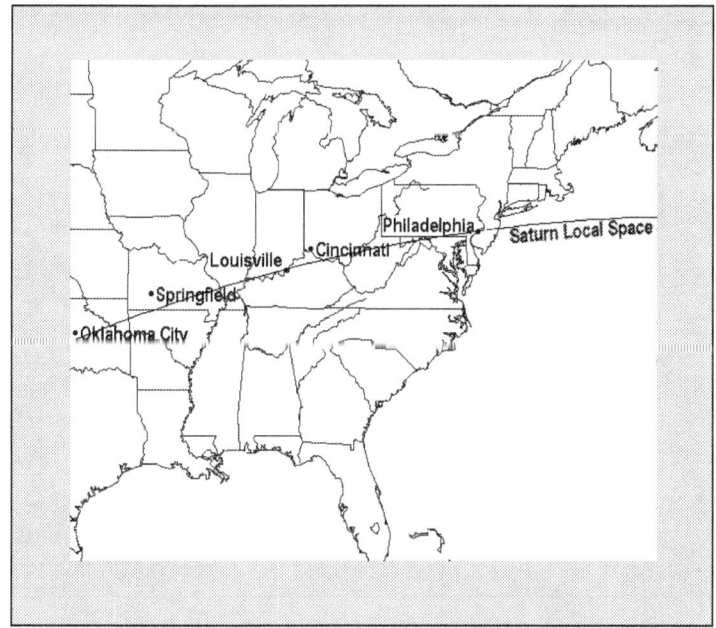

Figure 4 – USA Howland, Local Space Saturn line

independent capital city; one of the acts that precipitated the US Civil War. Montgomery was also the city where Rosa Parks refused to submit to segregation laws in what was to become the famous – and effective – bus boycott, 1955-56.[4]

Figure 4 is another view of the South Eastern USA. I removed some lines so we can focus on the Saturn LS line. Note how the LS Saturn line almost perfectly divides what were to become the warring Northern and Southern states of the Civil War, with much of the Saturn line actually right on the physical state boundaries themselves! Astrologically, we know that Saturn represents boundaries, and the Saturn line for this map delineates them.[5]

Mars too can give us insights about US relations. See Figure 5. Mars itself was almost directly overhead (zenith position) Havana, Cuba at the moment described by Howland's 11am USA chart. This obviously

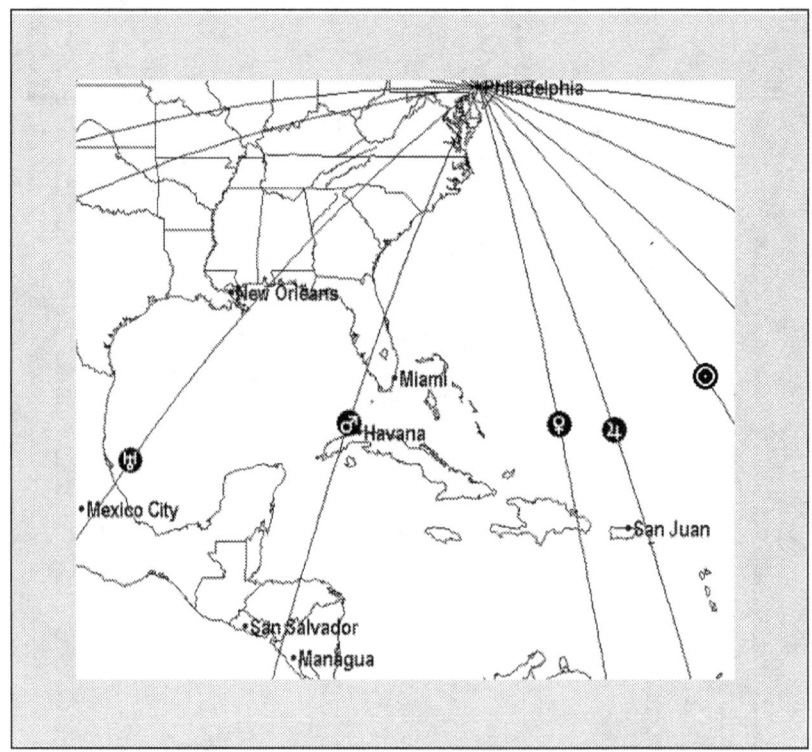

Figure 5 – USA Howland, Local Space detail with Zenith positions

Locality and the Question of the USA Birth Chart   225

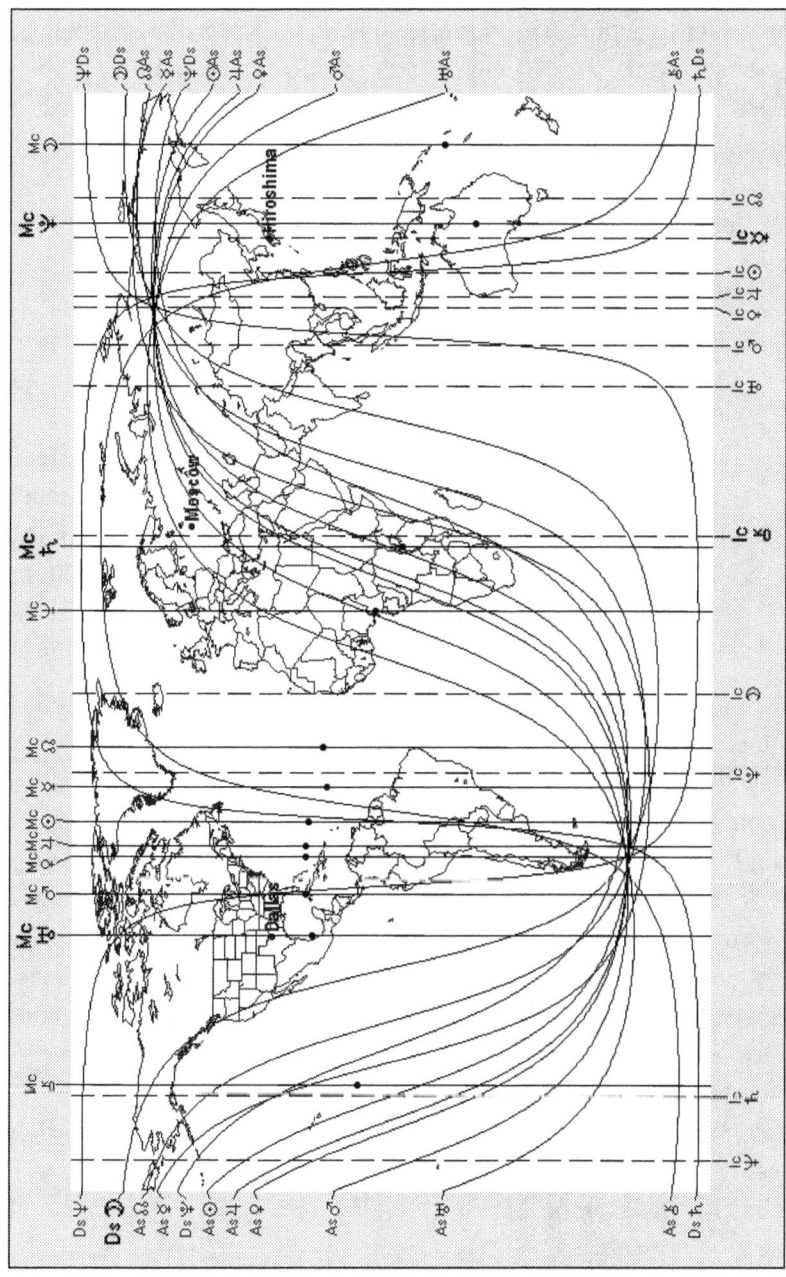

Figure 6 – USA Howland, A*C*G world map

implies tension there. The map also shows the LS Mars line running very close to Havana and Managua, both locations at which the USA had troops stationed in the past and where there are military undertones and tensions, some remaining to this day.

The interested reader is urged to review the corresponding A*C*G map for the 11am chart, as shown in Figure 6. In his book Howland points out significant historical correspondences, such as:

- The Pluto-MC line crosses over the southern tip of Japan, aptly describing the atomic bombs dropped there in 1945. After the war, American influence regenerated Japan, helping its transformation into one of the great industrial nations of the 20th century.
- The Saturn-MC line near Moscow describes the USA's chilly (inhibited) relations with Russia and her former 'Iron Curtain'.
- The Moon-Descending line runs alongside the most seismically active part of the US mainland, the San Andreas Fault in California. Howland reminds us that the Moon's connection with seismic phenomena is well known to both astrologers and seismologists.

I can add here that the A*C*G Uranus-MC runs within 70 miles of Oklahoma City, OK, the site of a devastating bomb blast, which was directed by anarchists against a US government building. That same Uranus-MC line is only 35 miles from Dallas, Texas, where US president John Kennedy was assassinated, and under 60 miles from Waco Texas, the location of what has been called the Waco massacre, involving government agents and the members of an anarchistic cult. In the USA Howland chart, the Rudhyar Sabian (degree) symbol for Uranus (8 degrees, 55 minutes of Gemini) has aggressive overtones: "A Quiver Filled with Arrows", and a keynote: "Man's aggressive relationship to natural life, as a basis for survival and conquest."[6]

Whatever one's preferred 04 July USA chart (11am or not), the locality indicators should show strong correlations with its history. The 11am chart looks to be a great fit!

© Martin Davis 1999.

America: 1776 to 1777: From a Declaration of Independence to The Creation of a Government Of, By, and For the Elite

Dale O'Brien

Since the late 1770s, there have always been two valid birth dates for the United States. One, of course, is July 4, 1776, popularly celebrated as the nation's birthday since the days of Thomas Jefferson and John Adams. On this date, in Philadelphia, at 'about eleven o'clock am', debate ended and a vote was taken. The Second Continental Congress verbally approved the final version of the Declaration of Independence – primarily written by Jefferson and most strongly advocated by Adams.

Although, at the time, Adams wrote excitedly about July 2nd, both he and Jefferson died on the same day, July 4, 1826. Each died considering July 4th to be highly significant. Jefferson described the Declaration as the "expression of the American mind." Americans have spoken fondly for years about 'the Spirit of '76'. We could call this chart the chart of the American people.

The second valid birth date is far less well known. In York, PA, in the 'early afternoon' (at, or just before their 1pm three-hour break) on November 15, 1777, the Continental Congress verbally approved *The Articles of Confederation and Perpetual Union*. The document declared the authority of the Continental Congress as the central government over the individual states. This was the birth of the United States government. In 1782, the essentially same Continental Congress would declare the bald eagle as the new nation's symbol. The 'Articles' chart reflects the American elite who quietly, but definitively, did, and very much still do, run America.

The late astrologer David Solté (1949–2002) was the first to bring this birth date to our attention.[7] He used a time of 12:46pm. I use a slightly later time of 1:00:30pm. David chose 12:46pm because it seemed to coincide with certain significant transits. However, I place the greatest significance on the Sabian Symbol Zodiacal degree images for the four angles of the chart of this long-established national government.

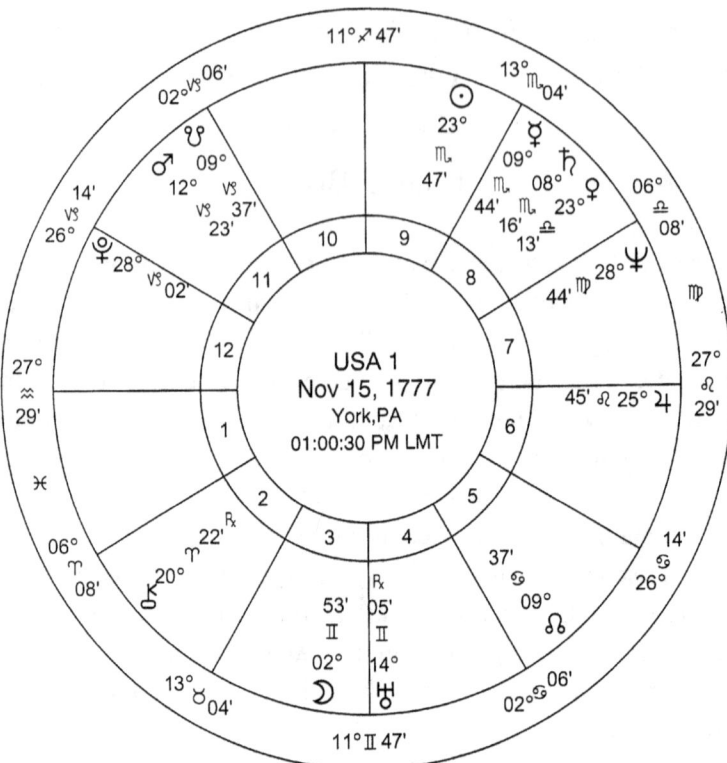

Figure 7 – USA 1 (for 1pm), birth chart

In York, at 1pm on November 15, 1777, the Sabian Symbol of the MC degree, at the top of the chart, is "A Flag Turns Into An Eagle; the Eagle Into a Chanticleer Saluting the Dawn." (See Figure 7). How could we *not* have a chart for the US government that did not exalt (MC) the ubiquitous USA flag and eagle? Similarly, the corresponding IC Sabian Symbol image also perfectly fits the chart. (A discussion of this follows.)

David's research uncovered "early afternoon". My own research determined a scheduled three-hour break starting at 1pm, less than fifteen minutes from David's estimate. (I choose the exact time to the half-minute to coincide with other appropriate Sabian Symbol degree images, especially the ascendant and descendant degrees.) Although the approximate Astro*Carto*Graphy of Solte's chart and what I like to call the 'USA 1 (for 1pm)' chart are essentially the same, the latter Astro*Carto*Graphy seems to work even more precisely as I will show in details to follow.

I will always treasure the great privilege of speaking often and at length and in depth with David about this chart. We agreed on almost everything regarding the validity and significance of the chart he called the 'Scorpionic America' chart. However, we disagreed when he insisted that there could be only one chart for America: his. Similarly, some proponents of this chart, years later, still want to negate the use of any July 4 chart.

It is interesting to me that there are about as many versions of the July 4 chart as there were colonies that became states. Just as the colonists saw themselves differently by region and colony turned state, so do different astrologers advocate different times and ascendants for their favorite July 4, 1776 chart. Similarly, the dominance-tending-towards-paranoia signature of the Nov 15, 1777 chart itself, seems to evoke a dominant, power-oriented, monopolistic attitude among some of its astrological adherents to this day.

Historic Context
To understand the context of the times, a little history is in order. 'The Boston Tea Party' of December 16, 1773 was an action taken not only against the king of England, but equally against the king's favoritism toward the British East India Company. Other rebellious actions against king- and royalty-favored corporations also went reasonably well for the discontent Americans before the Declaration of July 4, 1776.

Thomas Jefferson, predominantly, wrote the Declaration of Independence. Then, and later, Jefferson championed significant enactment of equality, democracy, freedom, and the rights of man. These values were so obvious to him that he described them in his document as "self-evident". As an Aries (cardinal) Sun sign, he was perfectly suited to initiate something new, declaring this new beginning when the Sun was also in an initiating sign, Cancer.

It Didn't Take Long for Things to Become as Serious as Scorpio!
Between July 4, 1776 and November 15, 1777, matters became less obvious, and far less easy. Newly appointed commanding General, George Washington and his army had suffered defeat after defeat. There was poor rank and file morale when the war did not end quickly and easily, as had naively been expected. The spirited voluntary populist militias of

'76 were replaced by pampered elite officers, leading and intimidating increasingly exploited and impoverished soldiers. (Some soldiers were without shoes even in winter; most were threatened with execution if they might try to go home. The term 'foot soldiers' had a particularly grim meaning at this time!)

The value of the currency by this point in 1777 was less than 25% of its face value! Members of the Continental Congress were told they would be executed if caught. The delegates to the Continental Congress, concerned for their lives and fortunes, had moved from city to city, driven by the impending threat of nearby British troops. Continental Congressman John Adams said that they were "chased like a covey of partridges" to York, a small Pennsylvania town. As if that wasn't bad enough, individual states, commoners and slaves (the latter about 20% of the population) were all threatening to take their own freedom. Even John Adams' beloved wife, Abigail, advocated freedom and equality for women, slaves, and free former slaves. Another very serious problem for the Congress members was the reluctance of both the people and their colonies/states to adequately pay for the war voluntarily.

Determined to overcome all of these challenges, these few men boldly created and exerted their authority. They confidently did so because they considered themselves politically, intellectually, economically, morally and spiritually superior to common men ('the rabble'), to women ('the lesser sex'), and most of all to slaves and the Native Americans. In 1774, the wealthiest 10% owned over 50% of the Caucasian population's wealth, America's wealth. The overwhelming majority of these men owned, or had owned, slaves, or benefited directly and significantly from slave-based commerce. They were mostly men who had previously, individually been dominant and successful. Now they were uncharacteristically failing, and were seriously, mortally threatened by the then dominant power of their former king and country.

Scorpion, Where Is Thy Sting?
On November 15, 1777, these few men came together literally and figuratively, and boldly defined themselves as a legally unified national governing body. Under these dire circumstances, they needed to do so immediately, in order to establish a desperately needed alliance with France against their then common enemy, England. John Adams (Sun in

Scorpio) strongly influenced them as they declared themselves a central government at a time when the Sun was also in Scorpio. They were determined to no longer feel like, in Adams' terms, "a covey of partridges" who had scurried from city to city, and now to this humble little town. Less than five years later, they would as a group identify themselves not as a flock of several vulnerable little birds, but instead they would be one great bird, the greatest of all, the American Eagle. The eagle, in its superior position, dominates the sky, the land, and the water (where it feeds). The eagle, as they saw it, rightfully dominates everyone and everything.

The Astro*Carto*Graphy of this 'USA 1' Chart

Geographic Relevance

One fair test of the validity of a chart of a nation should be reflected in its Astro*Carto*Graphy and/or Local Space lines. These geographic dynamics should be relevant throughout the nation's history. The nation's story in any era, anywhere, should make sense using the same techniques viable for a human individual, including Cyclo*Carto*Graphy.[8] Consider each A*C*G planetary line as a center point, with a range of relevance up to 500 miles in either direction if no other lines are present. Proximity of more than one line corresponds to an area of blended planetary energies. Parans, or latitude crossings, add more specific information.

A World of Difference! How the American People See and Express Themselves in contrast to How the American Controlling Elite See and Express Themselves

It's extremely impressive to see the Howland chart's (11am July 4th, 1776) Local Space Saturn line basically draw the Mason-Dixon line! (See Figure 4). Saturn, the planet associated with defining boundaries, divides the country in a way that makes sense. In every era, Americans have always divided themselves into Northerners ('Yankees') and Southerners. It also makes so much sense to follow the same July 4th chart's A*C*G Venus MH line from the Caribbean islands, where sugar and sugar-derived rum was shipped, closely parallel to the A*C*G Jupiter MH line through merchant-affluent New England. (See Figure 6).

Basic Location Information for the USA 1 Chart of November 15, 1777

IC: Before exploring Astro*Carto*Graphy for this chart, it is helpful to examine the natal chart's IC, including its fourth house story. (See Figure 7 for the chart). That story is essentially the same for both York, PA and the long time home of the US government, Washington, DC. Gemini at the IC implies more than one home for governing VIPs. This was true in the early stages, but since then as well. Presidents and legislators tend not to stay in DC all year round. Uranus here can indicate a discontent with weather conditions (DC's heat and humidity). Technology (Uranus) makes weathering the city tolerable, plus allows the ability to govern, via technology, from places as remote as Crawford, Texas.

Uranus at the IC opposes the Midheaven, an indicator of potential rebellion here. Remember (or learn for the first time) that thousands of veterans marched on and camped in the city during the Great Depression, demanding much-needed back pay for service in WWI. (Payments were to be delayed until 1945). When the Senate retained the same delay period, the United States' first millionaire president, Herbert Hoover ordered General Douglas MacArthur, his aide Eisenhower (a future Republican president), and George Patton to handle the discontent. The US military were involved in tear-gassing the veterans and their children, burning their shack shelters, and the shooting of two men.

Since 1800, Washington has been the home of the United States' government. For almost as long, DC has been, and it still is, predominantly an African-American city, (affectionately formerly described as 'Chocolate City'). There is much poverty. For the 1pm chart, the IC Sabian Symbol degree image is "A Black Slave-Girl Demands Her Rights of Her Mistress."[9] DC residents have only limited political self-representation, and for most of US history there was no political representation ('home rule'). From the beginning, the majority of the 'founding fathers' either were slaveholders or financially benefited from slave trade. Slaves were once traded in the Georgetown area of the city, today overwhelmingly white and affluent.

Political discontent and African-American issues combined in civil rights era marches on Washington and Martin Luther King's unforgettable 'I had a dream' speech (Gemini) before the Reflecting Pool. King was assassinated the same year that he was to lead a multi-racial Poor Peoples' March on Washington. His assassination occurred a year to the day that he spoke out against the war in Vietnam, a war that he saw as poor Americans killing poor Vietnamese in the interest of America's elite.

DC has also seen a variety of demonstrations of various discontented Americans, demonstrations with people carrying signs with various brief slogans (Gemini: saying things while walking, carrying written words).

Uranus at the IC can also indicate surprising disruptions in local residence, shaking the government at its very underpinnings. Uranus can be seen as Prometheus (see *Prometheus The Awakener*, by Richard Tarnas).[10] Prometheus, who stole fire from the gods, can be seen, in a less flattering light, as a simple thief. What older American can forget the Watergate break-in during the Nixon administration, as well as its ultimate consequences? What of Daniel Ellsberg and the Pentagon papers?

MH: So, who are these IC 'Slave' and 'Mistress' 'opposed' to? For the 1pm chart, the MH Sabian Symbol degree image is "A Flag Turns Into An Eagle; The Eagle into a Chanticleer Saluting The Dawn." In June 1782, this same dominance-oriented American elite chose the American bald eagle, an image of dominance, to represent themselves and their commander-in-chief – the eagle at the center of the Presidential Seal. In the late 1770s, *balde* meant white, the color of the feathers upon the bald eagle's head. (Perhaps the eagle's white head reminded them of the powdered wigs worn by some of the elite.) The eagle holds images of war in one claw, an image of peace in the other. The eagle looked toward the arrows until President Truman had it changed to face the olive branch. (Presumably that change was made after Truman ordered the aerial nuclear annihilation of Hiroshima and Nagasaki. Similarly, the Department of War became the Department of Defense, with the capacity to destroy the world many times over.) This image also fits the American government's worldwide reputation for rooster-like crowing and 'cockiness'.

Unprecedented Pluto Transit to the Midheaven
November 7, 2000: A Majority of America's Voters Choose Gore;
December 12, 2000: Five Very Important People Choose Bush: The Elite Win

2000 wasn't the first time that the people's choice was denied the presidency; however, it was the first time that the fourteenth amendment was used *against* recounting the votes of the African Americans that the amendment was meant to empower. Transiting Pluto was exactly conjunct the MC with transiting Chiron just five degrees away, exactly opposite to secondary progressed Uranus.

Thomas Jefferson not only enthusiastically favored democracy but also wanted the emerging nation to eliminate slavery. If he were alive in 2000, he might well repeat a quotation of his: "When the government fears the people, there is liberty. When the people fear the government, there is tyranny." Or perhaps he'd revise the sentiment to something like "When a government fears the people, an elitist government denies the people their liberty."

The USA's Worst Domestic Tragedy: 9/11/2001
Transiting Saturn conjunct USA 1 Uranus: legal restrictions on non-elitist people's free speech and 'right to know'; transiting Pluto opposite the same: austere, secretive 'top-down' policies suddenly (Uranus) to be put into place.

When the United States Were the Least United: "Brother Against Brother"
Civil war begins, 1861: secondary progressed Uranus in Gemini conjunct USA 1's IC. Transiting Mars in Gemini conjunct transiting Uranus, which is just about two degrees shy of the IC. Note that secondary progressed Moon was exactly conjunct USA 1's IC while conjunct the secondary progressed Uranus when Lincoln was elected five months earlier.

First Uranus Return: 1862: Slavery is abolished in DC; the war worsens; not enough volunteers eventually leads to the Conscription (draft) Act of March 03, 1863.

Emancipation Proclamation: 1863: Transiting Pallas Athena conjunct transiting North Lunar Node, opposite transiting South Lunar

Locality and the Question of the USA Birth Chart   235

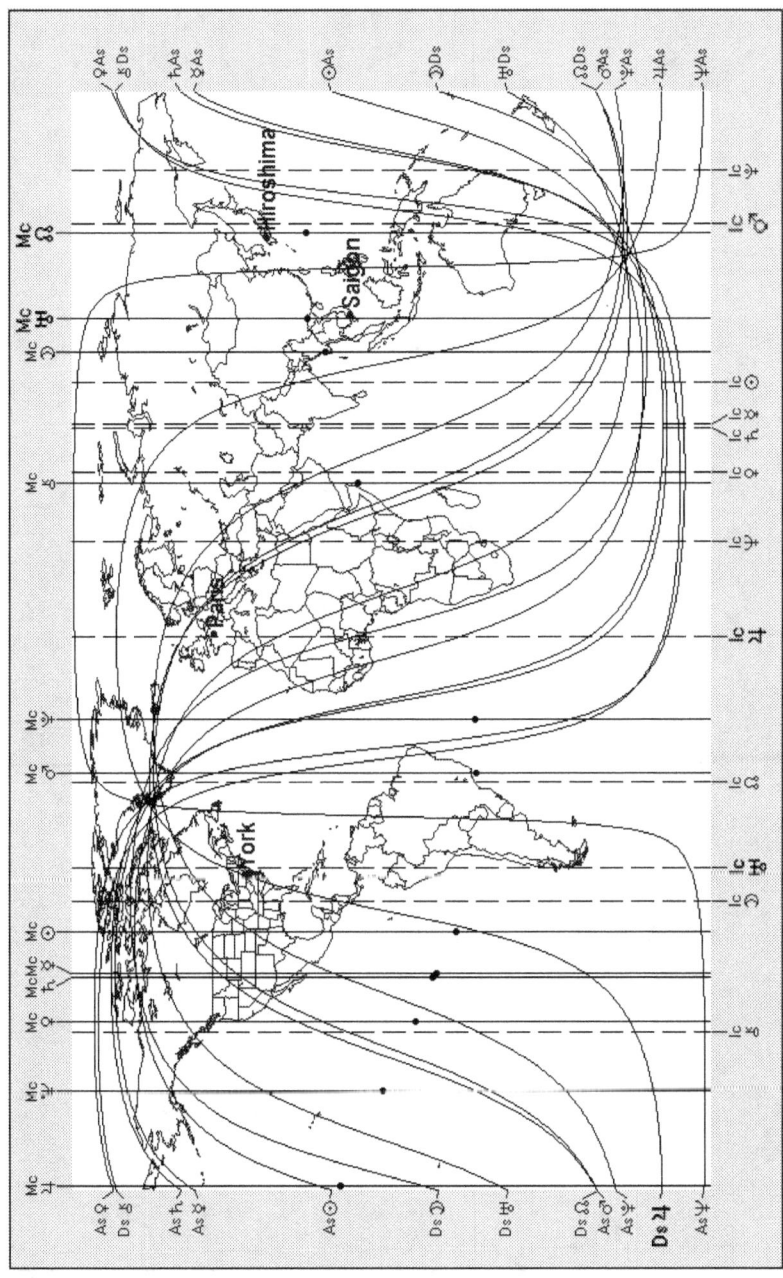

Figure 8 – USA 1, A*C*G world map

236 From Here to There

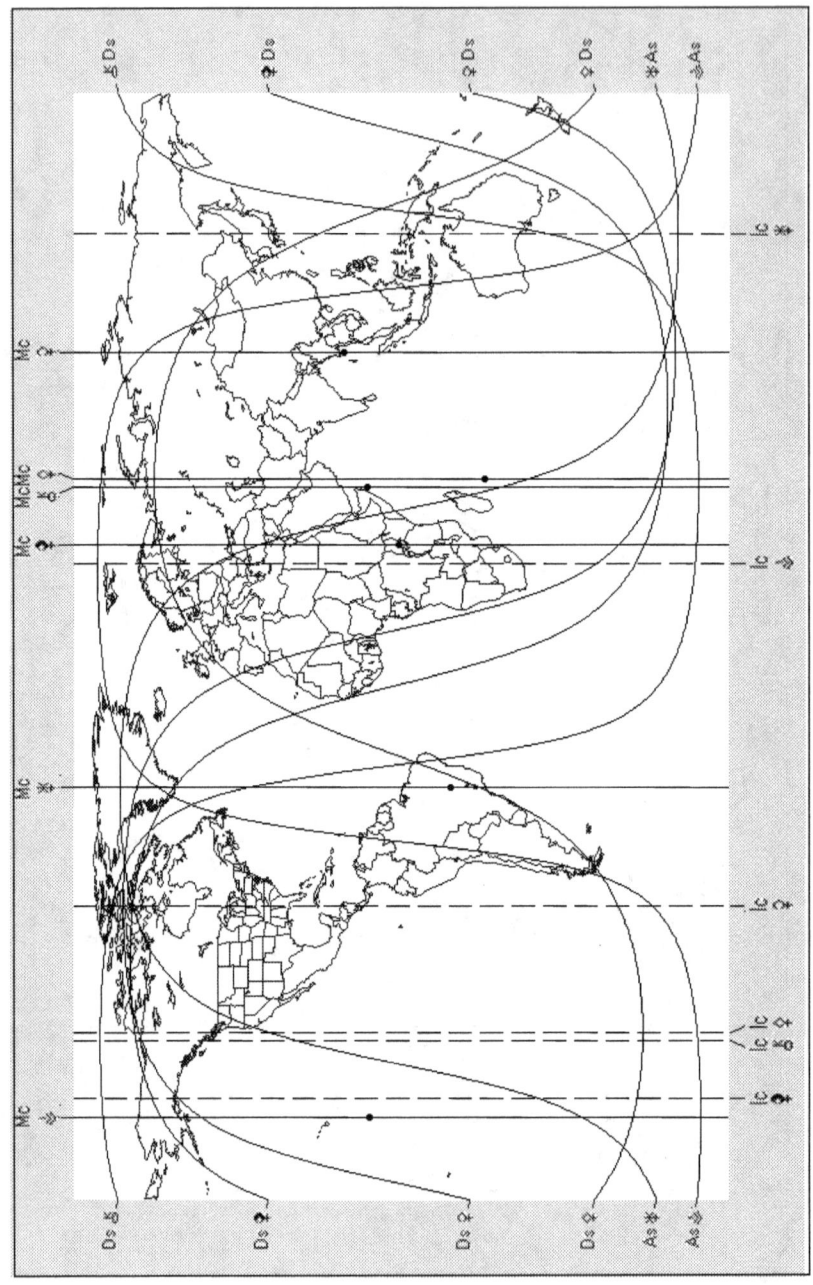

Figure 9 – USA 1, A*C*G world map, asteroids, Chiron and Lilith (Dark Moon)

Node, exactly conjunct USA 1's Uranus. The Proclamation granted freedom to most Southern slaves and gave them permission to attack the Southern insurgents. Pallas Athena is the ultimate strategist. The harmonious aspects indicate a plan that worked out just as intended.

Post War Uranus Transits; The Atomic Age
Transiting Uranus conjunct IC: April 25 to May 12, 1945 (exact May 9): Popular president, Franklin Delano Roosevelt is dead; war in Europe ends; communist challenge begins in earnest. For example, there was the coming partitioning of Berlin, June 5, 1945. (See also the first occurrence of the second Uranus Return, below).

Second Uranus Return: June18, 1945; January 11, 1946; March 31, 1946: UN charter: June 26,1945; Potsdam Conference and first atom bomb test: July16, 1945; Churchill ousted: July 26, 1945; Truman nuked Hiroshima August 6, 1945 and Nagasaki August 8, 1945. Note that the American people are shown no film, nor photos, nor reports of the Japanese civilians killed or horrifically injured by nuclear destruction. The CIA is established: January 22, 1946; 400,000 miners strike on April 1, 1946; Truman has the federal government take over the railroads to prevent a nationwide strike: May 17, 1946; The first FDR-influenced Supreme Court desegregation decision: June 3, 1946; The army was desegregated: July 26, 1946.

USA 1, Astro*Carto*Graphy: 'Lining Up' America's Controlling Elite
Both Figure 8 and Figure 9 are Astro*Carto*Graphy maps for November 15, 1777 at 1pm. Figure 8 shows the usual planets. Figure 9 depicts the positions of four asteroids, Chiron and Lilith (the dark Moon). All the points could be on one map but they are separated here for easier viewing. Interested readers are encouraged to review the details from their own computer software including the display of parans, which will be discussed soon. To assist with this the following list is provided:

Pallas Athena: Military, political and/or business strategy (especially involving a woman); the management of government (MH) or property/ defenses (IC); no nonsense; "taking care of business"

Juno: Allegiances, alliances, partnerships, co-operative ventures. (In the USA 1 chart, Juno conjunct Mars in Capricorn in the eleventh house indicates military alliances.)

Ceres (the first asteroid discovered, it is now considered a dwarf planet): Food, Farming, Finances: taking care of oneself and/or others. The provider is likely to be condescending in the treatment of the one benefiting from the provisions.

Vesta: Dedication to purpose and duty; selfless quiet devotion; conscientiousness; loyalty; integrity; the importance of doing what one is supposed to be doing.

Lilith: Refusal to be neither managed nor controlled; fiercely independent; 'wild'; may be seen as savage, primitive or backward by more cultured people/countries; the sometimes frightening wildness of 'Mother Nature' as storms, etc.

Chiron: Outsider, 'underdog' humans who, because they are different from others, may be denied their humanity. In the USA, this has included Native Americans, African slaves, free African Americans and the physically disabled. Chiron is also associated with environmentalists, environmental concerns and problems. Unlikely outsider-turned-insider mentor/advisor figures are also Chironic, including awkward 'nerds'. Chiron activities are neither 'strictly by the book' (Saturn) nor flagrantly violating laws (Uranus). Rather, there is unusual activity that is different from what the unimaginative would ordinarily expect.

York, PA: Where it all began
The closest line is Jupiter DSC (west of York): Having crossed the river from Lancaster on September 30, 1777, the Continental Congress felt safe enough to conduct business here.
Parans (in order of proximity, and therefore relevance):

Chiron ASC / Juno MH: Feeling vulnerable and misunderstood, but coming together cooperatively, compromising on central government vs states right issues. Presenting a collaborative structure – a unique hybrid of one government of United States.

Neptune IC / Juno DSC: uncertain base of operations; longing for an ally (the answer to their prayers).

Mars ASC / Saturn MH: Seriously organizing themselves in order to win national autonomy.

Mars DSC / N. Node ASC: (from Solar Maps): "…challenged to become assertive and focused…Independence and self confidence are keys…and it is important that you assert yourself. Under this influence you may find yourself thrust into leadership roles…"

Philadelphia, PA

The closest line is Uranus IC, the second closest is Jupiter DSC.

Parans the same as York, PA: Continental Congress's sudden displacement from Philadelphia, but Congress later return there.

New York City

The closest line is Uranus IC (very close): The Continental Congress had sudden relocations of their base of operations from here.

Parans the same as York, but Mars ASC/Sat MH is closest; Mars DSC/N. Node ASC is second closest, and Chiron Ascendant/Juno MH is third closest.

Boston

The closest line is Uranus IC.

Two of a few parans:

Neptune ASC / Pallas Athena DSC: Idealism challenged to be practical. During the earlier years of the pre-revolution and the early revolution prior to Nov 15, 1777, idealism drove Massachusetts like no other colony or state. Idealism met pragmatism as taxes and other challenges were imposed on the idealistically principled.

Mercury MH / Mars ASC: Powerful and potentially persuasive logic, but can be off-putting to the less intelligent (especially those outside of this geographic area).

Paris, France

The USA couldn't have existed without French initial support and cooperation. The closest line is Jupiter IC: Members of the Continental Congress were generously welcomed.

Exact paran:

Venus DSC / Mars MH: cultured French 'girlie men' with money help their American Continental Revolutionary ally. Peace treaty with England signed here. Parisian society ladies found Ben Franklin charming. Perhaps they put in a good word for the USA on his behalf?

Paris' parans within one degree orb:

Pluto in Capricorn ASC / Moon in Gemini IC: Culture shock, as the strange and secretive advocate(s) of a new government try to talk-up taking a stand against a common enemy, the King of England.

Pluto in Capricorn ASC / Ceres IC: Dire need for 'bread' (money) in their stance against the colonies' king, France's adversary.

Mars ASC / Lilith MH: Insistent persuasion of the French to help the unlikely new American government, but Congress' abandonment of French contact once they got what they wanted.

Neptune IC / Pluto DSC: In a most unfamiliar land, the challenge of Americans in Paris dealing with people very unlike themselves.

Jupiter MH / Lilith ASC: Freedom-loving people of the New World wilderness helped tremendously by a prosperous, generous French government.

Uranus ASC / Ceres ASC: Freedom to care for oneself; throwing off the need for a mother country; autonomy.

Vesta MH / Moon DSC: Dependence on the French to help sustain the tiny flame of their new government (the Continental Congress).

Venus ASC / Pluto IC: Culture shock: all dressed up and on best manners to stir up the French who have the power to bring their dominant adversary down.

Washington, DC - Capitol City since 1800, Essential Astro*Carto*Graphical Information

The closest line is Jupiter DSC, the second closest is Uranus IC:

Jupiter, under any line: (from the Astro Numeric Service (ANS) booklet)[11] "... prosperity, success, good luck, honor, and accomplishment ... self-important ... the best place for business ... growth through external addition, and thus under Jupiter, you grow and evolve, under the imagined protection of deities or forces favorable to self. Superstition and religion flourish under Jupiter, as one's luck and distinction from the mass are seen as the product of forces' or persons' favoritism ... Righteousness, leisure and bourgeois morals and pleasures triumph ..."

Jupiter DSC: (ANS booklet) "Here you attract influence and assistance from persons in high places ... others ... aid ... financially ... relate to people who are well off ... excellent location for a lawyer or salesperson, and any legal battles go best here ... business or dealings with the public prosper. Life seems guided by others and you usually get wide public sympathy and support, as well as material assistance ... one of the most fortunate areas possible, one in which forces beyond your control seem determined that you are to have an easy time of it."

Blending Jupiter & Uranus: (ANS booklet) " ... your extraordinary good luck zone. This is where wishing makes it so, and you are blessed by unusual good fortune. You become independent ... You are rescued from difficult circumstances, handle more money than is your custom, and learn to think on a broad scale ... Daring ideas work ... inventing your own idea of universal purpose. Reform can be successfully undertaken here, and you pattern yourself after your ideals, aided by the unusual luck that manifests from time to time ..."

Parans within one degree orb of Washington, DC's latitude: *Neptune IC/ Juno DSC:*

Neptune IC: City built on swampland, Potomac River, Reflecting pool; Tidal Basin; Anacostia River; Masonic architecture; monuments to Washington, Jefferson, Lincoln.

Juno DSC: Keywords: fairness, equality, consideration; location chosen as approximately midway between northern and southern states; the 'First Lady' and the White House mystique.

Neptune IC / Juno DSC: the mystique of certain monuments here, especially to three advocates of equality: Lincoln, Jefferson and FDR.

Sun MH / Pluto ASC: (interpretation from Solar Fire)[12] "You are intense, obsessive and have great personal power under this influence. You find it easy to rid yourself of the unwanted but may be intolerant of others less powerful. The use and abuse of power, either your own or other people's will become a focus…"

Also note the "Sun*Pluto" combination description from ANS booklet: " . . . there is a thirst for extreme individualism that manifests often in petty criminality, defiance of authority, passion, envy, and an overwhelming need for recognition and sexuality that hints at alienation and desperation ..."

About the Locational Dynamics of Significant Nations Involved in WW-II With or Against the US Government

Please refer again to Figure 8, the A*C*G map of this November 15 chart. Note the planetary lines and the cities they encompass:

Mars DSC = Berlin: A potential direct and open battlefield enemy threatens armed conflict. Here one's adversary will likely win, unless another army (the Russians) joins the battle.

Mars IC = Japan: The warrior who can viably attack one's land (e.g. Hawaii) via sneak attack. The challenging wrestler underneath.

Jupiter IC = London & Paris: The Allied 'family'; expansion of territory, safe home, the grand welcome of the US (e.g. the liberation of Paris).

Pallas Athena in Aries: (The armor-wearing goddess of military defense, i.e. Great Britain, The English Channel.) Strategically important area in war; armored amphibian landing at Normandy Beach. (See Figure 9.)

Partner Nations/Potential Partner Nations

Juno DSC (the nation's 'partner' line): Israel (especially Jerusalem) and Turkey. Note - because this US chart has Mars conjunct Juno, partnership almost invariably means military alliances.

Potentially the most dangerous area of the world for the US

This could be via military action and/or arming of those in the region, as well as for the enemies, allies, and innocents in this region:

Between Mars DSC and Pluto DSC: Here the American governing elite has either battle-to-the-death allies or, more frequently, perpetual dangerous enemies, in unending battles of revenge followed by revenge, fear of violence, or actually engaging in extreme violence and unending war, even nuclear conflict or suspicion of Weapons of Mass Destruction. No lasting peace with the US government and powers that be is ever likely here once hostilities have begun. The relevant area includes Iraq, Syria, Lebanon, and America's ally, Israel... See detail A*C*G map, Figure 10.

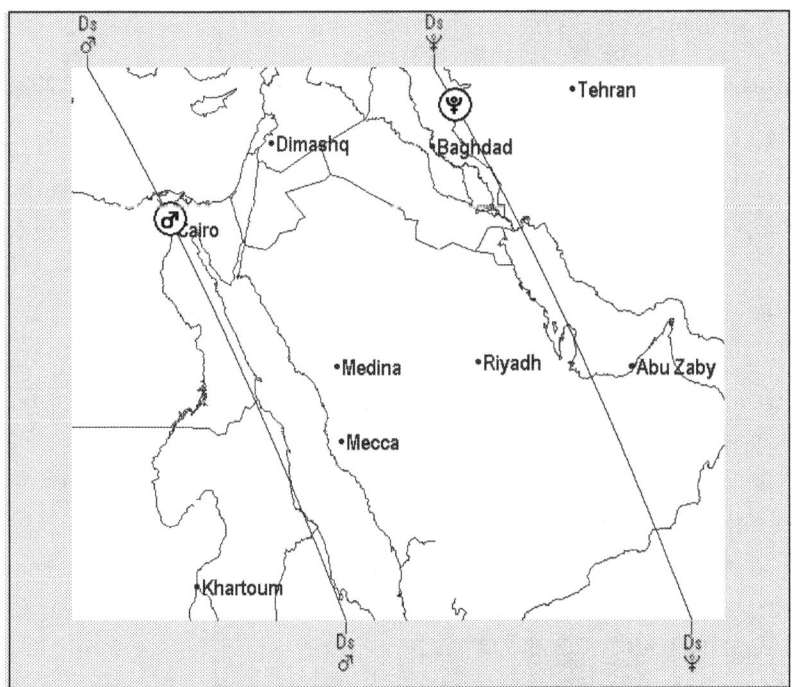

Figure 10 – USA 1, A*C*G detail, danger zone

Other telling lines

Sun MH: Houston, TX: An area from which power rules.

Pluto ASC: Oklahoma City, OK: Federal building bombing; largest munitions plant. Waco, TX: (Branch Davidians. Kansas City, MO: home to Truman, who nuked Japan. Crawford, TX: GW Bush ranch: hobby: vegetation destruction; near this line US V.P. Cheney nearly kills his friend and political ally.

Uranus MH: Hanoi; Saigon; Cambodia: Where the US government involved itself in revolutionary action; where a revolutionary government threatens the US government. Always expect the unexpected on a Uranus line!

Venus IC: Dubai: Place of tremendous wealth! The elite can even snow ski indoors in the midst of the desert outside. Effective 2007, Dubai became home to Haliburton, the multi-million dollar, formerly USA-based corporation previously headed by US Vice-President Dick Cheney. (Speaking of elite, note that when Cheney was tasked by the Republican party to choose their Vice Presidential candidate, he chose himself!)

Pallas Athena MH: goes through nearby Abu Dhabi = A Place of Strategy.

Pluto DSC nearby Dubai; Abu Dhabi. Secret powerful allies or secret powerful enemies.

Saturn IC: Kabul, Afghanistan; Tashkent, Uzbekistan. The weary burden of maintaining an occupied police state in order to prevent the social organization of an opposition. Look for approximately seven-year commitments, then reassessments.

Chiron MH: Tehran, Iran. Here the US government powers can take actions that are neither clearly legal, nor clearly illegal Solomon-like wisdom at best, regarding how the US interacts with the local government. Less wisely realized, flawed execution of intentions.

Pluto DSC: Iraq/Iran border; Kuwait; the Persian Gulf; United Arab Emirates; Oman: (from ANS booklet) "There is great danger under this line and the battle of selfhood is with a hostile world that seems intent on extinguishing you. The world withdraws from you, and leaves you to do battle with the very things or people that are closest to you ..."

Moscow

The city has very complex A*C*G indicators for the USA chart. Neptune IC and Pluto DSC lines are relevant, but neither is exceptionally close. This could be interpreted as a disliked opponent who is/seems religiously or ideologically opposed to the American government. Increasing the complexity, there are 14 relevant parans within plus or minus 1 degree, if parans involving Chiron, Pallas Athena, Juno, Ceres and Lilith are included. Hence, any juxtaposition of the US government and a Moscow based government is subject to change, at very least in emphasis. Similarly, any supposed assessment as either friend or foe is not realistic, even if the true complex dynamics are only obvious to the consummate insider (or perhaps also to some savvy locational astrologer!).

Changing Lines (C*C*G) Reflect a Changing Story

September 11, 2001

See A*C*G map detail, Figure 11. Coinciding with the first plane striking the WTC tower, Saturn IC and Pluto MH were either side of New York, with secondary progressed Mercury IC conjunct New York.

Meanwhile, a secondary-progressed paran of Pluto IC/Chiron DSC at 39N00 near DC and the Pentagon (in nearby northern Virginia) might indicate destruction of a government building and death of support personnel. However, a Lilith MH/Jupiter-IC secondary progressed paran, at within less than ½ degree of latitude from DC, might indicate a safe haven for high-level personnel. (Vice President Cheney and his 'shadow' government in 'an undisclosed secure location'?)

President Bush, in Florida at the time, was quite safe near the natal Jupiter DSC line, plus secondary progressed Jupiter DSC and secondary progressed Moon are running through Florida's panhandle.

Tertiary progressions are lunar-based, and can show motives for emotionally-based actions and reactions. On September 11th, tertiary progresseed Saturn DSC and Pluto DSC both went through Afghanistan (among other countries, like Pakistan). Bombing and occupation of Afghanistan immediately followed.

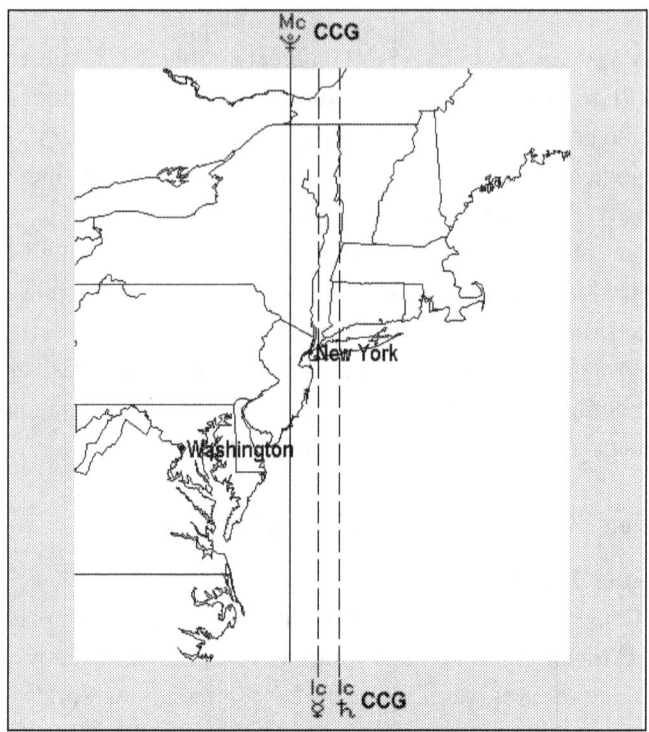

Figure 11 – USA 1, C*C*G detail, 9/11 attack

March 2003: Paris and London

France went from essential ally in the American Revolutionary War, courted by John Adams and others, to a distrusted participant by Articles of Confederation architect/US President John Adams, and others, only a few years later. Although France was a US ally again in WWI and WW II, this was not so for the US government action against Iraq.

England, adversary in the US war for independence, but an ally in WWI and WWII, was again an ally in the US government's military aggression against Iraq.

Paris and London, just before the US invasion of Iraq in March 2003: secondary progressed Mars ASC and North Node ASC near those cities indicated US pressure to support US military action. (The same lines appear near Rome also, but not as close.)

Paris: the two closest secondary progressed parans are Sun DSC/Saturn MH, plus Mercury DSC/Pallas Athena DSC: France as an important potential ally, or a VIP opponent, suggested appeal to a slower, more sober governing body – the UN; a call for defensive (Athenian) strategy, not Mars aggression.

London: Jupiter IC/North Node ASC indicates the support the US government had desired: a safe, hospitable staging area would also be probable (air bases, etc.)

Federal Government response to post-Hurricane Katrina, New Orleans and vicinity, early September 2005

The most telling story of how those at the highest level of the US federal government saw post-Katrina New Orleans and vicinity is reflected in tertiary progressions for that time. The hurricane of August 29, 2005 was first mistakenly thought to be "not that bad." Even after realizing the severity of the problem, federal response was limited and delayed (typically Saturnian adjectives). Although the media were there immediately, significant federal government presence was not. President Bush tried out a new guitar complete with a presidential seal, a gift of a country western star. *The National Enquirer* printed a story implying that the former alcohol abuser had fallen back to the bottle. (Supposedly the same *Enquirer* reporter who wrote this story was the first to tell the world of the Clinton-Lewinsky scandal.)

Once a federal presence was established, imposition of law and order was the priority. Since then, criminal charges sent liquor store looters to jail. A doctor and nurse in a nursing home accused of lethal injection mercy killings have been brought up on murder charges. The relevant tertiary progressions for August 29, 2005, 7:30am CDT, when the White House is notified of the levees being breached, show *Saturn and Chiron* emphasized by tertiary progression (the fastest moving form of Cyclo*Carto*Graphy, relevant for brief but dramatic events). The Node/Lilith paran is also relevant: the fierce power of nature.

The closest tertiary-progressed line, *Saturn IC,* was nearest New Orleans and nearby hurricane-damaged coastal Mississippi, west of New Orleans, indicating a serious domestic issue calling for order and responsibility. The issue: will the (Saturnian) boundaries/walls (levees) of the 'home' (the city of New Orleans) hold as they are supposed to, particularly in the poorer (Saturnine) neighborhoods. The outcome: Saturn can define the arbitrary imposition of domestic law and order on the Chironic, predominantly African-American poor people of the region. Mythologically, Chronos (or Saturn) ate his children, or tried to eat them. Chiron was his bastard offspring. When Saturn and Chiron aspect each other, the issue will be whether or not the poor and those often discriminated against will receive just or unjust treatment by the law. Unfortunately, usually the treatment received is unjust.

Adding to the complexity here is tertiary-progressed Chiron IC. Chiron IC can be seen as both the troubled/troublesome natural environment, and ecological issues, as well as regional people likely to be seen (by the prosperous economic elite at highest level of government) as less than human. Regarding the environmental issue: the ecologically-minded had unsuccessfully tried to warn the federal government (and others) about the danger of the ongoing destruction of the wetlands, particularly in the event of a serious hurricane. Global warming analysts (also Chiron IC) had also unsuccessfully tried to warn of the increasing probability of greater and more frequently occurring hurricanes due to global warming, also to no avail. Ever the underdog unheard Cassandra, such Chironic environmental advocates are particularly at a disadvantage when Saturn is involved. (Mythic Saturn would have eaten all of his children if he could, and Chiron was not only his son, but also a bastard son!)

Similarly, any advocates of the poor and unfortunate were/are at a great disadvantage here. Remember that the federal government saw their African-American ancestors, the slaves, as less than human. Legally the federal government saw the African-origin slaves as 3/5 human. Unfortunately, apparently not a lot had changed. Katrina victims who lost everything were given FEMA checks for up to $2,000. Supposedly because of allegations of fraud, in the next disaster, those applying for federal assistance must not only somehow prove that they did indeed reside in the devastated area. Even if able to do so, maximum cash benefits to be paid will, by law, be limited to no more than $500 each.

Post-Katrina African-American voices said that President Bush doesn't care about 'Black people'
The USA 1 chart and its Astro*Carto*Graphy imply the same, not only about the GW Bush administration, but about the collective American elite that have and still do run this country. Like their elite predecessors, the 1777 Continental Congress, these modern day elitists don't seem to care much about the ordinary people of other colors. By every economic measure, the richest of the rich have become significantly richer under the Bush administration, the middle class has shrunk, and the number of ordinary Americans living in poverty has significantly increased during the same time period. Note that the big astrological difference during this time period has been Pluto transiting into the USA 1 tenth house. The 'Plutocracy' is in charge, now more than ever in the United States.

© Dale O'Brien 2007.

Dale O'Brien is a full-time professional astrologer, A*C*G-certified by Jim Lewis in 1991. He has had articles in The Mountain Astrologer *and other magazines and has taught, lectured and performed for major astrological organizations such as UAC, ISAR, NCGR and ARC. O'Brien offers a wide variety of astrological services. He can be reached through his web site: www.docchiron.com, or by email: docchiron@yahoo.com, or by phone: 001 541 485 9772.*

NOTES

1. Poz Publications (1998). With over 500 charts, Howland's book is a feast of American charts and historical information – recommended. Howland can be reached at his email address roninlucya@yahoo.com
2. The Wessex Astrologer Ltd, UK, (1999), pages 119-128. Astrologers will note the Virgo rising with Neptune prominent, the Gemini Midheaven and the Aquarius Moon.
3. Interested readers will note that the LS Uranus line continues eastward from London near to Paris (the French supported the US in its War of I Independence), then it runs on between Jerusalem and Baghdad, two cities with a different 'special relationship' with the US to this very day.
4. Although the gains of the Montgomery bus boycott were small compared

with the gains blacks would later win, the boycott was an important start to the movement. The lasting legacy of the boycott, as Roberta Wright wrote, was that "It helped to launch a 10-year national struggle for freedom and justice, the Civil Rights Movement, that stimulated others to do the same at home and abroad."

5. Timothy Leary and revisionist historians have postulated that the real cause of America's Civil War was not the issue of slavery but the conflicting reality viewpoints of the industrial (the North) vs the agricultural (the South). Looking at the core issue of the war in this light also makes the Saturn line meaningful because it truly separates the industrial and agricultural sections of the country. Note that Saturn runs along the very southern (bottom) boundaries of the industrial states of (West to East): Illinois, Indiana, Ohio, and Pennsylvania, separating them from the more rural and agricultural states below them.
6. *An Astrological Mandala*, by Dane Rudhyar, Vantage Books, New York, 1974.
7. For a memorial to Solte, see http://www.solsticepoint.com/astrologersmemorial/solte.html
8. Cyclo*Carto*Graphy (C*C*G) lines are the moving transiting and progressed lines relative to the fixed lines of an A*C*G map. Both the names A*C*G and C*C*G are copyright to Jim Lewis's estate.
9. See *The Sabian Symbols as an Oracle*, by Lynda Hill, self-published, Australia, 2002. Also see: *360 Degrees of Wisdom*, by Lynda Hill, Plume (Penguin) USA, 2004.
10. Spring Publications, Connecticut, USA, 1995.
11. See http://www.astronumerics.com/
12. The Solar Fire and Solar Maps computer programs are products of Esoteric Technologies Pty. Ltd, South Australia. Text by Stephanie Johnson.

16

A History Lesson:
The A*C*G, Geodetics and Local Space of the George W Bush Presidency

Arielle Guttman

In conclusion, we have another piece by Arielle Guttman. We opened the book with her chapter from The Astro*Carto*Graphy Book of Maps, *written in 1988, which introduced A*C*G as a substantial biographical tool. Here, she deftly blends the three locality techniques of A*C*G, Local Space and Geodetics to give us a 'history lesson', one which is very close to her heart and, she says, was inspired by the late Jim Lewis.*

From working within the mythic and archetypal dimensions of astrology, we know that the planets act in accordance with their archetypal natures. In my mind, there is no better way to see these themes come alive than in locational astrology, where the living archetype plays out its drama on the landscape of our lives. People who use Astro*Carto*Graphy as a means of understanding their lives know that living on a Pluto, Venus, Mars or Mercury line does indeed bring that character to life in ways too numerous to count. The voices of some of these planets are gentle and loving; others absolutely scream at us. This puts us in a workable framework to best use Astro*Carto*Graphy. It is not a case of, "Is this a good place or a bad place for me to live?" The truer question becomes, "Does this planet serve my needs? Or, "Is this planet useful to me in my life theme at this stage?" We should remember that the planets (as shown in our birth charts) do not exist outside of ourselves, but are part of our own lives, residing in our own psyches.

The use of Astro*Carto*Graphy along with Geodetics (Geo-detics = geo = geography = Gaia) is another winning combination, especially when viewing situations and events that have a global impact. You could call Geodetics the astrology of planet earth. While this system lends itself well to A*C*G maps, the Geodetic placements on the map convey a more universal, global and archetypal view of the energy at hand, while the personal A*C*G map is just that: personal to its owner.

Nothing has had a greater global impact in recent years than the presidency of GW Bush. The November 2000 election itself was a case study in classic textbook astrology, especially regarding the Mercury retrograde phenomenon (delineated later in this piece), but also contained other juicy pieces of transit and eclipse tidbits which included a real-life drama of the nodes, Jupiter, Saturn, Neptune and Pluto as they made landfall over key geographical areas. Following the election was the 2001 Inauguration, which has proven to give us even greater insights into what we could expect with this administration and its key players.

The Astro*Carto*Graphy Map for the Election of 2000, set for November 7, 7pm EST (See Figure 1), contains a striking planetary signature, which includes the nine-month long opposition (September 2000 to May 2001) of Jupiter and Pluto that was peaking that year. This opposition occurred on the USA natal horizontal axis, giving it a much bigger impact on the country and its citizens than just any old Jupiter/Pluto aspect would have.

The space in-between any two planetary A*C*G lines can be treated as the boundary of operational field energies for that particular planetary pairing or aspect. In this case it was Washington DC and Florida. Jupiter, you will note from the A*C*G map, is placed over Florida and it was the first time in US history that an election was based on a *selection*, first by the Florida Court, then by the US Supreme Court in Washington (where Pluto, among others, sits), and where the will of the people casting the ballots of the candidates of their choice was all but ignored and rendered insignificant. A precedent-setting presidential (s)election, indeed.

There are two ways to project the planets on a map with A*C*G. The map featured in Figure 1 is the *In Mundo* version, which places the planets in a truer relationship to the horizon of any location by considering how far off the ecliptic that particular planet rises or sets. It was Jim Lewis' preferred way of projecting the planets. There is also a *Zodiac* projection, which is used in Figure 2. This method ignores the ecliptic

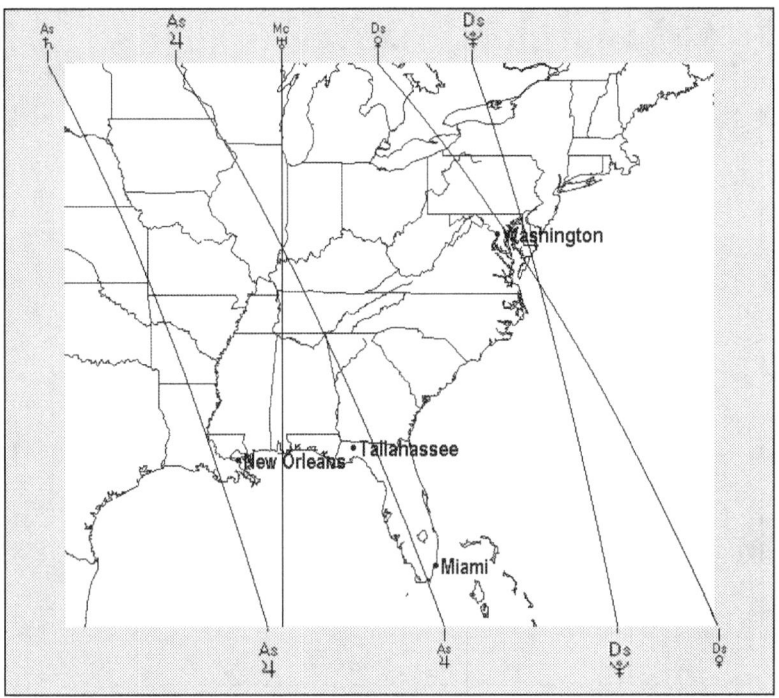

Figure 1 - A*C*G Map of Election Night 2000 – In Mundo

and simply projects the planets in zodiac order on the degree they are occupying at that moment.

What's particularly striking about the true Zodiac version of this map (Figure 2) is that the afore-mentioned Jupiter/Pluto opposition precisely straddles the state of Florida. Pluto sits over Dade County (Miami and West Palm Beach); voters there were treated to a very real-life Pluto on the Descendant drama when illegal seizure of power occurred. Add to this the opposition of Jupiter (over Tallahassee – Florida's capitol and the seat of its high court), in its fallen sign and retrograde, where scandalous impropriety from the highest places reigned down upon the people – so uncharacteristic for a US election that one would have thought this was a military take-over in a banana republic. (Minus the bananas; recent history has proven this to be true).

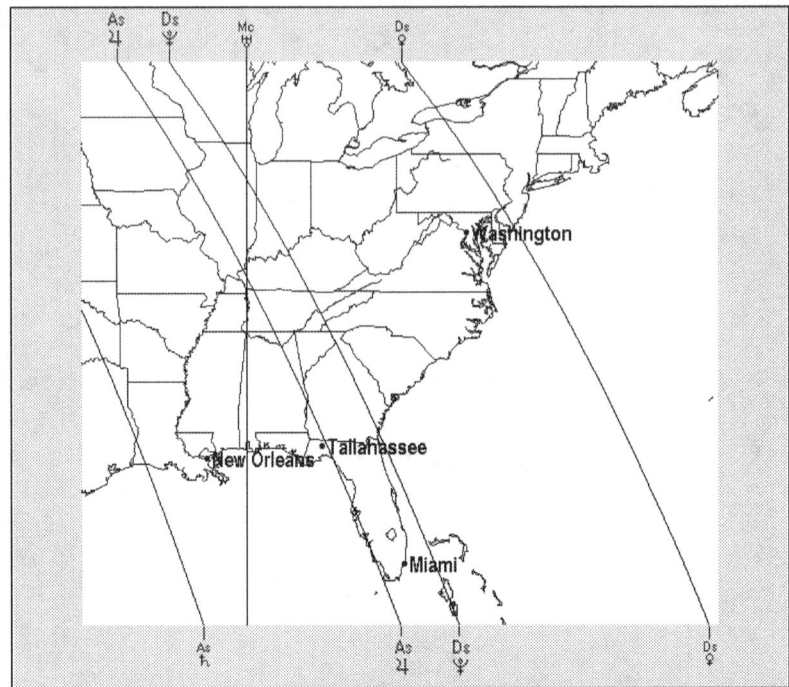

Figure 2 - A*C*G Map of Election Night 2000 – In Zodiac

Astrology as a science involves capturing the planets in a particular pose of the moment and freezing it, much like a photograph. The birth chart of election night will not go away. Though it 'happened one night' it is something that impacted for a four-year minimum, leading toward eight and beyond. It lives on for the extent of its life.

For those who don't recollect clearly the details of what happened that night, here is a summary. Voters in Dade County, particularly the aforementioned places, were treated to a nightmare of confusion, including ballots so skewed they couldn't be read and Gore's name couldn't be located. Then, when a voter believed he was casting a vote for Gore, it turned out that the vote was registered for Pat Buchanan or Bush. At this point in the story it would be a good idea to introduce the concept of Mercury retrograde.

Mercury, the single most 'tricksy' planet was in the single most trickster position it could be in on Election Day 2000. Forever in my memory as an astrologer, this event will carry the signature of the most retrograde of all Mercury retrograde events I have witnessed in my lifetime.

Mercury retrograde is a message that blazes to the astrologically literate to: *read the fine print carefully before making a decision that is irrevocable.* The ironic part of this is that Mercury was stationary on Election Day, about to turn direct that night, but before it did, it had to traverse a dramatic shift of signs and directions that even the most astute navigator would have found mind-boggling. Within 24 hours of the election, Mercury was ordered to leave Scorpio, enter Libra, turn direct from retrograde, then re-enter Scorpio. As the rules of engagement for each direction, station and sign placement for Mercury are different, even the usually bright and competent over-soul of Mercury, Hermes himself, was befuddled and confused by all of this. As he himself has been pegged with the most trickster energy of any of the planetary players, you could say we were all in for one of the biggest tricks of all. It's interesting to recall at this point that Mercury is the planet that disposits Jupiter in Gemini for this event, and that Mercury is clearly the communication channel. Those remembering this particular election night will recall how the news media were changing their tunes by the hour and by the minute, embarrassingly and awkwardly attempting to keep up with the changing charade of events that Mercury itself was going through that fated night.

So much for the event. Now, who were the planetary players for this particular dramatization? The starring planet in both candidates' charts was none other than Neptune, as both Al Gore and GW Bush have Ascendants of early Leo rising. There was Neptune, straight on opposition to both of them. If you think the people were confused, imagine being in their shoes. They, no doubt, were the most confused of all that night, as the orchestration of these events was clearly in the hands of the Jupiter/Pluto police force, behind closed doors in a steamy, murky underworld setting. Both of these political figures (Gore and Bush) have their natal Neptune lines occurring over the East Coast, and specifically Florida in their natal A*C*G maps Let's start with a review of Al Gore's natal ACG map. See Figure 3.

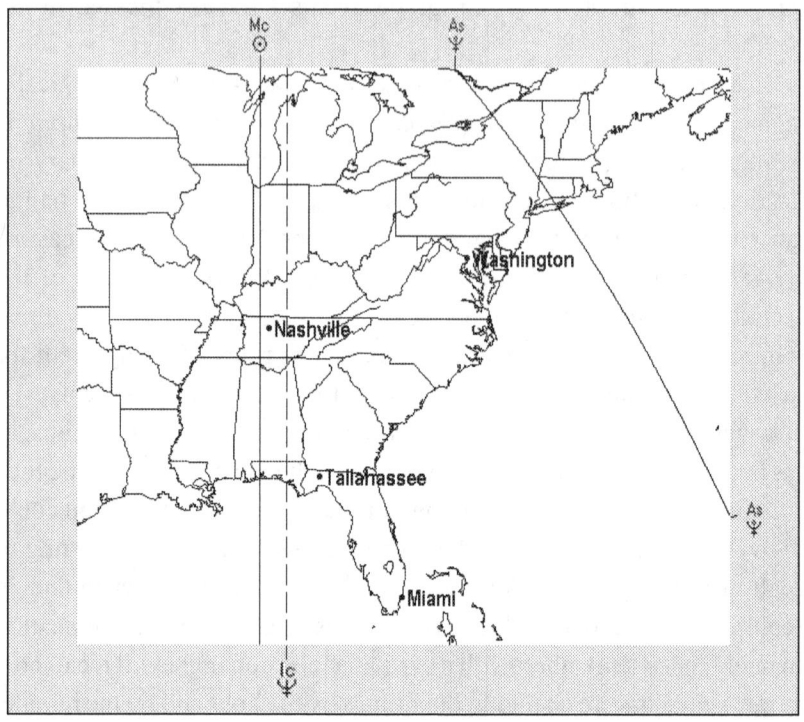

Figure 3 - Al Gore A*C*G Map

Bad news for Gore: notice the Sun/Neptune opposition in the birth map, playing out near Tallahassee Florida, where the Court decided to select the President rather than observe constitutional US law to let its citizens elect the President. With Pluto Ascending close enough to Washington to be dangerous, Gore was pushed into a corner of the ring and forced to accept defeat, even knowing there was no evidence proving that outcome. The Sun MH position for Gore, one that indicates fame and glory, passes through the state of Tennessee, his home state.

Now, let's look at Al Gore's A*C*G map in the Geodetic zodiac, Figure 4.

His Sun, Neptune and the asteroid Pallas all congregate over Florida. The Sun-Ascending, precisely over Florida, suggests a victory in that state. But Neptune, in opposition to the Sun, is literally producing a tidal wave over Miami, and Gore wound up being affected even more than Bush by the Florida ballot fiasco and court decision because of that

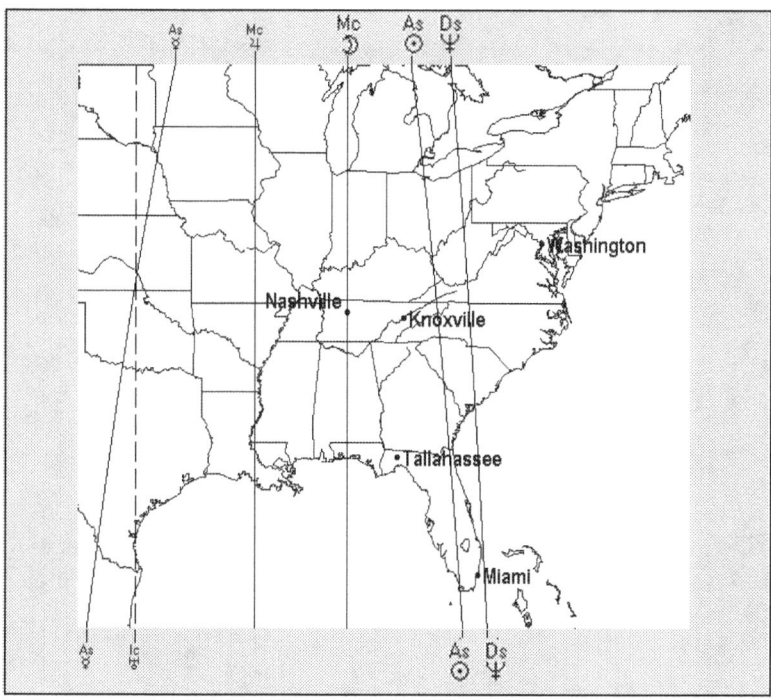

Figure 4 - Al Gore Geodetic A*C*G Map

placement. As for the presidency, Gore's Sun is close to Washington but not close enough. The asteroid Pallas is close to Washington, but not close enough. Neptune is close to Washington, but as a politician there, you probably wouldn't want it any closer than it is. Neptune is shadowed in Gore's chart (in an opposition to his Sun). That's a situation that asks, "What just happened?" or "What is it I'm not seeing?" or "How could I have fallen for that one?" And that's why, if you're afraid of Neptune – and it's astounding to me how many people are – it comes down to just that. The shadow side of Neptune is that it resides in the shadows, in the fog, but oh what seduction! It's not seen because people don't want to see it. Then, when they come out of it, they wonder how they didn't see it. And further, it's as if the entire country didn't see it.

Gore was actually influenced by three Neptune positions on Election Day 2000: transiting Neptune opposite natal Ascendant, Neptune in the A*C*G map of Florida, and Neptune in the Geodetic map of Florida. That's just too much Neptune to make any sense out of the events as they

258   *From Here to There*

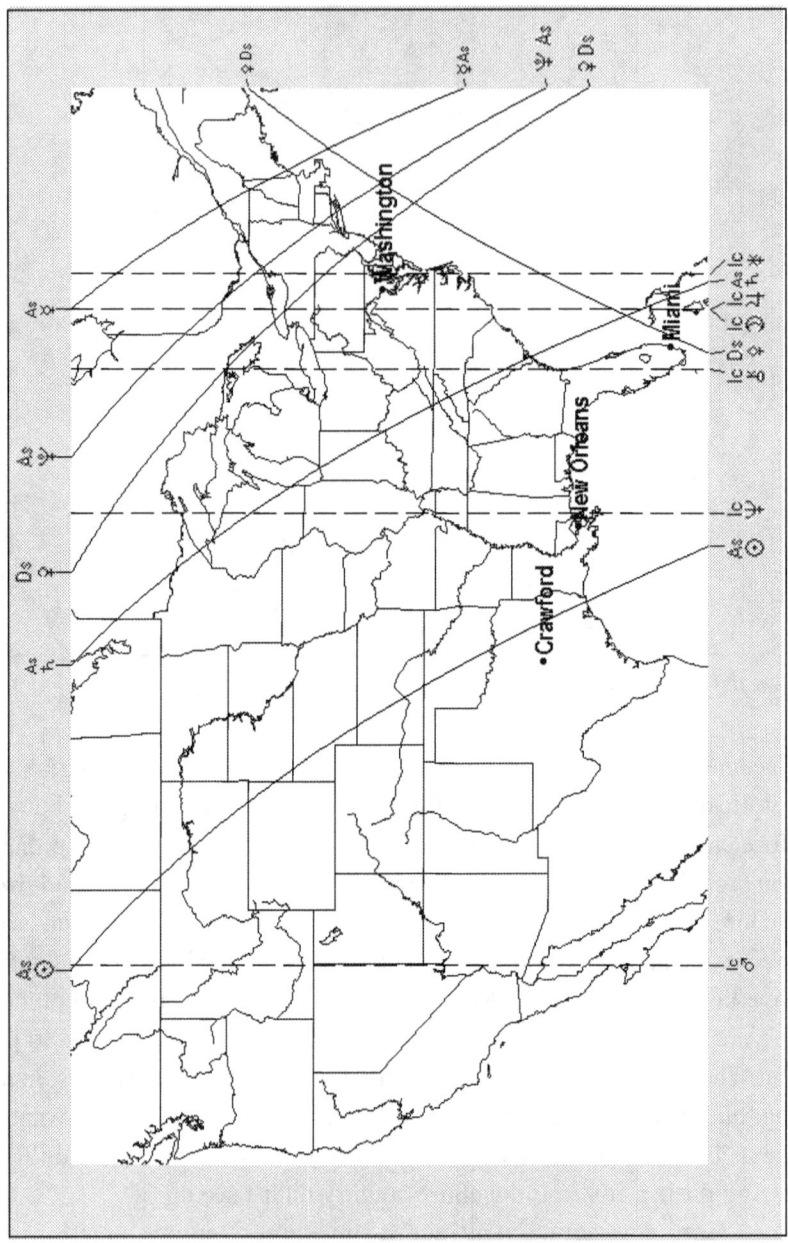

Figure 5 - George W Bush A*C*G Map

occurred and to give any real understanding to the situation at hand. It literally means there's a leak in the boat, but we can't see it; we just know we're sinking fast.

Now for the GW Bush map and the Election of 2000. See Figure 5. Like Gore, Bush has his Sun passing through his home state of Texas. For a politician, the Sun line is important. For anyone, the Sun lines on the map are important, especially the visible areas of the Sun: where it rises and where it culminates. This harkens back to its astrological rulership of Leo, the sign of the King or the young prince. In cases like this you often have an archetypal shadowing overruling the facts. That is, people perceive the person with the Sun in a given place to be the true leader or winner of the prize or position: the one who deserves the most fame, the highest rank and victory over their competitors, even if they are less skilled, less intelligent or less qualified for the job. With the Sun-Asc passing through Texas, Bush would shine as its representative on the national scene, especially with his particular family backing and support. But Washington is even better for him. Clearly, with this many planets hugging the nation's capital (seven in highly angular positions), there would be few people with this amount of planetary clout to challenge him. And it gets even stronger when taking into consideration the Geodetics. See Figure 6.

Here we have a case of five to seven planets (depending upon your use of orbs) affecting Washington DC and Florida. Again, we have the Sun (in this case occupying the lesser visible position, the IC) precisely over Washington. And in this case the Sun therein suggests a position of receptivity and some obfuscation, as we never see the Sun at midnight. The circumstance of an individual having so many Geodetic positions over Washington puts that person in a position of great power, using the rule of Will as their mode of operation. The combination of planetary power over both maps literally gives the individual *carte blanche* to do what he wants with little concern for how it affects the nation. It's the rule of the King, the tradition of which comes down from former times as: "if it's good for me, it's good for everyone else." Between the two maps, it was as if destiny carried Bush to Washington in a carpeted, canopied hand-basket with an entourage, much like Cleopatra's entrance

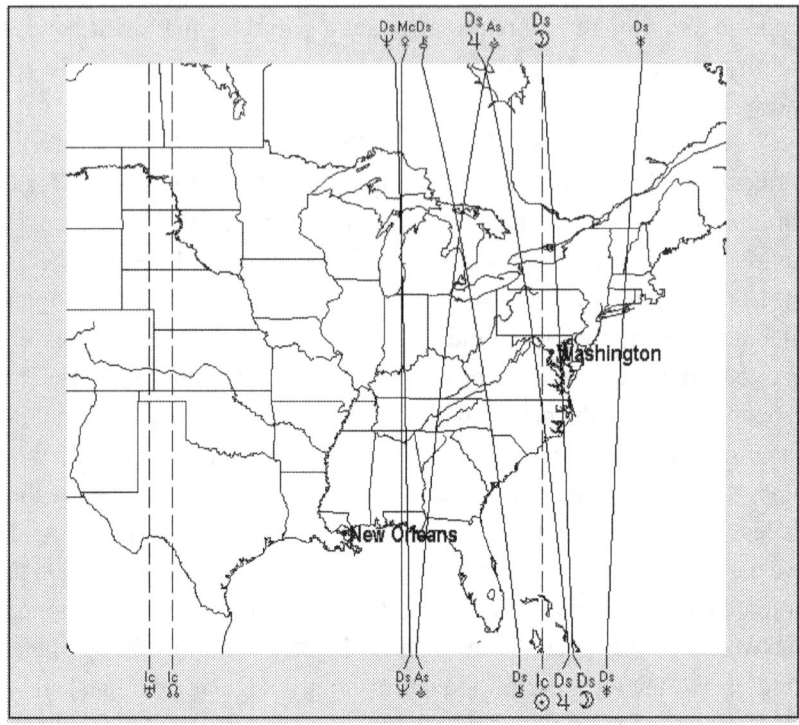

Figure 6 - George W. Bush Geodetic A*C*G Map

into Rome. And he himself had little to do with it, apart from showing up and smiling for the cameras.

What's interesting from an astrological point of view, regarding both candidates' maps, is that they are both about the same age, they both have an early degree of Leo rising, they both were having a Neptune opposition to their natal Ascendant, they both have personal and Geodetic Neptune over the state of Florida and they both had the Sun representing them from their home state. It was a difficult election for astrologers to call. Most picked Gore to win this election, and if the ballots had been cast and read properly, I believe he would have won Florida, thus winning the US because, at that point, Florida was the critical mass that would turn the tide one way or the other. Though I believe he would have won Florida, I had to use some amount of objectivity in picking who I thought would wind up as President, and based on A*C*G and Geodetic map renderings, I had to conclude Bush would wind up in the White House. The powerful vortex of planets surrounding Washington for him in both maps forces him to act out some kind of destiny or pre-written script there. The force of planets that cushions him represents the interests of the people and corporations he is cloistered by, leaving him little room to deviate from the script.

In the weeks following the election, Mercury became direct in Scorpio and the news media could not stop headlining the story of the Florida vote, the Florida re-count, the Florida court decision and, finally, the US Supreme Court Decision. In early December, Mercury left Scorpio to enter Sagittarius, and the die was cast. We were now to forget everything we just heard; Neptune was still casting its hypnotic effects. The new King had been announced, orders were issued for the news media to stop running this story and get on with other pressing business, such as the annual glorification of holiday time and shopper alerts, lest business suffer

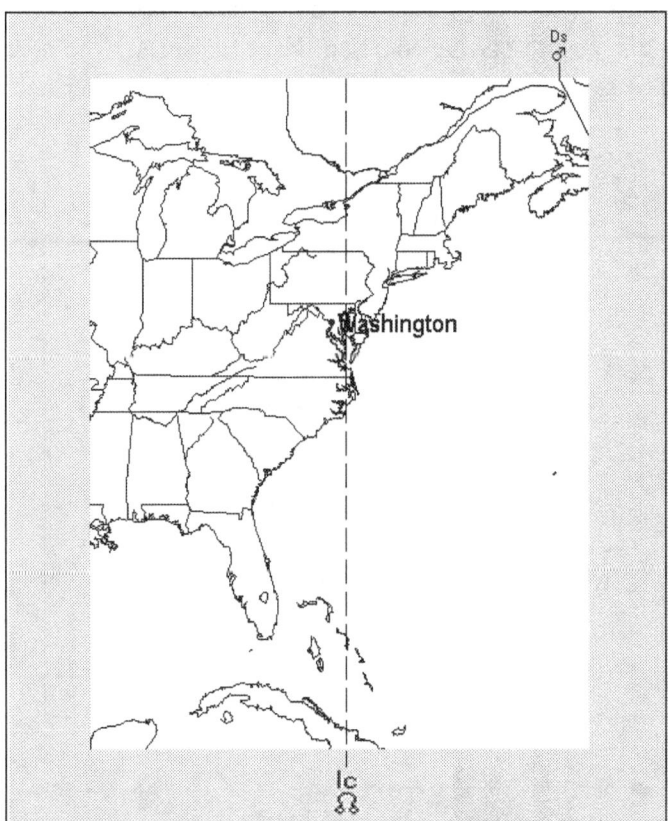

Figure 7 - Inauguration 2001 Geodetic A*C*G Map

from such uncertainty in leadership; and so that America would not suffer from the humiliating exposure that this totally unconstitutional, unlawful, unprecedented, but especially, unresolved take-over might mean for its innocent citizens.

On election day 2000 the transiting lunar nodes, which are always related to nearby eclipses, were featured in the Geodetic map, just off the East Coast of America. In the year 2000, there was an unprecedented number of eclipses (six – the usual being four per year). These eclipse and node degrees occurred on or around the US natal Sun (13° Cancer), the US natal Geodetic MH (12° Capricorn) and the natal Sun of GW Bush (13° Cancer). On Inauguration Day 2001, when King George would be crowned, the South lunar node was conjunct the nation's capital. See Figure 7.

Such a placement indicates what we had in store for us: a harkening back to the past to resolve some unfinished business. The new cabinet contained seven members of GW Bush's father's former cabinet and

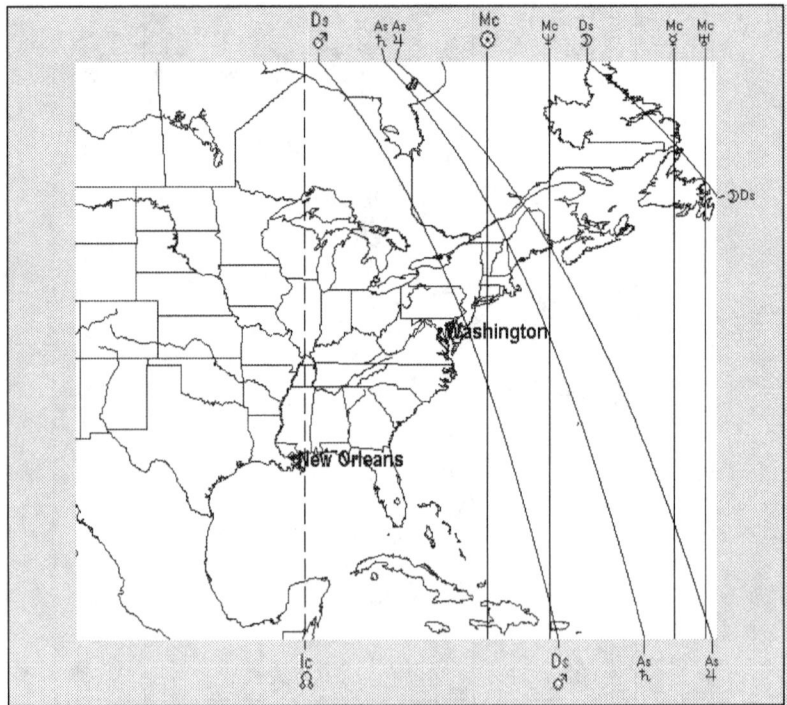

Figure 8 - The A*C*G Map of the Inauguration of GW Bush

A History Lesson   263

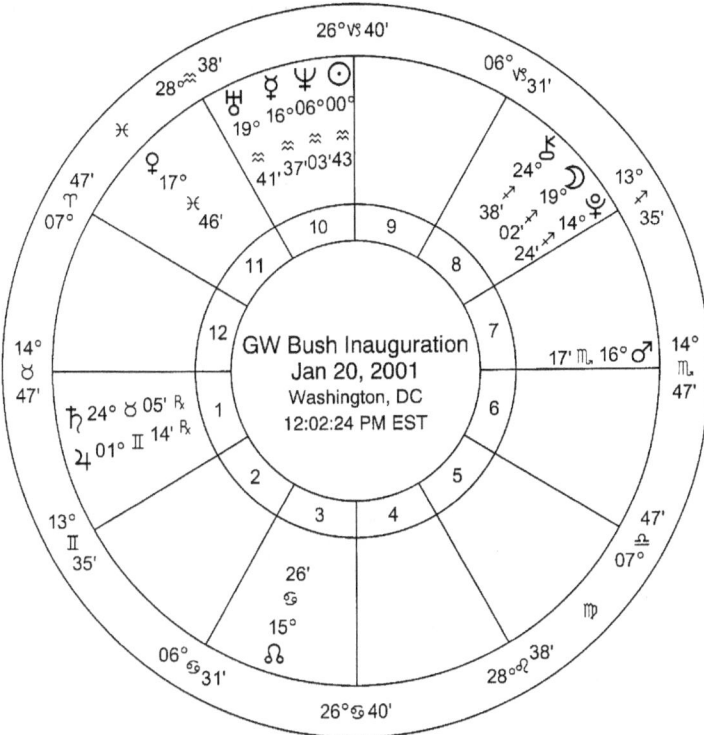

Figure 9 - Chart of the Inauguration

would take the country backwards in time to the pre-Clinton era, virtually erasing every gain and accomplishment Clinton had produced in his eight year term.

The A*C*G Map of the actual Inauguration (12:02:24 pm on January 20, 2001) is even more telling. See Figure 8 for the map. Also see Figure 9, the inauguration chart.

Here, what clearly stands out is an angular Mars on the Descendant position of the map and chart of the event. Mars, powerfully placed in its own sign of Scorpio and in an angular position of the chart, gives that planet strength and power above all else. To make matters worse, Mars in this chart is square Mercury, square Uranus and in a wide opposition to Saturn, indicating a shadowed effect. Mars so highly amplified gives, first and foremost, an aggressive, warrior stance, and also gives the military the rule of law. Mars on the Descendant in any chart can indicate hostile relations with partners, open enemies, and in the house of peace

264 *From Here to There*

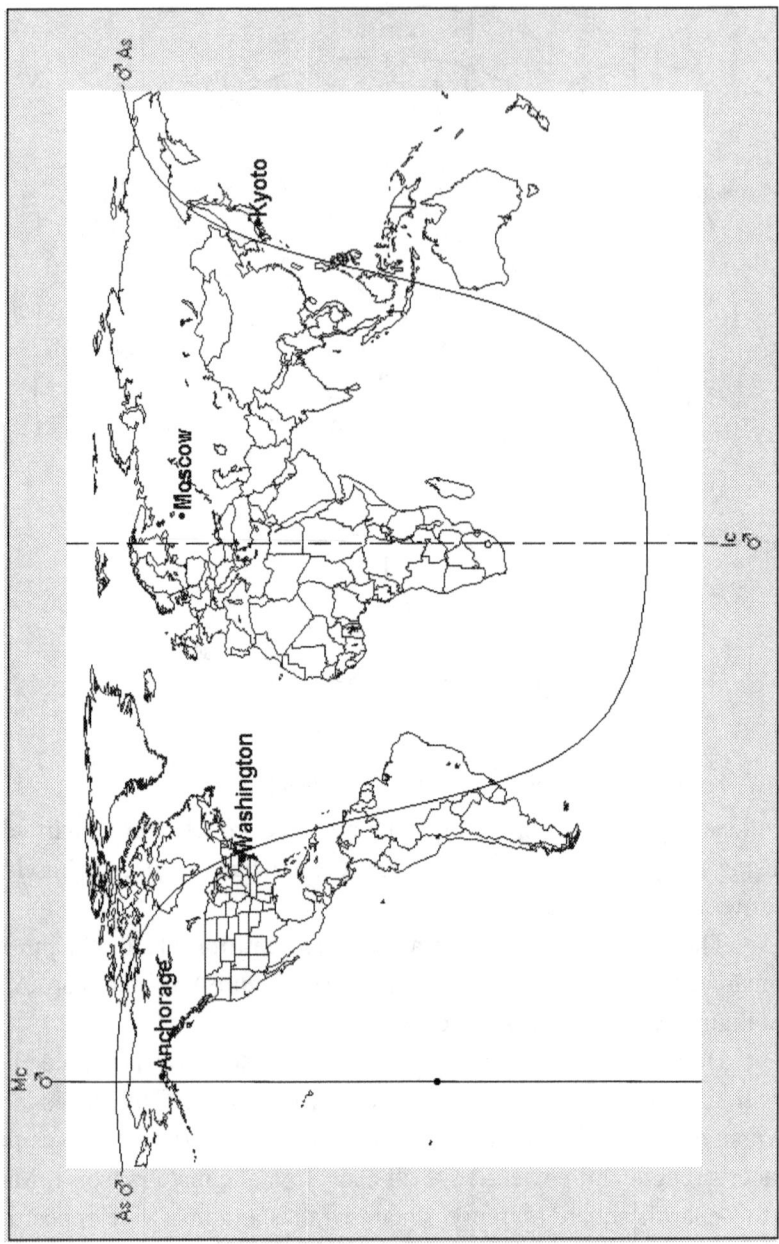

Figure 10 - Mars lines for the Inauguration of GW Bush

can actually mean war. There was no doubt in analyzing the chart of this event that we would be faced with four years of a warrior national stance, emanating from the White House. Guns and state-of-the-art weaponry pointing out from the White House Oval Office would make its residents feel secure. But, clearly, with Mars Descending over Washington, this location is where Bush is in the greatest danger himself!

Jim Lewis used to say, "US Presidents love making war on their Mars lines." In this case, between the chart of George Bush personally and the Inauguration Chart, the Mars spreads itself out pretty much over the world, including his own residence.

The Inauguration A*C*G map Mars culminates over Alaska, and in the first days of his presidency Mr. Bush asserted that the Arctic Wildlife Refuge was non-essential and open game to oil drilling. Another Mars line in this map falls between China and Japan; in the first few weeks of Bush's office, Asian relations quickly deteriorated. But the ongoing assault to Japan has been his and his administration's complete disregard for the Kyoto Agreement, which sets limiting goals on greenhouse gases. Though other industrial nations have signed up to the agreement, Bush chose to reject it, questioning the validity of any limits. See Figure 10 which is an A*C*G map of the Inauguration showing just the Mars lines.

Within six months of the Inauguration, the most pronounced full-moon eclipse for the country and its president was experienced on July 5, 2001 at 13° Capricorn, portending a crisis situation for both country and president in the weeks and months that followed. At the same time, the Saturn/Pluto opposition was coming into place across the US natal horizontal axis. (Sibly chart, July 4th, 1776, 5:10pm, LMT)

Some very clear examples of this 'Mars effect' will also come from Bush's Local Space map. See Figure 11.

The Local Space map gives us another picture of planetary projection. In this case, all planets emanate from the birth place out to the horizon in whatever direction they happened to be pointing. A very sharp image of this extended Mars for Bush shoots itself to the Persian Gulf, encompassing Iran, Iraq and Saudi Arabia but practically screaming down the streets of downtown Baghdad. Bush's Pluto Local Space line (the higher octave planet of Mars) passes through Paris, France, where chilly, if not downright hostile relations soon surfaced with French

266 From Here to There

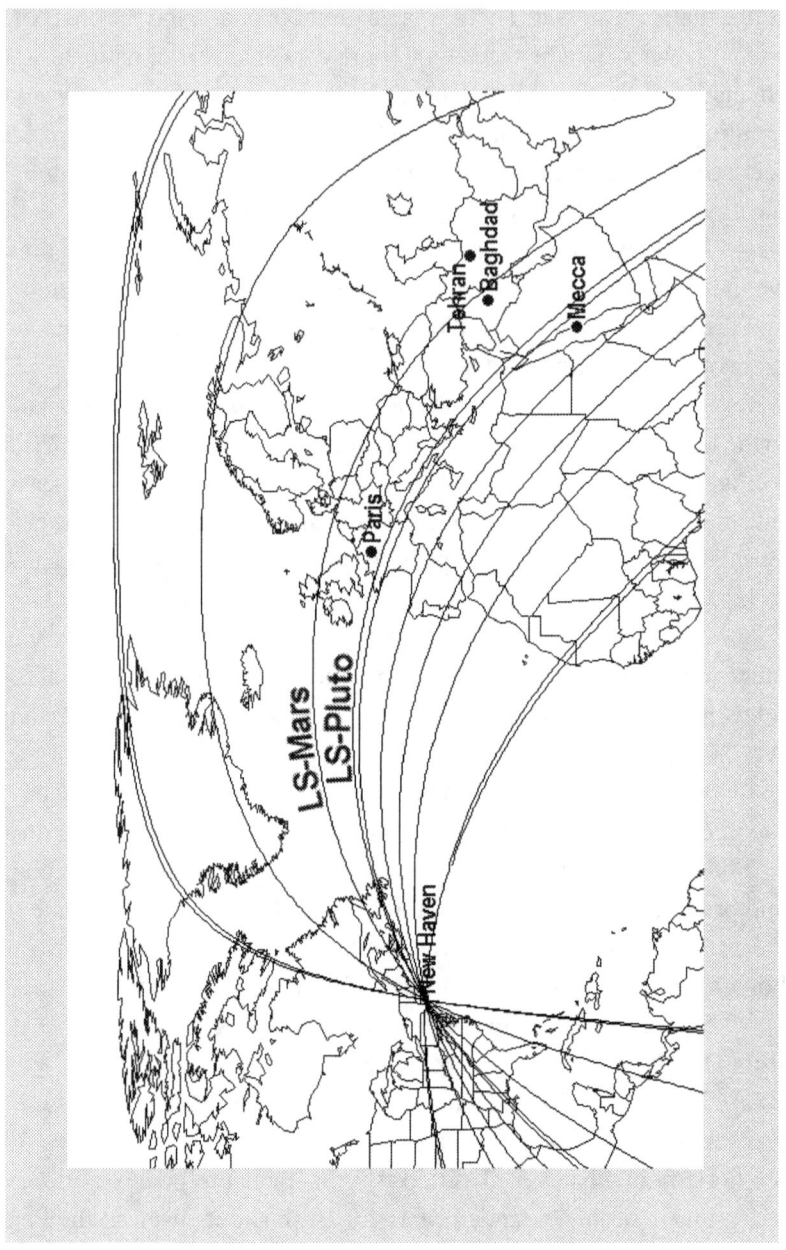

Figure 11 - George W Bush Local Space Map

president Jacques Chirac regarding the US invasion of Iraq. Pluto and Venus pass close to Mecca as well, symbolizing both Plutonian conflict with the Muslim world and possibly the desire for their oil riches.

By the end of 2006, transiting Saturn triggered all the planets in the fixed T-square of the 2001 Inauguration Chart (see Figure 9). It fell into a first-quarter square to itself from Leo, a third-quarter square to Mars and an opposition to Mercury and Uranus. Saturn reached the nadir of the chart in 2005, indicating a low point for this chart at the same time it reached its own first quarter phase of the cycle. That would give the project at hand a sense of extreme challenge and potential crisis, while at the same time indicating attempts to elicit support from friends and allies who question the aims and sanity of pursuing such a direction. Themes

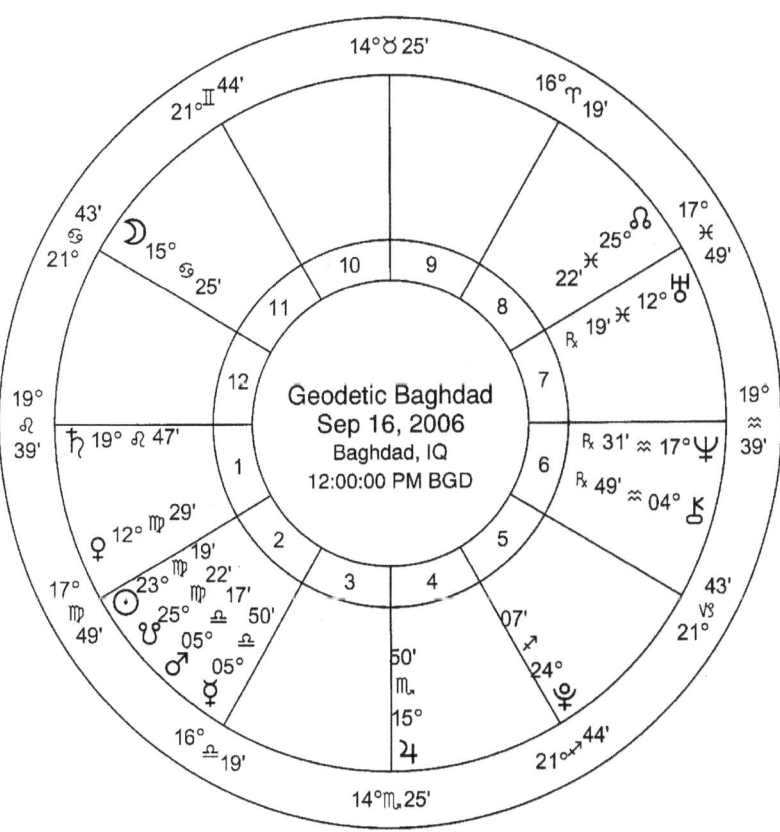

Figure 12 - The Geodetic chart for Baghdad, September 2006.

of failure, particularly in leadership and management face the individual at this stage in the cycle. Bush's former allies and supporters of his military campaign began to question the mission and its purpose. Also, in September-October 2006 transiting Saturn arrived at the ascendant degree (19° Leo 39) of the Geodetic chart for Baghdad. See Figure 12.

This would indicate a show-down in Iraq, creating a brick wall or a ring-pass-not situation. Saturn spoke by warning this administration that it wouldn't be possible to push forward any more with the mission in Iraq as outlined previously. To succeed from this point, a completely new direction would have to be defined and practiced, or stalling and stalemating of any activity would transpire. (Note: within a few months, on December 06, 2006, the Iraq Study Group released its official report to the President, Congress and the public, affirming this need for new approaches.)

Keep in mind that personal horoscopes operate differently from event horoscopes and mundane considerations. You and I have free will to determine how we will best make use of our planets, whether they are consciously directed or shadowed. It is clear from the above example that destiny had a hand in playing out these events which became much bigger on the world stage than the situations and events of the average individual. But what is also clear is that the A*C*G, Geodetic and Local Space maps are excellent tools for understanding how energies play out on the world stage. We as astrologers can make use of our understanding of planetary archetypes and make our own choices. Right?

© Arielle Guttman 2006 [excerpts from NCGR lecture, 2001.]

This article is dedicated to the memory of Jim Lewis, whose voice spoke during its preparation.

Index

A

Astro*Carto*Graphy
    accident 83, 84
    Book of Maps 9, 25
    business 203, 208, 214
    fixed stars 168, 173
    Geodetic 114, 119, 126, 257, 260, 261
    introduction, 3, 78, 89, 143, 144, 145
    Jyotish locality 142
    mundane 39, 40, 42, 44, 67, 69, 70, 72, 225, 235, 236, 243, 246, 253, 254, 258, 262, 264
    parans 4, 38, 79, 86, 104, 111, 166
    rectification 50, 51, 52, 53
    reincarnation 93, 96, 100, 102, 104, 107, 109, 111
    relocation 31, 32, 33, 36, 37, 38, 52, 59, 69, 72, 78, 79, 125, 135, 155, 157, 208
    reports 9
    Solar Return 196, 200, 201
    synastry 46, 47, 48, 49
    USA 220, 225, 235, 236, 243, 246, 253, 254, 256, 258, 262, 264

B

Baigent, Michael 7
Blair, Tony 72
Bonaparte, Napoleon 98, 99, 100,
Bradley, Donald 2
Brady, Bernadette 168, 194
Bush, GW 43, 58, 59, 67, 69, 70, 72, 186, 189, 258, 260, 261, 262, 263, 264, 266

C

Campion, Nicholas 7
Cassidy, Kathryn 162, 167
Chavez, Hugo 39
CONTINUUM 13, 14, 92
Cossar, Faye 203, 218, 219
Cozzi, Steve 10
Cunningham, Donna 14, 130, 140, 141
Currey, Robert 13, 16, 58, 75
Cyclo*Carto*Graphy
    examples 49, 50, 58, 83, 84, 166, 246
    introduction 7

D

Davis, Martin 1, 10, 15, 17, 31, 35, 36, 51, 52, 220.
Destiny Point 10, 35, 36, 44, 46, 47, 48, 52
Duncan, Gary 2

E

Earhart, Amelia 123, 125, 126
Erlewine, Michael 4, 5, 10, 89
Esoteric Technologies 12, 14

F

Fagan, Cyril 2
Fenton, Sasha 15
Firebrace, Roy 2
Flaherty, Dennis 14, 142, 155, 157, 160

G

Geodetic charts 118, 122, 267
Geodetic World Map 11, 113, 114, 119, 126

Gore, Al 256, 257
Graves, Robert 103, 104
Guttman, Arielle 8, 15, 25, 29, 251, 268

H
Hand, Robert 9, 15
Harding, Michael 11
Harvey, Charles 4, 7, 8, 11
Hathaway, Edith 12
Heyerdahl, Thor 95, 96, 97
Hillary, Sir Edmund 117
Howe, Gregg 3, 8
Howland, Ronald 220, 221, 223, 224, 225

I
Irving, Kenneth 14

J
Jawer, Jeff 8
Jayne, Charles 2, 4, 6
Johndro, Edward 1, 4
Jolie, Angelina 47
Jyotish locality 142

K
KLM charts 207, 209, 211, 212

L
Lewis, Jim 2, 8, 12, 13, 16, 25, 143, 268
Lincoln, Abraham 182
Lindbergh, Charles 31, 32, 33
Local Space 5, 6, 10, 11, 31, 34, 53, 89, 97, 100, 102, 104, 107, 109, 165, 210, 211, 212, 220, 221, 223, 224, 266
compass 211, 212

M
MacLise, Ossian 108, 109
Mann, A.Tad 93, 111
Mann, Thomas 101, 102
Mar, Maya del 8
Matrix Software 5, 9,12, 16
McCauley, Karen 13, 14
McRae, Chris 11, 113, 128
Meadows, David 15, 196, 202
Michelson, Neil F. 8

N
Nixon, Richard 185

O
O'Brien, Dale 220, 227, 249
Onassis, Jacqueline 26

P
Picasso, Pablo 105, 106, 107
Pitt, Brad 47

R
Relocation issues 130

S
Sepharial 1
Shivdasani, Sonu 37, 38
Smith, Captain Edward 53
Solté, David 227, 229
Studio Schrofer 213, 214
Sullivan, Erin 15

T
Thatcher, Margaret 41, 42, 43
Thompson, Angel 13, 14, 87, 92

U
USA birth chart 220, 228, 235, 236, 243

V

Verdi, Guiseppe 110, 111

W

Washington, George 178
White, Maya 76, 78, 79, 83, 84, 86

Other books by The Wessex Astrologer

The Essentials of Vedic Astrology
Lunar Nodes - Crisis and Redemption
Personal Panchanga and the Five Sources of Light
Komilla Sutton

Astrolocality Astrology
Martin Davis

The Consultation Chart
Wanda Sellar

The Betz Placidus Table of Houses
Martha Betz

Astrology and Meditation
Greg Bogart

Patterns of the Past
Karmic Connections
Judy Hall

The Book of World Horoscopes
Nicholas Campion

The Moment of Astrology
Geoffrey Cornelius

Life After Grief - An Astrological Guide to Dealing with Loss
Darrelyn Gunzburg

You're not a Person - Just a Birthchart
Declination ; The Steps of the Sun
Paul F. Newman

The Houses: Temples of the Sky
Deborah Houlding

Temperament: Astrology's Forgotten Key
Dorian Geiseler Greenbaum

Astrology, A Place in Chaos
Bernadette Brady

Astrology and the Causes of War
Jamie Macphail

Flirting with the Zodiac
Kim Farnell

The Gods of Change
Howard Sasportas

Astrological Roots: The Hellenistic Legacy
Joseph Crane

www.ingramcontent.com/pod-product-compliance
Lightning Source LLC
Chambersburg PA
CBHW050341230426
43663CB00010B/1939